NINJA FOODI GRILL
COOKBOOK 2021-2022

1000-Day Mouth-Watering & Easy Indoor Grilling and Air Frying Recipes for Beginners and Advanced Users

Loreen Swanson

Table of Contents

Ninja Foodi Grill is one of the revolutionary cooking appliances that come from Ninja Foodi Manufacturers. It is versatile cooking appliance used for grilling, air frying, baking, roasting and dehydrating purposes. It never burns or overcooks your food and maintains inside temperature as per recipe settings to give you fast and even cooking results. The best part of the Ninja Foodi Grill is its flip lid. You can easily flip the lid to check your food at any time. The Ninja Foodi Grill gives you an outdoor cooking experience in your kitchen without compromising the taste and texture of outdoor cooking. It cooks your healthy food without filling your kitchen with smoke. While cooking your food into Ninja Foodi Grill it helps to maintain the aroma and natural flavors of the ingredients. The Ninja Foodi Grill requires 1760 Watt power to generate a maximum 500°F temperature to cook your food faster.

This cookbook contains 80 delicious and healthy Ninja Foodi Grill Recipes from different categories like breakfast, snacks, appetizers, vegetables, sides, fish, seafood, poultry, beef, lamb, porkand desserts. The recipes written in this cookbook are well-prepared and made up from easily available ingredients. All the recipes are written in easy and understandable language. The recipes start with their preparation and cooking time followed by step-by-step cooking instructions. At the end of each recipe, nutritional value information is written. The nutritional value information will help to keep track of daily calorie intake. There are various books available in the market on this topic, thanks for choosing my cookbook. I hope you love and enjoy all the Ninja Foodi Grill Recipes written in this book.

What is Ninja Foodi Grill?

Ninja Foodi Grill is one of the advanced multi-functional cooking appliances specially designed for indoor cooking. It comes in a 4-quart cooking capacity and is made up of stainless steel material.

Ninja Foodi Grill is 5-in-1 cooking appliance and not only use for grilling but also usedfor air crisping, baking, roasting and dehydrating your favorite foods. The Ninja Grill comes with cooking accessories like a cooking pot, crisper tray, non-stick grill grate and cleaning brush to make your daily cooking process fast and easy. The inner pot of the Ninja Foodi Grill is made up of a non-stick surface.

The Ninja Foodi Grill works on cyclonic grilling technology to circulate very hot (500°F) air around your food to give you fire-grilled and crispier cooking results. Using low, medium, high and max temperature settings you can cook a variety of dishes without filling your kitchen with smoke. The Foodi Grill also allows cooking of your frozen food directly into the grill without defrosting. Using a Ninja Foodi Crisper Basket you can air fry your favorite food using very few fats and oils as compared with the deep-frying method. It makes your favorite food crisper from the outside and juicy tender from the inside without changing the taste and texture like deep-fried food.

Benefits of Ninja Foodi Grill

Ninja Foodi Grill is one of the advanced and innovative cooking appliances having lots of benefits. Some of the Ninja Foodi Grill benefits are mentioned as follows.

1. **Multifunctional 5-in-1 Appliance:** The Ninja Foodi is one of the multi-functional cooking appliances used for grilling, air frying, baking, roasting and dehydrating your favorite food. You never need to buy separate cooking appliances for a single cooking function.
2. **Faster and Even Cooking:** Ninja Foodi Grill is an advanced cooking machine that uses cyclonic air circulation technology to circulate very hot (500°F) air around the food. It cooks your food faster and also gets even cooking results every time.
3. **Compact and Easy to Operate:** The Ninja Foodi comes in compact size and shape. It is easily fitted on your kitchen countertop. The Ninja Foodi Grill comes with a large size digital control panel system. All the functions are given on the control panel system. You just need to choose an appropriate function and set Time/Temperature settings as per your recipe needs.
4. **Crisp and Brown Cooking Results:** The Ninja Foodi Grill cooks your food by circulating hot cyclonic air around the food. It makes your food crispy crunchy from the outside and juicy and tender from the inside. It gives a nice brown texture to your food.
Healthy Cooking: Using the Air Crisp function you can cook your food with very little fat and oils. It takes 80 to 85% fewer fats and oil compare with the traditional deep frying method. Fewer fats and oil means less calorie intake and good health.

Functions of Ninja Foodi Grill

The Ninja Foodi comes with 5-in-1 functions. These functions are mentioned as follows.

- **Grill:** This function is used to convert your Ninja Foodi into the grill. It allows grilling you your favorite food like meat, steak, chicken breast, and more. While using this function use grill grates for better cooking results and make nice char-grill marks on your food. Grilling your food in Ninja Foodi makes your food crispier and gives a nice brown texture over your food.
- **Air Crisp:** This function is ideal for air frying your favorite foods like French fries, chicken wings, onion rings and more. Air frying is one of the healthiest methods of cooking your food by using very little fat and oils. It makes your food crunchy, crisper from the outside and juicy tender from the inside.
- **Roast:** Using this function you can roast your favorite foods like small cuts of meat, vegetables and more. Roasting food gives a nice brown texture to your food and makes it tender and juicy with a nice crust.
- **Bake:** Ninja Foodi comes with an eight inch baking pan. You can easily bake cake, cookies and more using Ninja Foodi. Using this function you can quickly make homemade desserts with less effort.
- **Dehydrate:** This function is ideal for dehydrating your favorite food; vegetable and meat slices. Using this function you can easily dehydrate your food and store them for a longer time. Slice of an apple takes approximately seven hours to dry completely.

How to Clean and Maintain

1. The unit should be cleaned thoroughly after every use.

2. Before cleaning, unplug the unit from the outlet.

3. **Never** put the cooker base in the dishwasher or submerge it in water or other liquid.

4. Wipe the cooker base and control panel clean with a clean damp cloth.

5. The dishwasher is safe for the cooking pot, silicone ring, reversible rack, Cook & Crisp Basket, and detachable diffuser.

6. Water and dish soap can be used to clean the pressure lid, including the pressure release valve and anti-clog cap. **Do not** use the dishwasher to clean the pressure lid or any of its components, and **do not** disassemble the pressure release valve or red float valve assembly.

7. After the heat shield has cooled, wipe down the crisping lid with a wet cloth or paper towel.

8. If there is food residue on the cooking pot, reversible rack, or Cook & Crisp Basket, fill it with water and soak it before cleaning. **Scouring pads should not be used**. Scrub with a non-abrasive cleanser or liquid dish soap and a nylon pad or brush if necessary.

9. After each use, air-dry all parts or use a soft dry towel.

Grilled Huli Huli Chicken

Prep time: 5 minutes.
Cook time: 12 minutes.
Serves: 8

Ingredients
- 6-8 Chicken Legs
- ½ tsp fresh ginger, minced or crushed
- 1 tsp garlic, minced or crushed
- ¼ cup brown sugar
- 3 Tbsp ketchup
- 4 Tbsp soy sauce
- 2 Tbsp chicken stock, as needed

Preparation
1. In a bowl, add ketchup, soy sauce, garlic, ginger, and brown sugar. Mix well and slowly add in the chicken stock. thin up the marinade a bit to make it easier to cover the chicken.
2. In a container or bag add your chicken legs and pour ½ of the marinade sauce all over the chicken. Cover and let marinate at least 2 hours to overnight.
3. Once the chicken is marinated, preheat your Ninja Foodi Grill or another grill after selecting the GRILL mode at HIGH heat. When it hot toss your chicken legs on, leaving space between each.
4. Cook 4-6 minutes on each side, basting with the remaining marinade. Cook until the internal temperature reaches 165 degrees F internal temperature.
5. Remove the Huli Huli chicken from the grill, let the rest 5 minutes then serve with your favorite sides.

Serving Suggestion: Serve with mashed potatoes or grilled veggies as side.

Variation Tip: use chopped cilantro for garnish.

Nutritional Information Per Serving:
Calories 509 | Carbohydrates 8g | Protein 63g | Fat 23g | Sodium 752mg| Fiber 0g

Marinated London Broil

Prep time: 5 minutes.
Cook time: 8 minutes.
Serves: 4

Ingredients
- 1 ½ lbs London Broil
- ¼ cup red wine vinegar
- 1 Tbsp olive oil
- 1½ Tbsp spicy mustard
- 2 cloves garlic minced
- 1 Tbsp Worcestershire sauce
- 1-2 tsp rosemary fresh
- 1 tsp sea salt
- 1 tsp onion powder
- 1 tsp dried thyme
- ½ tsp black pepper

Preparation
1. Tenderize each side with a meat tenderizer.
2. Mince the garlic cloves and finely chop the rosemary. Combine all the marinade ingredients into a large plastic, sealable bag. Add the steak and seal the bag. Mix the marinade all around so the ingredients combine with each other. Then squeeze the air out of the bag and refrigerate for 2-4 hours.
3. Remove the steak from the fridge, leave it in the bag and let it sit at room temp for 30 minutes.
4. Remove the steak from the bag and blot off the marinade.
5. Select GRILL mode, adjust the temperature to MAX heat and preheat. When it says "ADD FOOD" lays the steak on the grill surface and presses the steak down onto the grill surface.
6. Grill on max grill for 4 minutes and then flip. Grill on max grill another 2-4 minutes for medium rare. Remove from grill and let the steak rest for 5-10 minutes.

Serving Suggestion: Slice thinly across the grain. Serve & Enjoy!

Variation Tip: use fresh herbs.

Nutritional Information Per Serving:
Calories 265 | Carbohydrates 2g | Protein 40g | Fat 9g | Sodium 798mg| Fiber 1g

Greek Chicken with Tzatziki Sauce

Prep time: 10 minutes.
Cook time: 15 minutes.
Serves: 4
Ingredients
For the grilled chicken breasts:
- 4 chicken breasts
- ¼ cup extra-virgin olive oil
- 2 tsp dried oregano
- 1 tsp garlic powder
- Juice of one medium lemon
- Sea salt and freshly cracked pepper to taste

For the tzatziki sauce:
- ½ cup finely grated cucumber
- 1 cup of Greek yogurt
- 2 tsp of apple cider vinegar
- Juice of one medium lemon
- 1 tbsp of garlic powder

Preparation
1. For the chicken marinade, whisk together the lemon juice, olive oil, oregano, salt, pepper, and garlic powder in a medium bowl.
2. Pour into a Ziploc bag or container with the chicken to marinate in the refrigerator for at least 2 hours.
3. Meanwhile, make the tzatziki sauce by first grating the cucumbers.
4. Add in the Greek yogurt, vinegar, garlic, lemon juice, and sea salt to taste in a bowl. Chill in the refrigerator until ready to serve.
5. Select the "GRILL" function and adjust temperature to "HI", set the time to 15 minutes and preheat your Ninja Foodi Grill.
6. Add the marinated chicken.
7. Cook the chicken breasts for about 5-7 minutes per side, depending on thickness. Remove from grill and allow the cooked chicken to rest.

Serving Suggestion: To serve, plate sliced chicken over a bed of rice top with the creamy tzatziki sauce and a lemon wedge. Enjoy!
Variation Tip: serve along with pita bread also.
Nutritional Information Per Serving:
Calories 521 | Carbohydrates 26g | Protein 59g | Fat 20g | Sodium 448mg | Fiber 2g

Minted Tomato, Onion & Glazed Tofu Kebabs

Prep time: 15 minutes
Cook time: 40 minutes
Servings: 4
Ingredients
- 1 14-ounce package extra-firm water-packed tofu, drained
- 1 tablespoon lime juice
- 16 fresh mint leaves
- 4 plum tomatoes, quartered and seeded
- 1 tablespoon reduced-sodium soy sauce
- 1 tsp minced fresh ginger
- 1 onion, peeled, quartered and separated into layers
- 2 jalapeño peppers, seeded and cut into ½-inch pieces
- ¼ cup Kecap manis

Preparation
1. Insert Grill Grate. Select the GRILL mode, adjust temperature to LOW and time to 10 minutes. Preheat the Ninja Foodi Grill..
2. Cut the tofu in half horizontally, cutting 2 large slices about one inch thick. Take a kitchen towel and put it on the cutting board. Set the tofu on the towel. Put another clean folded towel over the tofu.
3. Put a flat and heavyweight thing like a skillet on top; Drain it for 15 minutes; then remove the weight and cut the tofu into 1½-inch pieces.
4. Combine the lime juice, soy sauce, and ginger in a bowl. Add the tofu and toss it to coat. Cover it and marinate in the refrigerator for 15 minutes.
5. Tuck in a mint leaf into every tomato quarter and thread them onto four or 8 skewers alternatively with onion, tofu, and jalapenos.
6. Add the food to the Grill Grate and close the hood. Cook for 10 minutes.

Serving Suggestion: Serve with mint sauce.
Variation Tip: use lemon for tanginess.
Nutritional Information Per Serving:
Calories 412 | Carbohydrates 64.3g | Protein 16.1g | Fat 10.1g | Sodium 895mg | Fiber 2g

Steak and Potatoes

Prep time: 15 minutes.
Cook time: 45 minutes.
Serves: 4

Ingredients
- 3-4 potatoes russet
- 3 steak
- ¼ cup avocado oil
- 2 tbsp steak seasoning
- 1 tbsp sea salt

Preparation
1. Wash potatoes, dry, and poke with a fork all over them.
2. Rub avocado oil all over each one so they are well saturated. Sprinkle salt on outsides and put into air fryer basket.
3. Close lid and set to 400 degrees F, AIR CRISP function, cook for 35 minutes. Flip, then cook for an additional 10 minutes or until middle is fork tender when poked.
4. Remove potatoes and cover with foil to keep them warm. Remove Crisper Basket and replace with grill piece inside machine. Select the "GRILL" function and adjust temperature to "HI" and preheat.
5. Sprinkle both sides of steak with seasoning and press down so it sticks well.
6. When Ninja Foodi Grill is done preheating it will say lift adds food. Add steaks now.
7. Sirloins cooked 8 minutes, flipping halfway through; filet cooked for 6 minutes, flipping after 4 minutes.
8. Remove once you feel it is done to your liking. Allow to rest for at least 5 minutes to maintain juiciness before cutting.

Serving Suggestion: Serve with potatoes as side.

Variation Tip: use chopped dill for garnish.

Nutritional Information Per Serving:
Calories 572 | Carbohydrates 21g | Protein 38g | Fat 38g | Sodium 1849mg| Fiber 4g

BBQ Beef Short Ribs

Prep time: 5 minutes.
Cook time: 50 minutes.
Serves: 2

Ingredients
- 2 Beef Short Ribs
- ¼ c Red Wine
- ¾ c Beef Stock
- ¼ c Diced Onion
- ½ c BBQ sauce

Seasoning
- Seasoning salt
- Garlic Powder
- Onion Powder
- 1 Tbsp Cornstarch

Preparation
1. Season the beef ribs with the seasonings.
2. Add the onion, wine, and broth to the bottom of the Foodi cooking bowl.
3. Close the toggle switch to sealing.
4. Pressure cook on manual, high, for 40 minutes.
5. Do a natural release for 10 minutes, and then carefully release any remaining pressure until the pin drops and its safe open the lid.
6. Remove the ribs to a plate.
7. Generously brush the BBQ sauce over the entire surface of the ribs. Place the ribs back into the pot, on the top rack of the air crisping rack.
8. Air crisps the ribs for 10 minutes at 350 degrees F. Feel free to flip them halfway through.
9. Remove the ribs to rest and take out the rack.
10. Mix up the slurry and pour into the pan juices in the pot to thicken.
11. Spoon over the ribs and enjoy!

Serving Suggestion: Serve warm with slurry.

Variation Tip: use chicken drumsticks as same but avoid pressure cook.

Nutritional Information Per Serving:
Calories 906 | Carbohydrates 78g | Protein 50g | Fat 22g | Sodium 2667mg| Fiber 3g

Steak Kabobs

Prep time: 10 minutes.
Cook time: 8 minutes.
Serves: 2

Ingredients

- 1-2 steaks
- 1 onion
- 1 bundle mushrooms
- 10-12 cherry tomatoes
- 1 bell pepper
- 2 - 2 ½ cup Italian Dressing
- Wooden or Metal Skewers

Preparation

1. Cut steaks about 1-inch strips. Soak wooden skewers in water for at least 30 minutes. Or they will burn up.
2. Pour Italian dressing over the steak and let it marinate while prep vegetables.
3. Wash and prep vegetables. The mushrooms whole and tomatoes whole and sliced the pepper and onions in around 1-inch pieces.
4. Once skewers have been soaked in water, if using wood, start pushing steak and vegetables onto the skewers.
5. Place in a dish and then pour the dressing over the top of the veggies and meat. Then cover and let marinate for 3-4 hours in the fridge.
6. Preheat Ninja Foodi Grill. Select the GRILL setting and MAX heat. Let it preheat, it takes about 12 minutes.
7. Once the grill is hot, carefully place your steak kabobs onto the grill. And you should cook 4-5 at a time.
8. Close lid and select 8 minutes. Flip at the 4-minute mark.
9. Cook steaks until it reaches your desired doneness. At 8 minutes our medium-well to well done. If you want rarer, cook for a bit less.
10. Once your steak skewers are done, remove with tong, and then remove from skewers and serve.
11. Enjoy these easy and delicious Ninja Foodi Grill steak kabobs any day of the week, and rain or shine.

Serving Suggestion: Serve delicious ranch sauce.

Variation Tip: use chicken and taste will be the same.

Nutritional Information Per Serving:
Calories 416 | Carbohydrates 17g | Protein 12g |

Fat 33g | Sodium 1191mg| Fiber 1g

Juicy Stuffed Bell Peppers

Prep time: 10 minutes
Cook time: 15 minutes
Servings: 4

Ingredients

- 4 slices bacon, cooked and chopped
- 4 large eggs
- 1 cup cheddar cheese, shredded
- 4 bell peppers, seeded and tops removed
- Chopped parsley for garnish
- Salt and pepper to taste

Preparation

1. Divide cheese and bacon equally and stuff into your bell pepper.
2. Add eggs into each bell pepper. Season with salt and pepper.
3. Pre-heat your Ninja Foodi by pressing the "AIR CRISP" option and setting it to "390 Degrees F."
4. Set the timer to 15 minutes.
5. Let it pre-heat until you hear a beep.
6. Transfer bell pepper to your cooking basket and transfer to Ninja Foodi Grill.
7. Lock lid and cook for 10-15 minutes.
8. Cook until egg whites are cooked well until the yolks are slightly runny.
9. Remove peppers from the basket and garnish with parsley.
10. Serve and enjoy!

Serving Suggestion: Serve with parsley garnishing or enjoy as it is.

Variation Tip: use chopped dill for garnish.

Nutritional Information Per Serving:
Calories 326 | Carbohydrates 10g | Protein 22g | Fat 23g | Sodium 781mg| Fiber 2g

Chicken Satay

Prep time: 40 minutes.
Cook time: 6 minutes.
Serves: 3

Ingredients
- 1½ lbs chicken breast boneless, skinless

Marinade
- ½ cup coconut milk
- 2 cloves garlic minced
- 2" piece ginger grated
- 2 tsp turmeric
- 1 tsp sea salt
- 1 Tbsp Lemongrass Paste
- 1 Tbsp Chili Garlic Sauce
- 2 tsp Lemon Juice

Optional Garnishes
- chopped cilantro
- chopped peanuts
- peanut sauce

Preparation
1. If using bamboo skewers, soak them in water for at least 30 minutes before using.
2. Mix all the ingredients in the marinade in a medium size bowl.
3. Slice chicken breast into ½" strips and place into the marinade. Allow to marinate at room temp for 30 minutes.
4. Turn the Ninja Foodi Grill on and select the GRILL function and MAX temp. Make sure the Grill Grate that came with the grill is inside during the preheat. While the NF preheats, assemble your chicken skewers.
5. Take a strip and weave it onto a skewer.
6. When the Ninja Foodi Grill has preheated it will tell you to "ADD FOOD." Add about 6 skewers to the Grill Grate surface. Add more if they will fit, but don't overlap them or they won't cook evenly.
7. Close the lid and set the time for 6 minutes. Grill for 3 minutes and flip the skewers. Grill an additional 2-3 minutes
8. Garnish with fresh cilantro and chopped peanuts.

Serving Suggestion: serve with peanut sauce.

Enjoy

Variation Tip: Add your favorite seasoning for taste.

Nutritional Information Per Serving:
Calories 177 | Carbohydrates 3g | Protein 25g | Fat 75g | Sodium 622mg| Fiber 1g

Peach BBQ Chicken Thighs

Prep time: 15 minutes.
Cook time: 15 minutes.
Serves: 6

Ingredients
- 4- 6 chicken thighs bone-in
- ¾ cup barbecue sauce
- 4 Tbsp peach preserve
- 1 ½ Tbsp Lemon Juice
- Salt and Pepper to taste

Preparation
1. Start by mixing peach preserves, barbecue sauce, lemon juice, and salt and pepper in a bowl. Whisk until well incorporated.
2. Place your chicken thighs in the marinade for 4 hours at a minimum.
3. Once chicken is done marinating, select GRILL mode and adjust the temperature to HI and preheat your Ninja Foodi Grill for 10 minutes. Toss chicken thighs on the grill, skin down.
4. Cook 4-5 minutes per side or until the chicken is nice and brown. Once get a nice grill mark on them, drop the heat down to medium.
5. Then finish cooking until the chicken reaches an internal temperature of 165 degrees F.
6. Remove chicken and place on a plate, and lightly cover with aluminum foil.
7. Let chicken rest 5 minutes before serving.

Serving Suggestion: Serve with salad on side.
Variation Tip: use vinegar instead of lemon.
Nutritional Information Per Serving:
Calories 342| Carbohydrates 15g | Protein 31g | Fat 18g | Sodium 639mg| Fiber 0g

Carne Asada Street Tacos

Prep time: 3 minutes.
Cook time: 20 minutes.
Serves: 8

Ingredients

- 2 tsp sea salt
- 2 tsp cumin
- 2 tsp smoked paprika
- 1 tsp garlic powder
- 1 tsp onion powder
- ¼ tsp chipotle
- ½ cup orange juice fresh squeezed
- ¼ cup lime juice
- 4 garlic cloves about ½ Tbsp
- 1 Ancho chili pepper dry
- 1 cup cilantro I use the stems

Carne Asada

- 1 ½ pounds skirt steak
- 1 cup beef stock
- 16 corn tortillas
- 4 ounces cotija cheese
- Cilantro for garnish
- ½ cup radishes sliced.
- 1 cup onion diced

Preparation

1. Mix up the spices and add to a medium size sealable bag.
2. Slice the steak against the grain into thin strips and place into baggy with the dry spices. Shake to coat meat and then add the remaining marinade ingredients. Leave at room temp for 30 minutes or refrigerate for 4 hours or overnight.
3. Dump the steak and the marinade into the inner pot. Add 1 cup of beef stock. Set the pressure on high for 10 minutes. Allow the Ninja Foodi to release its pressure for 10 minutes then immediately release the remaining pressure.
4. Select the "Air Crisp" function of the Ninja Foodi Grill at 360 Degrees F for 5 minutes.
5. Put the rack in the high position and lay the corn tortillas over 2 rungs in the rack. Spritzing with oil will help them be more pliable.
6. Air Crisp the Tortillas for 3 minutes or until they become warm and slightly crispy.
7. Double the corn tortillas and stuff with carne a Sada meat and top with crumbled cheese, cilantro, onion, and sliced radishes. Serve & Enjoy!

Serving Suggestion: Serve with your favorite dipping sauce.
Variation Tip: use chopped dill for garnish.
Nutritional Information Per Serving:
Calories 308 | Carbohydrates 34g | Protein 24g | Fat 9g | Sodium 731mg| Fiber 5g

Moroccan Roast Chicken

Prep time: 5-10 minutes
Cook time: 22 minutes
Servings: 4

Ingredients

- 3 tbsp plain yogurt
- 4 skinless, boneless chicken thighs
- 4 garlic cloves, chopped
- ½ tsp salt
- ⅓ cup olive oil
- ½ tsp fresh flat-leaf parsley, chopped
- 2 tsp ground cumin
- 2 tsp paprika
- ¼ tsp crushed red pepper flakes

Preparation

1. Take your food processor and add garlic, yogurt, salt, oil and blend as well.
2. Take a mixing bowl and add chicken, red pepper flakes, paprika, cumin, parsley, garlic, and mix well.
3. Let it marinate for 2-4 hours.
4. Pre-heat Ninja Foodi by pressing the "ROAST" option and setting it to "400 degrees F" and timer to 23 minutes.
5. Let it pre-heat until you hear a beep.
6. Arrange chicken directly inside your cooking pot and lock lid, cook for 15 minutes, flip and cook for the remaining time.

Serving Suggestion: Serve and enjoy with yogurt dip.
Variation Tip: use ranch sauce for extra flavor.
Nutritional Information per Serving:
Calories: 321| Carbohydrates: 6 g | Protein: 21 g | Fat: 24 g | Sodium: 602 mg |Fiber: 2 g

Ninja Foodi Grill Steak

Prep time: 5 minutes.
Cook time: 7 minutes.
Serves: 2

Ingredients
- 2 steaks
- 1 tbsp kosher salt
- ¼ tsp corn starch
- ½tsp chili powder
- 2 tsp brown sugar
- ¼tsp onion powder
- 1 tsp black pepper
- ¼ tsp Turmeric
- ½ tsp smoked paprika

Preparation
1. Mix up all steak seasonings in a bowl.
2. Once steaks are rubbed down with the spices on all sides, wrap or cover and store in the fridge. Store for 30 minutes to 2 hours.
3. Select GRILL mode, set the temperature to MAX and time to 8-12 minutes. Press START/STOP to preheat the Ninja Foodi Grill.
4. Once the preheat is done take your steaks and place them on the grill.
5. You will cook your steaks to the doneness you desire.
6. Once steaks are done, allow resting on a plate for 5 minutes that is tented in aluminum foil.

Serving Suggestion: Serve with grilled veggies as side.

Variation Tip: differ seasoning allows unique taste.

Nutritional Information Per Serving:
Calories 319 | Carbohydrates 3g | Protein 29g | Fat 21g | Sodium 1654mg| Fiber 0g

Grilled Chicken Bruschetta

Prep time: 10 minutes.
Cook time: 15 minutes.
Serves: 3

Ingredients
- 3 Chicken Breasts
- Roasted Garlic and Bell Pepper Seasoning
- Salt and Pepper, to taste
- Cooking Oil Spray for Grill
- 1 cup Basil Pesto
- Fresh Mozzarella Cheese, Sliced
- 2 Roma Tomatoes, diced

Preparation
1. Place the chicken in gallon size bag and then use a meat mallet to pound the chicken to around ¼" thick.
2. Remove from bag and place raw chicken on a platter and season with the Roasted Garlic and Bell Pepper Seasoning.
3. For the Ninja Foodi Grill, select the AIR CRISP setting and adjust the temperature to 400 degrees F.
4. Grill the chicken for 15 minutes, while cooking after 5 minutes, place some pesto on top of each chicken breast, then slice and lay out some fresh mozzarella on each slice of chicken.
5. Remove your grilled bruschetta chicken from the Ninja Foodi Grill and top with diced roma tomatoes, add extra pesto, basil leaves and serve as desired.

Serving Suggestion: Serve with diced tomatoes.

Variation Tip: use salt and pepper for seasoning and it taste yummy.

Nutritional Information Per Serving:
Calories 359 | Carbohydrates 6g | Protein 25g | Fat 5g | Sodium 399mg| Fiber 1g

Chicken & Bacon Caesar Salad

Prep time: 35 minutes.
Cook time: 30 minutes.
Serves: 4

Ingredients
Marinated Chicken Breasts
- 1 lb chicken breasts
- ⅛ cup balsamic vinegar
- ⅛ cup olive oil
- ¼ tsp garlic powder
- ¼tsp black pepper
- ¼ tsp salt

Caesar Dressing
- ⅔ cup mayo
- 4 anchovies in oil
- 2 small cloves garlic
- 2.5 tbsp lemon juice
- 2 tbsp nutritional yeast
- ½ tsp dijon mustard
- ½ tsp coconut amino
- ¼ tsp apple cider vinegar
- ½ tsp salt
- ¼ tsp pepper

Salad & Toppings
- 8 cups romaine lettuce
- 4 eggs soft or hard boiled
- 8 oz. sugar free bacon cooked
- 1 tsp nutritional yeast

Preparation
1. Prepare the Chicken Breasts: Put one chicken breast inside a zip lock bag Gently pound the chicken using a meat tenderizer or heavy rolling pin until it's even in thickness. Repeat for the other chicken breasts.

2. Whisk together the marinade ingredients and pour it over the chicken, turning to coat. Marinate for 30-60 minutes.

3. Select the GRILL function of the Ninja Foodi Grill and adjust the temperature to MEDIUM and preheat. Turn your grill to medium and allow preheating. Add the chicken breasts to the grill, cooking for about 12 minutes, turning once. Remove from the heat and let the chicken on the rest before slicing.

4. **Prepare the Salad Toppings**: Wash and chop the lettuce. Cook the bacon and allow it to cool, and then roughly chop it. Boil the eggs however you like them and slice them into halves or quarters.

5. Make the Caesar Salad Dressing: Using an immersion blender set to low, mix together all the ingredients, smash the garlic clove and finely chop the anchovies, then whisk all ingredients together in a bowl.

6. Season to taste with salt and pepper. Keep it covered in the refrigerator for up to 5 days.

7. Assemble the Salad: Divide the lettuce among four large bowls. Top each bowl with nutritional yeast, salad dressing, chicken, eggs, and bacon.

8. Sprinkle each salad with cracked black pepper and enjoy.

Serving Suggestion: Serve with dill garnishing or enjoy as it is.

Variation Tip: For a low carb / keto option, simply omit the tomatoes.

Nutritional Information Per Serving:
Calories 631 | Carbohydrates 12g | Protein 42g | Fat 46g | Sodium 1461mg| Fiber 3g

Simple Zucchini Egg Muffins

Prep time: 5-10 minutes
Cook time: 7 minutes
Servings: 4

Ingredients
- 4 whole eggs
- 2 tbsp almond flour
- 1 zucchini, grated
- 1 tsp butter
- ½ tsp salt

Preparation
1. Take a small-sized bowl and add almond flour, salt, zucchini. Mix well.
2. Take muffin molds and grease them gently, add the zucchini mix.
3. Arrange your molds in Ninja Foodi Grill and cook on "AIR CRISP" mode for 7 minutes at a temperature of 375 degrees F.
4. Serve and enjoy the meal once complete!

Serving Suggestion: Serve in breakfast.
Variation Tip: Add mushroom for taste.
Nutritional Information per Serving:
Calories: 94|Fat: 8 g| Carbohydrates: 2 g| Fiber: 0.5 g| Sodium: 209 mg |Protein: 7 g

Homely Zucchini Muffin

Prep time: 5-10 minutes
Cook time: 7 minutes
Servings: 4

Ingredients
- 4 whole eggs
- 1 zucchini, grated
- 2 tbsp almond flour

- ½ tsp salt
- 1 tsp butter

Preparation
1. Add zucchini, salt, and almond flour into a mixing bowl.
2. Mix them well.
3. Grease muffin molds with butter.
4. Add zucchini mixture to them.
5. Arrange muffin tins in your Ninja Foodi Grill.
6. Then close the lid and cook on "AIR CRISP" mode for 7 minutes at 375 degrees F.

Serving Suggestion: Serve warm with tea.
Variation Tip: use cheese inside the muffin for fun.
Nutritional Information per Serving:
Calories: 94| Fat: 8 g| Carbohydrates: 2 g| Fiber: 0.5 g| Sodium: 209 mg| Protein: 7 g

Coffee Glazed Bagels

Prep time: 15 minutes.
Cook time: 4 minutes.
Serves: 4

Ingredients:
- 4 bagels split in half
- ¼ cup coconut milk
- 1 cup fine sugar
- 2 tablespoons black coffee
- 2 tablespoons coconut flakes

Preparation:
1. Preheat the Ninja Foodi Grill on the "Grill Mode" at LOW-temperature settings.
2. When the grill is preheated, open its hood and place the bagels in it.
3. Cover the grill's hood and grill for 2 minutes.
4. Flip the bagel and continue grilling for another 2 minutes.
5. Grill the remaining bagels in a similar way.
6. Whisk the rest of the ingredients in a bowl well.
7. Drizzle this sauce over the grilled bagels.
8. Serve.

Serving Suggestion: Serve the bagels with chocolate syrup.
Variation Tip: Cut the bagels in half and layer them with cream cheese.
Nutritional Information Per Serving:
Calories 412 | Fat 25g |Sodium 132mg | Carbs 44g | Fiber 3.9g | Sugar 3g | Protein 18.9g

Breakfast Burger

Prep time: 15 minutes.
Cook time: 26 minutes.
Serves: 4

Ingredients:
- 1 lb. ground beef
- 1 tbsp. Worcestershire sauce
- 1 tsp. Montreal steak seasoning
- ½ tsp. salt
- ½ tsp. pepper
- 3 tbsp. butter
- 8 Texas toast slices
- 2 tbsp. canola oil
- 2- ½ cups hash brown potatoes, shredded
- 4 American cheese slices
- 8 cooked bacon strips

Preparation:
1. Mix beef with ¼ tsp. black pepper, ¼ tsp. salt, steak seasoning and Worcestershire sauce in a bowl.
2. Make 4-½ inch thick patties out of this beef mixture.
3. Select the "Grill" Mode, set the temperature to MED.
4. Press the START/STOP button to initiate preheating.
5. Once preheated, place the patties in the Ninja Foodi Grill.
6. Cover the hood and allow the grill to cook.
7. Transfer the patties to a plate.
8. Brush the toast slices with butter and grill them for 2 minutes from both the sides.
9. Similarly, grill the hash browns for 6 minutes per side.
10. Divide the patties, hash brown, cheese and bacon strip in the grilled toasts.
11. Serve.

Serving Suggestion: Serve the burgers with fried eggs.

Variation Tip: Add chopped parsley to the patty mixture.

Nutritional Information Per Serving:
Calories 859 | Fat 49g |Sodium 595mg | Carbs 55g | Fiber 6g | Sugar 13g | Protein 45g

Prosciutto Egg Panini

Prep time: 15 minutes.
Cook time: 15 minutes.
Serves: 4

Ingredients:
- 3 large eggs
- 2 large egg whites
- 6 tbsp. fat-free milk
- 1 green onion, thinly sliced
- 1 tbsp. Dijon mustard
- 1 tbsp. maple syrup
- 8 slices sourdough bread
- 8 thin prosciutto slices
- ½ cup sharp cheddar cheese, shredded
- 8 tsp. butter

Preparation:
1. Sauté onion with butter in a skillet for 1 minute.
2. Beat eggs with egg whites, mustard, and maple in a bowl.
3. Pour this mixture into the skillet, stir and cook for 5 minutes.
4. Pour it over half of the bread slices.
5. Add ham, and cheddar cheese on top and place remaining bread slices on top.
6. Select the "Grill" Mode, set the temperature to MED.
7. Use the arrow keys to set the cooking time to 10 minutes.
8. Press the START/STOP button to initiate preheating.
9. Once preheated, place the sandwich in the Ninja Foodi Grill.
10. Cover the hood and allow the grill to cook.
11. Flip the sandwiches once cooked halfway through.
12. Slice and serve warm.

Serving Suggestion: Serve the panini with crispy bacon on top.

Variation Tip: Top panini with chopped fresh herbs.

Nutritional Information Per Serving:
Calories 228 | Fat 10g |Sodium 640mg | Carbs 21g | Fiber 4g | Sugar 8g | Protein 13g

Scrambled Egg Bread

Prep time: 15 minutes.
Cook time: 14 minutes.
Serves: 4

Ingredients:
- 1 loaf (1 lb.) sliced French bread
- 2 tbsp. butter, softened

Filling:
- 2 tbsp. butter
- 1 small onion, chopped
- 1 cup cubed fully cooked ham
- 1 large tomato, chopped
- 6 large eggs
- ⅛ tsp. pepper
- 1-½ cups cheddar cheese, shredded

Preparation:
1. Cut the bread in half, crosswise then cut each half lengthwise.
2. Hollow 2 pieces of the cut bread to get ½ inch shells and dice the inner portion of the bread into cubes.
3. Toss the bread cubes with 1 tbsp. butter in a bowl.
4. Sauté onion with 1 tbsp. butter in a skillet for 4 minutes.
5. Stir in tomatoes and ham then mix well.
6. Beat eggs with pepper and remaining butter in a bowl.
7. Pour them over the ham mixture and add 1 cup cheese and bread cubes on top.
8. Cook this mixture for 5 minutes until the eggs are set.
9. Place the bread shells on a foil sheet and stuff each with egg mixture.
10. Add remaining cheese on top.
11. Select the "Bake" Mode, set the temperature to 350 degrees F.
12. Use the arrow keys on the display to select time to 4 minutes.
13. Press the START/STOP button to initiate preheating.
14. Cover the hood and let the appliance cook.
15. Serve warm.

Serving Suggestion: Serve the bread with a glass of apple smoothie.

Variation Tip: Add sautéed ground chicken or pork on top of eggs.

Nutritional Information Per Serving:
Calories 297 | Fat 15g |Sodium 548mg | Carbs 15g | Fiber 4g | Sugar 1g | Protein 19g

Mushroom Pepper

Prep time: 10 minutes
Cook time: 10 minutes
Servings: 4

Ingredients
- 4 cremini creminis mushrooms, sliced
- 4 large eggs
- ½ cup cheddar cheese, shredded
- ½ onion, chopped
- ¼ cup whole milk
- Sea salt
- ½ bell pepper, seeded and diced
- Black pepper

Preparation
1. Add eggs and milk into a medium bowl.
2. Whisk them together.
3. Add mushrooms, onion, bell pepper, and cheese.
4. Mix them well.
5. Preheat by selecting the "BAKE" option and setting it to 400 degrees F.
6. Set the timer for 10 minutes.
7. Pour the egg mixture into the baking pan and spread evenly.
8. Let it pre-heat until you hear a beep.
9. Then close the lid.
10. Cook for 10 minutes.
11. Serve and enjoy!

Serving Suggestion: Serve and enjoy.

Variation Tip: add melted cheese for extra flavor.

Nutritional Information Per Serving:
Calories 153 | Carbohydrates 5g | Protein 11g | Fat 10g | Sodium 494mg| Fiber 1g

Grilled Bruschetta

Prep time: 15 minutes.
Cook time: 4 minutes.
Serves: 4

Ingredients:
- 1 cup celery, chopped
- 1-lb. tomatoes, seeded and chopped
- 3 tablespoons balsamic vinegar
- ¼ cup basil, minced
- 3 tablespoons olive oil
- ½ teaspoon salt
- 2 garlic cloves, minced
- 3 tablespoons Dijon mustard

Mustard Spread
- 1 tablespoon green onion, chopped
- ¼ cup Dijon mustard
- 1 garlic clove, minced
- ¾ teaspoon dried oregano
- ½ cup mayonnaise
- 1 French loaf bread, sliced

Preparation:
1. Take the first eight ingredients in a bowl and mix them together.
2. Cover this prepared topping and refrigerate for about 30 minutes.
3. Now take mayonnaise, onion, garlic, oregano, and mustard in a bowl.
4. Mix them well and prepare the mayonnaise spread.
5. Preheat the Ninja Foodi Grill on the "Grill Mode" at MEDIUM-temperature settings.
6. When the grill is preheated, open its hood and place the bread slices on the grill.
7. Cover the grill's hood and grill for 2 minutes.
8. Flip the bread slices and grill again for 2 minutes.
9. Top the grilled bread with mayonnaise spread and tomato relish.
10. Serve fresh.

Serving Suggestion: Serve the Bruschetta with crispy bacon on the side.

Variation Tip: Add a layer of garlic mayonnaise to the bruschetta.

Nutritional Information Per Serving:
Calories 284 | Fat 7.9g |Sodium 704mg | Carbs 46g | Fiber 3.6g | Sugar 6g | Protein 18g

Grilled Chicken Tacos

Prep time: 15 minutes.
Cook time: 14 minutes.
Serves: 4

Ingredients:
- 2 teaspoons sugar
- ⅓ cup olive oil
- ⅓ cup lime juice
- ⅓ cup red wine vinegar
- 2 teaspoons salt
- 2 teaspoons pepper
- 1 cup fresh cilantro, chopped
- 2 tablespoons chipotle in adobo sauce, chopped
- 2 lbs. boneless skinless chicken thighs
- Taco Wraps:
- 8 flour tortillas
- 4 poblano peppers
- 1 tablespoon olive oil
- 2 cups shredded Jack cheese

Preparation:
1. Take the first six ingredients in a blender jug and blend them together.
2. Once blended, mix with chipotles and cilantro.
3. Mix chicken with this cilantro marinade and cover to refrigerate for 8 hours.
4. Grease the poblanos with cooking oil and keep them aside.
5. Preheat the Ninja Foodi Grill on the "Grill Mode" at MEDIUM-temperature settings.
6. When the grill is preheated, open its hood and place the peppers on the grill.
7. Cover the grill's hood and grill for 5 minutes.
8. Flip the peppers and then continue grilling for another 5 minutes.
9. Place the chicken in the Ninja Foodi grill and cover the lid.
10. Now peel and slice the peppers in half, then also slice the chicken.
11. Spread each tortilla and add half cup chicken, half peppers, and ¼ cup cheese.
12. Fold the tortilla and carefully place it in the Ninja Foodi grill and cover its lid.
13. Grill each for 2 minutes per side on the medium temperature setting.
14. Serve.

Serving Suggestion: Serve the tacos with crumbled crispy bacon on top and warm bread on the side

Variation Tip: Add chopped carrots and cabbage to the chicken filling.

Nutritional Information Per Serving:
Calories 134 | Fat 4.7g |Sodium 1mg | Carbs 54.1g | Fiber 7g | Sugar 3.3g | Protein 26g

Grilled French Toast

Prep time: 15 minutes.
Cook time: 6 minutes.
Serves: 6

Ingredients:
- 3 eggs
- 1-quart strawberries, quartered
- 2 tablespoons aged Balsamic vinegar
- Juice of 1 orange and 2 teaspoons orange zest
- 1 sprig of fresh rosemary
- ¾ cup heavy cream
- 2 tablespoons honey
- 1 teaspoon vanilla extract
- Salt to taste
- 6- 1-inch challah bread slices
- Fine sugar, for dusting

Preparation:
1. Spread a foil sheet on a working surface.
2. Add strawberries, Balsamic, orange juice, rosemary and zest.
3. Fold the foil edges to make a pocket.
4. Whisk egg with cream, honey, vanilla, and a pinch of salt.
5. Dip and soak the bread slices in this mixture and shake off the excess.
6. Preheat the Ninja Foodi Grill on the "Grill Mode" at MEDIUM-temperature settings.
7. When the grill is preheated, open its hood and place the bread slices and foil packets in it.
8. Cover the grill's hood and grill for 3 minutes.
9. Flip the bread slices and continue grilling for another 3 minutes.
10. Serve the bread with the strawberry mix.
11. Enjoy.

Serving Suggestion: Serve the French toasts with maple syrup.
Variation Tip: Replace honey with maple syrup.
Nutritional Information Per Serving:
Calories 217 | Fat 3g |Sodium 114mg | Carbs 23.1g | Fiber 1g | Sugar 10g | Protein 10g

Portobello Mushrooms Bruschetta

Prep time: 15 minutes.
Cook time: 8 minutes.
Serves: 6

Ingredients:
- 2 cups cherry tomatoes, cut in half
- 3 tablespoons red onion, diced
- 3 tablespoons fresh basil, shredded
- Salt and black pepper to taste
- 4 tablespoons butter
- 1 teaspoon dried oregano
- 6 Portobello Mushrooms caps

Balsamic Glaze
- 2 teaspoons brown sugar
- ¼ cup balsamic vinegar

Preparation:
1. Start by preparing the balsamic glaze and take all its ingredients in a saucepan.
2. Stir, cook this mixture for 8 minutes on medium heat, then remove from the heat.
3. Take the mushrooms and brush them with the prepared glaze.
4. Stuff the remaining ingredients into the mushrooms.
5. Preheat the Ninja Foodi Grill on the "Grill Mode" at LOW-temperature settings.
6. When the grill is preheated, open its hood and place the stuffed mushrooms in it with their cap side down.
7. Cover the grill's hood and grill for 8 minutes.
8. Serve.

Serving Suggestion: Serve the mushrooms with fried eggs and crispy bacon.
Variation Tip: Add chopped parsley to the mushrooms
Nutritional Information Per Serving:
Calories 331 | Fat 2.5g |Sodium 595mg | Carbs 19g | Fiber 12g | Sugar 12g | Protein 8.7g

The Broccoli and Maple Mix

Prep time: 5-10 minutes
Cook time: 10 minutes
Servings: 4

Ingredients
- 2 heads broccoli, cut into florets
- 4 tbsp soy sauce
- 2 tsp maple syrup
- 4 tablespoons balsamic vinegar
- 2 tsp canola oil
- Red pepper flakes and sesame seeds for garnish

Preparation
1. Take a shallow mixing bowl and add vinegar, soy sauce, oil, maple syrup.
2. Whisk the whole mixture thoroughly.
3. Add broccoli to the mix.
4. Keep it aside. Set your Ninja Foodi Grill to GRILL mode at MAX heat.
5. Set the timer to 10 minutes.
6. Once you hear the beep, add prepared broccoli over Grill Grate.
7. Cook for 10 minutes.
8. Serve and enjoy!

Serving Suggestion: Serve topped with sesame seeds, pepper flakes.
Variation Tip: use your favorite vegetables.
Nutritional Information per Serving:
Calories: 141| Fat: 7 g, Fat: 1 g, Carbohydrates: 14 g, Fiber: 4 g, Sodium: 853 mg, Protein: 4 g

Sausage with Eggs

Prep time: 15 minutes.
Cook time: 10 minutes.
Serves: 4

Ingredients:
- 4 sausage links
- 2 cups kale, chopped
- 1 sweet yellow onion, chopped
- 4 eggs
- 1 cup mushrooms
- Olive oil

Preparation:
1. Preheat the Ninja Foodi Grill on the "Grill Mode" at LOW-temperature settings.
2. When the grill is preheated, open its hood and place the sausages n the Ninja grill.
3. Cover the grill's hood and grill for 2 minutes.
4. Flip the sausages and continue grilling for another 3 minutes
5. Now spread the onion, mushrooms, sausages, and kale in an iron skillet.
6. Crack the eggs in between the sausages.
7. BAKE this mixture for 5 minutes in the grill at 350 degrees F.
8. Serve warm and fresh.

Serving Suggestion: Serve the sausages with crispy bread toasts.
Variation Tip: Add chopped tomatoes to the mixture before baking.
Nutritional Information Per Serving:
Calories 212 | Fat 12g |Sodium 321mg | Carbs 14.6g | Fiber 4g | Sugar 8g | Protein 17g

Veggie Packed Egg Muffin

Prep time: 5-10 minutes
Cook time: 7 minutes
Servings: 4

Ingredients
- 4 whole eggs
- 2 tbsp almond flour
- 1 tsp butter
- 1 zucchini, grated
- ½ tsp salt

Preparation
1. Add almond flour, zucchini, and salt into a mixing bowl.
2. Mix them well.
3. Grease muffin molds with butter.
4. Adds zucchini mixture to them.
5. Arrange muffin tins in your Ninja Foodi Grill and lock the lid.
6. Cook on "AIR CRISP" mode for 7 minutes at 375 degrees F.

Serving Suggestion: Serve warm.
Variation Tip: use chopped dill for taste.
Nutritional Information per Serving:
Calories: 94| Fat: 8 g| Carbohydrates: 2 g| Fiber: 0.5 g| Sodium: 209 mg| Protein: 7 g

Bacon-Herb Grit

Prep time: 15 minutes.
Cook time: 10 minutes.
Serves: 4
Ingredients:
- 2 teaspoons fresh parsley, chopped
- ½ teaspoon garlic powder
- ½ teaspoon black pepper
- 3 bacon slices, cooked and crumbled
- ½ cup cheddar cheese, shredded
- 4 cups instant grits
- Cooking spray

Preparation:
1. Start by mixing the first seven ingredients in a suitable bowl.
2. Spread this mixture in a 10-inch baking pan and refrigerate for 1 hour.
3. Flip the pan on a plate and cut the grits mixture into 4 triangles.
4. Preheat the Ninja Foodi Grill on the "Grill Mode" at MEDIUM-temperature settings.
5. When the grill is preheated, open its hood and place the grit slices in it.
6. Cover the grill's hood and grill for 5 minutes per side.
7. Serve warm.
Serving Suggestion: Serve these grits with hot sauce or any other tangy sauce you like.
Variation Tip: Add sautéed ground chicken or pork.
Nutritional Information Per Serving:
Calories 197 | Fat 15g |Sodium 548mg | Carbs 59g | Fiber 4g | Sugar 1g | Protein 7.9g

Cinnamon Oatmeal

Prep time: 10 minutes
Cook time: 30 minutes
Serves: 8
Ingredients:
- 2 eggs
- 3 cups rolled oats
- ¼ cup butter, melted
- ½ cup maple syrup
- 1 ½ cups unsweetened almond milk
- 1 teaspoon ground cinnamon
- 1 teaspoon vanilla
- 1 ½ teaspoon baking powder
- Pinch of salt

Directions:
1. Place the cooking pot in the Ninja Foodi Grill main unit.
2. In a bowl, whisk eggs with milk, cinnamon, vanilla, baking powder, butter, maple syrup and salt. Add oats and stir well.
3. Pour oat mixture into the greased baking pan.
4. Press Bake mode, set the temperature to 350°F, and set time to 30 minutes. Press Start.
5. Once Ninja Foodi Grill is preheated then place your own baking pan in the cooking pot.
6. Cover with lid and cook for 30 minutes.
Serving Suggestion: Top with some milk and serve.
Variation Tip: You can use any non-dairy milk.
Nutritional Information per Serving:
Calories 245 | Fat 9.5g |Sodium 114mg | Carbs 35.2g | Fiber 3.5g | Sugar 12.2g | Protein 5.7g

Spinach Tater Tot Casserole

Prep time: 10 minutes
Cook time: 40 minutes
Serves: 8
Ingredients:
- 8 eggs
- 15 ounces frozen tater tots
- 1 ½ cup cheddar cheese, shredded
- 4 ounces fresh spinach, chopped & sautéed
- 1 cup roasted red peppers, chopped
- Pepper
- Salt

Directions:
1. Place the cooking pot in the Ninja Foodi Grill main unit.
2. In a bowl, whisk eggs with pepper and salt. Add cheese, roasted peppers and spinach and stir well.
3. Place the tater tots into the greased baking dish. Pour egg mixture over tater tots.
4. Press Bake mode, set the temperature to 350°F, and set time to 40 minutes. Press START.
5. Once a unit is preheated then place baking dish in the cooking pot.
6. Cover with lid and cook for 40 minutes.
Serving Suggestion: Serve warm.
Variation Tip: Add your choice of seasonings.
Nutritional Information per Serving:
Calories 254 | Fat 16g |Sodium 680mg | Carbs 15g | Fiber 1g | Sugar 680g | Protein 12g

Ninja Foodi Bean

Prep time: 5 minutes
Cook time: 10 minutes
Servings: 4
Ingredients
- Fresh ground black pepper
- Flaky sea salt
- Pinch of pepper
- 1 lemon, juiced
- 2 tablespoon oil
- 1-pound green bean, trimmed
Preparation
1. Take a medium bowl and add the green bean.
2. Mix and stir well.
3. Select the GRILL mode, adjust temperature to MAX and time to 10minutes. Press START/STOP to preheat.
4. Wait until you hear a beep. Transfer beans to the grill grate, cook for 8-10 minutes.
5. Toss well to ensure that all sides cooked evenly.
6. Squeeze a bit of lemon juice on the top.
7. Season with salt, pepper and pepper flakes according to your taste.
8. Enjoy!
Serving Suggestion: Serve with bread.
Variation Tip: use chopped dill for garnish.
Nutritional Information Per Serving:
Calories 100 | Carbohydrates 10g | Protein 2g | Fat 7g | Sodium 30mg| Fiber 4g

Kale and Sausage Delight

Prep time: 10 minutes

Cook time: 10 minutes
Servings: 4
Ingredients
- Olive oil as needed
- 1 cup mushrooms
- 2 cups kale, fine chopped
- 4 sausage links
- 4 medium eggs
- 1 medium yellow onion, sweet
Preparation
1. Open the lid of your Ninja Foodi Grill and arrange the Grill Grate.
2. Pre-heat your Ninja Foodi Grill to HIGH and set the timer to 5 minutes with GRILL mode.
3. Once you hear the beeping sound, arrange sausages over the grill grate.
4. Cook for 2 minutes, flip and cook for 3 minutes more.
5. Take a baking pan and spread out the kale, onion, mushroom, sausage and crack an egg on top. Cook on BAKE mode on 350 degrees F for about 5 minutes more.
6. Serve and enjoy!
Serving Suggestion: Serve with bread.
Variation Tip: use fresh baked vegetables as side.
Nutritional Information Per Serving:
Calories 236 | Carbohydrates 17g | Protein 18g | Fat 12g | Sodium 369mg| Fiber 4g

Butternut Squash with Italian Herbs

Prep time: 5-10 minutes
Cook time: 16 minutes
Servings: 4
Ingredients
- 1 medium butternut squash, peeled, seeded, and cut into ½ inch slices
- 1 tsp dried thyme
- 1 tablespoon olive oil
- 1 and ½ tsp oregano, dried
- ¼ tsp black pepper
- ½ tsp salt
Preparation
1. Add all the Ingredients into a mixing bowl and mix it.

2. Pre-heat your Ninja Foodi by pressing the "GRILL" option and setting it to "MEDIUM.".

3. Set the timer to 16 minutes.

4. Allow it to pre-heat until you hear a beep.

5. Arrange squash slices over the grill grate.

6. Cook for 8 minutes.

7. Flip them and cook for 8 minutes more.

8. Serve and enjoy!

Serving Suggestion: Serve with your favorite drink.

Variation Tip: use chopped dill for garnish.

Nutritional Information Per Serving:
Calories 238 | Carbohydrates 36g | Protein 158g | Fat 12g | Sodium 128mg| Fiber 3g

Stuffed up Bacon and Pepper

Prep time: 10 minutes
Cook time: 15 minutes
Servings: 4

Ingredients

- Chopped parsley, for garnish
- Salt and pepper to taste
- 4 whole large eggs
- 4 bell pepper, seeded and tops removed
- 4 slices bacon, cooked and chopped
- 1 cup cheddar cheese, shredded

Preparation

1. Take the bell pepper and divide the cheese and bacon evenly between them.

2. Crack eggs into each of the bell pepper.

3. Season the bell pepper with salt and pepper.

4. Pre-heat your Ninja Food Grill in AIR CRISP mode with temperature to 390 degrees F.

5. Set timer to 15 minutes.

6. Once you hear the beep, transfer the bell pepper to cooking basket.

7. Transfer your prepared pepper to Ninja Foodi Grill and cook for 10-15 minutes until the eggs are cooked, and the yolks are just slightly runny.

Serving Suggestion: Serve, Garnish with a bit of parsley.

Variation Tip: use chopped dill for garnish.

Nutritional Information per Serving:
Calories: 326| Fat: 23 g| Carbohydrates: 10 g| Fiber: 2 g| Sodium: 781 mg| Protein: 22 g

Epic Breakfast Burrito

Prep time: 5-10 minutes
Cook time: 30 minutes
Servings: 4

Ingredients

- 12 tortillas
- Salt and pepper to taste
- 2 cups potatoes, diced
- 3 cups cheddar cheese, shredded
- 10 whole eggs, beaten
- 1 pound breakfast sausage
- 1 tsp olive oil

Preparation

1. Pour olive oil into a pan over medium heat.

2. Cook potatoes and sausage for 7 to 10 minutes, stirring frequently.

3. Spread this mixture on the bottom of the Ninja Foodi Grill pot.

4. Season with salt and pepper.

5. Pour the eggs and cheese on top.

6. Select BAKE setting. Cook at 325 degrees F for 20 minutes.

7. Top the tortilla with the cooked mixture and roll.

8. Sprinkle cheese on the top side. Add Crisper basket to Ninja Foodi Grill.

9. AIR CRISP the Burritos for 10 minutes at 375 degrees F.

10. Serve and enjoy!

Serving Suggestion: Serve with your favorite sauce.

Variation Tip: use variation with vegetables.

Nutritional Information Per Serving:
Calories: 400| Fat: 20 g| Carbohydrates: 36 g| Fiber: 5 g| Sodium: 675 mg| Protein: 22 g

Energetic Bagel Platter

Prep time: 5-10 minutes
Cook time: 8 minutes
Servings: 4
Ingredients
- 4 bagels, halved
- 2 tbsp coconut flakes
- 1 cup fine sugar
- 2 tbsp black coffee, prepared and cooled down
- ¼ cup of coconut milk
Preparation
1. Take your Ninja Foodi Grill and open the lid.
2. Arrange grill grate and close top.
3. Pre-heat Ninja Foodi by pressing the "GRILL" option and setting it to "MEDIUM.".
4. Set the timer to 8 minutes.
5. Let it pre-heat until you hear a beep.
6. Arrange bagels over grill grate and lock lid.
7. Cook for 2 minutes.
8. Flip sausages and cook for 2 minutes more.
9. Repeat the same procedure to grill remaining Bagels.
10. Take a mixing bowl and mix the remaining Ingredients Pour the sauce over grilled bagels
11. Serve and enjoy!
Serving Suggestion: Serve with sauce.
Variation Tip: add fried egg for taste.
Nutritional Information Per Serving:
Calories 300 | Carbohydrates 42g | Protein 18g | Fat 23g | Sodium 340mg| Fiber 4g

Morning Frittata

Prep time: 10 minutes

Cook time: 10 minutes
Servings: 4
Ingredients
- 4 large eggs
- 4 c cremini mushrooms, sliced
- ½ bell pepper, seeded and diced
- ½ cup shredded cheddar cheese
- ½ onion, chopped
- ¼ cup whole milk
- Salt and pepper to taste
Preparation
1. Add eggs and milk into a medium-sized bowl.
2. Whisk it and then season with salt and pepper.
3. Then add bell pepper, onion, mushroom, cheese. Mix them well.
4. Pre-heat Ninja Foodi Grill by pressing the "BAKE" option and setting it to "400 Degrees F."
5. Set the timer to 10 minutes.
6. Let it pre-heat until you hear a beep.
7. Pour Egg Mixture in your bake pan, spread well.
8. Transfer to Grill and lock lid.
9. Bake for 10 minutes until lightly golden.
10. Serve and enjoy!
Serving Suggestion: Serve warm with tea.
Variation Tip: use your favorite vegetables for taste.
Nutritional Information per Serving:
Calories: 153| Fat: 10 g| Carbohydrates: 5 g| Fiber: 1 g| Sodium: 177 mg| Protein: 11 g

Breakfast Potato Casserole

Prep time: 10 minutes
Cook time: 35 minutes
Serves: 10
Ingredients:
- 7 eggs
- 8 ounces cheddar cheese, grated
- 1 pound sausage, cooked
- 20 ounces frozen hash browns, diced
- ½ cup unsweetened almond milk
- 1 onion, chopped and sautéed
- Pepper
- Salt
Directions:
1. Place the cooking pot in the Ninja Foodi Grill main unit.

2. In a bowl, whisk eggs with milk, pepper and salt. Add remaining ingredients and mix well.
3. Pour egg mixture into the greased baking dish.
4. Press Bake mode, set the temperature to 350°F, and set time to 35 minutes. Press Start.
5. Once a unit is preheated then place the baking dish in the cooking pot.
6. Cover with lid and cook for 35 minutes.
Serving Suggestion: Serve warm.
Variation Tip: You can use any non-dairy milk.
Nutritional Information per Serving:
Calories 446 | Fat 30.7g |Sodium 743mg | Carbs 21.6g | Fiber 2.1g | Sugar 1.7g | Protein 20.2g

Avocado Eggs

Prep time: 15 minutes.
Cook time: 8 minutes.
Serves: 2
Ingredients:
- 2 eggs
- 1 ripe avocado
- 1 pinch of barbecue rub
- Salt and pepper, to taste

Preparation:
1. Slice the avocado in half and remove its pit.
2. Remove some flesh from the center.
3. Drizzle barbecue rub, salt, and black pepper on top.
4. Preheat the Ninja Foodi Grill on the "Grill Mode" at LOW-temperature settings.
5. When the grill is preheated, open its hood and place the avocados in it with their skin-side down.
6. Cover the grill's hood and grill for 8 minutes.
7. Flip the avocados once grilled halfway through.
8. Crack an egg into each half of the avocado.
9. Serve.
Serving Suggestion: Serve the avocado cups with crispy bacon on top.
Variation Tip: Top egg with chopped bell pepper and fresh herbs.
Nutritional Information Per Serving:
Calories 322 | Fat 12g |Sodium 202mg | Carbs 14.6g | Fiber 4g | Sugar 8g | Protein 17.3g

Bistro Breakfast Sandwiches

Prep time: 10 minutes.
Cook time: 12 minutes.
Serves: 2
Ingredients:
- 2 tsp. butter
- 4 large eggs, beaten
- 4 hearty Italian bread slices
- ⅛ tsp. salt
- ⅛ tsp. black pepper
- 4 oz. smoked Gouda, cut in 4 slices
- 1 medium pear, sliced
- 4 strips of Canadian bacon, cooked and sliced
- ½ cup fresh baby spinach

Preparation:
1. Sauté eggs with 1 tsp. butter in a skillet on medium heat.
2. Spread the eggs on top of 2 bread slices.
3. Add black pepper, salt, cheese slices, pear slices, spinach and bacon on top of the egg.
4. Then place the other bread slices on top.
5. Select the "Grill" Mode, set the temperature to MAX.
6. Use the arrow keys on the display to select the time to 8 minutes.
7. Press the START/STOP button to initiate preheating.
8. Once preheated, place the sandwiches in the Ninja Foodi Grill.
9. Flip the sandwiches once cooked halfway through.
10. Slice and serve warm.
Serving Suggestion: Serve the sandwiches with a glass of green smoothie.
Variation Tip: Add some black pepper for more taste.
Nutritional Information Per Serving:
Calories 629 | Fat 33g |Sodium 1510mg | Carbs 44g | Fiber 3.9g | Sugar 3g | Protein 38g

Delicious Banana Bread

Prep time: 10 minutes
Cook time: 40 minutes
Serves: 12
Ingredients:
- 4 ripe bananas, mashed
- ¼ cup butter, melted
- 1 teaspoon baking soda
- 1 teaspoon baking powder
- 1 ¼ cups flour
- 1 teaspoon vanilla
- 1 cup sugar
- ½ teaspoon salt

Directions:
1. Place the cooking pot in the Ninja Foodi Grill main unit.
2. In a mixing bowl, mix flour, baking soda, sugar, baking powder and salt.
3. Add mashed bananas and vanilla and mix until well combined.
4. Pour batter into the greased loaf pan.
5. Press Bake mode, set the temperature to 350°F, and set time to 40 minutes. Press Start.
6. Once a unit is preheated then place loaf pan in the cooking pot.
7. Cover with lid and cook for 40 minutes.
Serving Suggestion: Slice and serve.
Variation Tip: You can also use melted vegan butter.
Nutritional Information per Serving:
Calories 181 | Fat 3g |Sodium 4mg | Carbs 35g | Fiber 1g | Sugar 21g | Protein 1g

Banana Oat Muffins

Prep time: 10 minutes
Cook time: 20 minutes
Serves: 12
Ingredients:
- 1 egg
- 1 cup banana, mashed
- 2 ¼ cups old-fashioned oats
- ½ teaspoon cinnamon
- 1 teaspoon baking powder
- 1 teaspoon vanilla
- ¼ cup honey
- ¾ cup milk
- ¼ teaspoon salt

Directions:
1. Place the cooking pot in the Ninja Foodi Grill main unit.
2. In a bowl, mix oats, cinnamon, baking powder and salt and set aside.
3. In a separate bowl, whisk egg with honey, vanilla, milk and mashed banana.
4. Add oat mixture into the egg mixture and mix until well combined.
5. Pour oat mixture into the greased silicone muffin molds.
6. Press Bake mode, set the temperature to 350°F, and set time to 20 minutes. Press Start.
7. Once a unit is preheated then place muffin molds in the cooking pot.
8. Cover with lid and cook for 20 minutes.
Serving Suggestion: Allow to cool completely then serve.
Variation Tip: You can also use almond milk instead of milk.
Nutritional Information per Serving:
Calories 103 | Fat 1.8g |Sodium 64mg | Carbs 19.9g | Fiber 1.9g | Sugar 8.5g | Protein 3g

Delicious Berry Oatmeal

Prep time: 10 minutes
Cook time: 20 minutes
Serves: 4
Ingredients:
- 1 egg
- 2 cups old-fashioned oats
- ½ cup strawberries, sliced
- ¼ cup maple syrup
- 1 ½ cups milk
- 1 cup blueberries
- ½ cup blackberries
- 1 ½ teaspoon baking powder
- ½ teaspoon salt

Directions:

1. Place the cooking pot in the Ninja Foodi Grill main unit.
2. In a bowl, mix oats, salt and baking powder.
3. Add egg, vanilla, maple syrup and milk and stir well. Add berries and stir well.
4. Pour mixture into the greased baking dish.
5. Press Bake mode, set the temperature to 375° F, and set time to 20 minutes. Press Start.
6. Once a unit is preheated then place the baking dish in the cooking pot.
7. Cover with lid and cook for 20 minutes.
Serving Suggestion: Allow to cool completely then serve.
Variation Tip: Add almond milk instead of milk.
Nutritional Information per Serving:
Calories 461 | Fat 8.4g |Sodium 353mg | Carbs 80.7g | Fiber 10.1g | Sugar 23.4g | Protein 15g

Greek Egg Muffins

Prep time: 10 minutes
Cook time: 20 minutes
Serves: 12
Ingredients:
- 8 eggs
- 1 cup spinach, chopped
- ⅓ cup Feta cheese, crumbled
- ½ cup sun-dried tomatoes, sliced
- 1 tablespoon basil leaves, chopped
- ¼ cup milk
- ½ onion, diced
- Pepper
- Salt

Directions:
1. Place the cooking pot in the Ninja Foodi Grill main unit.
2. In a bowl, whisk eggs with milk, pepper and salt. Add remaining ingredients and stir well.
3. Pour egg mixture into the greased silicone muffin molds.
4. Press Bake mode, set the temperature to 350°F, and set time to 20 minutes. Press Start.
5. Once a unit is preheated then place muffin molds in the cooking pot.
6. Cover with lid and cook for 20 minutes.
Serving Suggestion: Serve warm.
Variation Tip: Add ¼ teaspoon Italian seasoning for more flavor.
Nutritional Information per Serving:
Calories 59 | Fat 3.9g |Sodium 104mg | Carbs 1.5g | Fiber 0.3g | Sugar 1g | Protein 4.7g

Breakfast Skewers

Prep time: 15 minutes.
Cook time: 8 minutes.
Serves: 4
Ingredients:
- 1 package (7 oz.) cooked sausage links, halved
- 1 can (20 oz.) pineapple chunks, drained
- 10 medium fresh mushrooms
- 2 tbsp. butter, melted
- Maple syrup

Preparation:
1. Toss sausages, pineapple, and mushrooms with butter and maple syrup in a bowl.
2. Thread these ingredients on the wooden skewers.
3. Select the "Grill" Mode, set the temperature to MED.
4. Use the arrow keys to set the cooking time to 8 minutes.
5. Press the START/STOP button to initiate preheating.
6. Once preheated, place the skewers in the Ninja Foodi Grill.
7. Cover the hood and allow the grill to cook.
8. Flip the skewers once cooked halfway through.
9. Serve warm.
Serving Suggestion: Serve the skewers with bacon and keto bread.
Variation Tip: Drizzle red pepper flakes on top for a tangier taste.
Nutritional Information Per Serving:
Calories 246 | Fat 20g |Sodium 114mg | Carbs 13g | Fiber 1g | Sugar 10g | Protein 7g

Campfire Hash

Prep time: 10 minutes.
Cook time: 31 minutes.
Serves: 4

Ingredients:
- 1 large onion, chopped
- 2 tbsp. canola oil
- 2 garlic cloves, minced
- 4 large potatoes, peeled and cubed
- 1 lb. smoked kielbasa sausage, halved and sliced
- 1 can (4 oz.) green chiles, chopped
- 1 can (15- ¼ oz.) whole kernel corn, drained

Preparation:
1. Sauté the onion with canola oil in a skillet for 5 minutes.
2. Stir in garlic and sauté for 1 minute then transfer to a baking pan.
3. Toss in potatoes and kielbasa then mix well.
4. Select the "Bake" Mode, set the temperature to 400 degrees F.
5. Use the arrow keys to set the cooking time to 20 minutes.
6. Press the START/STOP button to initiate preheating.
7. Once preheated, place the baking pan in the Ninja Foodi Grill.
8. Cover the hood and allow the grill to cook.
9. Serve warm.

Serving Suggestion: Serve the hash with crispy bread toasts.
Variation Tip: Add chopped tomatoes to the hash before baking.
Nutritional Information Per Serving:
Calories 535 | Fat 26g |Sodium 1097g | Carbs 46g | Fiber 4g | Sugar 8g | Protein 17g

Grilled Honeydew

Prep time: 15 minutes.
Cook time: 6 minutes.
Serves: 4

Ingredients:
- ¼ cup peach preserves
- 1 tbsp. lemon juice
- 1 tbsp. crystallized ginger, chopped
- 2 tsp. lemon zest, grated
- ⅛ tsp. ground cloves
- 1 medium honeydew melon, cut into cubes

Preparation:
1. Mix peaches preserves with lemon juice, ginger, lemon zest, and cloves in a bowl.
2. Thread the honeydew melon on the wooden skewers.
3. Brush the prepared glaze over the skewers liberally.
4. Select the "Grill" Mode, set the temperature to MED.
5. Use the arrow keys to set the cooking time to 6 minutes.
6. Press the START/STOP button to initiate preheating.
7. Once preheated, place the skewers in the Ninja Foodi Grill.
8. Cover the hood and allow the grill to cook.
9. Flip the skewers once cooked halfway through.
10. Serve.

Serving Suggestion: Serve the skewers with muffins on the side.
Variation Tip: Add some salt to season the honeydew.
Nutritional Information Per Serving:
Calories 101 | Fat 0g |Sodium 18mg | Carbs 26g | Fiber 3.6g | Sugar 6g | Protein 1g

Zesty Grilled Ham

Prep time: 15 minutes.
Cook time: 10 minutes
Serves: 4

Ingredients:
- ⅓ cup packed brown sugar
- 2 tbsp. prepared horseradish
- 4 tsp. lemon juice
- 1 (1 lb.) fully cooked bone-in ham steak

Preparation:
1. Boil brown sugar, lemon juice and horseradish in a small saucepan.
2. Soak the ham slices in this mixture and coat well.
3. Select the "Grill" Mode, set the temperature to MED.
4. Press the START/STOP button to initiate preheating.
5. Once preheated, place the ham in the Ninja Foodi grill.
6. Cover the hood and allow the grill to cook.
7. Serve warm.

Serving Suggestion: Serve the ham with crumbled crispy bacon on top and fried eggs on the side

Variation Tip: Soak the ham in salt brine to cure (soak in the juices) overnight, then grill for a juicer texture.

Nutritional Information Per Serving:
Calories 180 | Fat 5g |Sodium 845mg | Carbs 20g | Fiber 0g | Sugar 3g | Protein 14g

Ninja Foodi Breakfast Sausages

Prep time: 10 minutes
Cook time: 20 minutes
Serves: 6

Ingredients:
- 2 teaspoons chili flakes

- 2 teaspoons dried thyme
- 1 teaspoon cayenne
- 4 teaspoons tabasco
- 3 pounds ground sausage
- 1 teaspoon paprika
- 4 teaspoons brown sugar
- 2 teaspoons onion powder
- 6 teaspoons garlic, minced
- Salt and black pepper, to taste

Preparation:
1. Install grill grate in the unit and close hood. Select GRILL, set temperature to HIGH, and set time to 20 minutes for medium-cooked burgers. Select START/STOP to begin preheating.
2. Meanwhile, add ground sausage, tabasco sauce, herbs, and spices in a large bowl. Mix well.
3. Make sausage-shaped patties out of the mixture and set them aside.
4. When the unit beeps to signify it has preheated, and shown Message "Add Food" place patties on the grill grate, gently pressing them down to maximize grill marks.
5. Flip halfway through and take out the sausages.
6. Serve and enjoy!

Serving Suggestions: Serve with bread.
Variation Tip: Brown sugar can be replaced with white sugar.

Nutritional Information per Serving:
Calories: 787 |Fat: 64.5g|Sat Fat: 20.7g|Carbohydrates: 4.2g|Fiber: 0.5g|Sugar: 2.4g|Protein: 44.5g

Ninja Foodi Swiss-Cheese Sandwiches

Prep time: 10 minutes
Cook time: 18 minutes
Serves: 4

Ingredients:
- 6 tablespoons half and half cream
- 2 eggs
- ¾ cup Swiss cheese, sliced
- 1 teaspoon powdered sugar
- 2 teaspoons butter, melted
- 4 bread slices
- ½ teaspoon vanilla extract
- ¼ pound deli turkey, sliced
- ¼ pound deli ham, sliced

Preparation:
1. Insert grill grate in the unit and close hood. Select GRILL, set temperature to MED, and set time to 18 minutes. Select START/STOP to begin preheating.

2. In a separate bowl, combine half and half cream and vanilla essence. Mix thoroughly.
3. Layer ham, turkey, and Swiss cheese slices between 2 slices of bread.
4. Place the remaining bread slices on top and dip them in the egg mixture.
5. When the unit has beeps to signify it has preheated, and the shown message "Add Food "place the sandwich to grill grate. Close hood and grill for 18 minutes.
6. After 9 minutes, flip the sandwich, then close the hood and continue cooking for 9 more minutes.
7. Dish out and top with powdered sugar.
8. Serve and enjoy!
Serving Suggestions: Top with raspberry jam before serving.
Variation Tip: Powdered sugar can be omitted.
Nutritional Information per Serving:
Calories: 260 |Fat: 15.9g|Sat Fat: 8g|Carbohydrates: 10.8g|Fiber: 0.7g|Sugar: 2.7g|Protein: 18.1g

Ninja Foodi Bacon Bombs

Prep time: 5 minutes
Cook time: 7 minutes
Serves: 2
Ingredients:
- 2 eggs, lightly beaten
- 1 tablespoon cream cheese, softened
- ½ cup whole-wheat pizza dough, freshly prepared
- 2 bacon slices, crisped and crumbled
- ½ tablespoon fresh chives, chopped

Preparation:
1. Insert grill grate in the unit and close hood. Select BAKE, set temperature to 350 degrees F. and set time to 6 minutes. Select START/STOP to begin preheating.
2. In the meantime, crack eggs into a nonstick pan and stir-fry for 1 minute.
3. Combine the chives, bacon, and cream cheese in a mixing bowl. Set aside after thoroughly stirring.
4. Cut the pizza dough in half and roll each half into a round.
5. Fill the dough pieces with the bacon mixture and bind the edges with water.
6. When the unit beeps to signify it has preheated and Grill shows "Add Food", place the dough pieces in it and bake for about 6 minutes.
7. Take out, serve and enjoy!
Serving Suggestions: Serve with chopped cilantro on the top.
Variation Tip: Use jalapenos to enhance taste.
Nutritional Information per Serving:
Calories: 216 |Fat: 14.2g|Sat Fat:

5.6g|Carbohydrates: 6.8g|Fiber: 1g|Sugar: 1.1g|Protein: 14.5g

Ninja Foodi Bread and Bacon Cups

Prep time: 12 minutes
Cook time: 10 minutes
Serves: 4
Ingredients:
- 4 bread slices
- 8 tomato slices
- 4 eggs
- ¼ teaspoon balsamic vinegar
- 2 bacon slices, chopped
- 2 tablespoons shredded mozzarella cheese
- ¼ teaspoon maple syrup
- ½ tablespoon fresh parsley, chopped
- Salt and black pepper, to taste

Preparation:
1. Arrange the bread slices in ramekins that have been lightly buttered and topped with tomato and bacon strips.
2. Add cheese, eggs, and maple syrup to the top of the mixture.
3. Drizzle with vinegar and season with salt, pepper, and parsley.
4. In the meantime, place the "Crisper Basket" in the Ninja Foodi Grill's cooking pot and close the hood.
5. Press the "AIR CRISP" button, then set the temperature to 320°F and the timer to 10 minutes.
6. To begin preheating, press START/STOP.
7. When the Ninja Foodi Grill says "Add Food," place the ramekins in the "Crisper Basket."
8. Remove from the oven after around 10 minutes of cooking.
9. Finally, serve and enjoy!
Serving Suggestions: Top with mayonnaise before serving.
Variation Tip: Add chopped bell pepper to enhance taste.
Nutritional Information per Serving:
Calories: 185 |Fat: 11.2g|Sat Fat: 4.2g|Carbohydrates: 7g|Fiber: 0.6g|Sugar: 1.8g|Protein: 14g

Ninja Foodi Breakfast Frittata

Prep time: 15 minutes
Cook time: 10 minutes
Serves: 6
Ingredients:
- 1 cup grated parmesan cheese, divided
- 2 bacon slices, chopped
- 2 tablespoons olive oil
- 12 cherry tomatoes, halved
- 6 eggs
- 12 fresh mushrooms, sliced
- Salt and black pepper, to taste

Preparation:
1. Insert grill grate in the unit and close hood. Select GRILL, set temperature to MED, and set time to 10 minutes. Select START/STOP to begin preheating.
2. Meanwhile, add tomatoes, bacon, mushrooms, black pepper, and salt in a large bowl. Mix well.
3. Take another bowl and beat eggs and cheese in it.
4. When the unit beeps to signify it has preheated and Ninja Foodi Grill shows "Add Food", place the bacon mixture and top with eggs mixture on grill grate. Close hood and cook for 5 minutes.
5. After 5 minutes, flip it, then close hood and continue cooking for 5 more minutes.
6. Dish out and serve hot.
Serving Suggestions: Top with chopped cilantro before serving.
Variation Tip: You can also use canola oil instead of olive oil.
Nutritional Information per Serving:
Calories: 204 |Fat: 13.3g|Sat Fat: 3.6|Carbohydrates: 11.4g|Fiber: 3.3g|Sugar: 7.4g|Protein: 12.7g

Ninja Foodi Cinnamon Buttered Toasts

Prep time: 10 minutes
Cook time: 5 minutes
Serves: 6
Ingredients:
- ½ cup sugar
- 1½ teaspoons vanilla extract
- ½ cup salted butter, softened
- 1½ teaspoons ground cinnamon
- ¼ teaspoon freshly ground black pepper
- 12 whole-wheat bread slices

Preparation:
1. In a large mixing bowl, combine the vanilla, sugar, black pepper, cinnamon, and butter. Mix until you have a smooth batter.
2. Place the bread slices on top of the mixture and set them aside.
3. Meanwhile, in a Ninja Foodi Grill, place the "Crisper Basket" and close the lid.
4. Select "AIR CRISP," set the temperature to 400°F and the timer to 5 minutes.
5. To begin preheating, press START/STOP.
6. Place the bread slices in the "Crisper Basket" and cook for 5 minutes when the Ninja Foodi Grill says "Add Food."
7. Remove from the unit and serve.
Serving Suggestions: Cut the slices diagonally before serving.
Variation Tip: You can omit black pepper.
Nutritional Information per Serving:
Calories: 353 |Fat: 17.3g|Sat Fat: 10.2g|Carbohydrates: 42.1g|Fiber: 5g|Sugar: 20.3g|Protein: 7.5g

Ninja Foodi Eggs with Ham

Prep time: 15 minutes
Cook time: 13 minutes
Serves: 4
Ingredients:
- 4 teaspoons unsalted butter, softened
- 8 eggs, divided
- 4 tablespoons heavy cream
- 6 tablespoons grated parmesan cheese
- ¼ pound ham, thinly sliced
- ¼ teaspoon smoked paprika
- 4 teaspoons fresh chives, minced
- Salt and black pepper, to taste

Preparation:
1. Insert crisper basket in the unit. Select AIR CRISP, set temperature to 320°F, and set time to 13 minutes. Select START/STOP to begin preheating.
2. In the meantime, grease the bottom of a baking pan and arrange the ham pieces on top.

3. In a large mixing bowl, whisk together two eggs, cream, salt, and black pepper. Whisk everything together thoroughly.

4. Pour the mixture over the ham slices and top with the remaining eggs.

5. Sprinkle with paprika, cheese, and chives, then pop the baking pan into the Ninja Foodi Grill's "Crisper Basket" and the shown message "Add Food."

6. Remove from the oven after 13 minutes at 320 degrees F.

7. Cut into slices and serve.

Serving Suggestions: Top with jalapenos before serving.

Variation Tip: Mozzarella cheese can also be used.

Nutritional Information per Serving:
Calories: 393 |Fat: 29.6g|Sat Fat: 15.4g|Carbohydrates: 3.8g|Fiber: 0.5g|Sugar: 0.7g|Protein: 29.7g

Ninja Foodi Pumpkin Bread

Prep time: 15 minutes
Cook time: 25 minutes
Serves: 8

Ingredients:
- ½ cup coconut flour
- 2 teaspoons baking powder
- ½ teaspoon ground cinnamon
- ½ cup chopped pumpkin
- 4 tablespoons unsweetened almond milk
- 1½ teaspoons pumpkin pie spice
- 4 eggs
- 2 teaspoons vanilla extract
- Salt, to taste

Preparation:
1. In a large mixing basin, combine flour, spices, salt, and baking powder. Mix thoroughly.

2. In a separate dish, whisk together the eggs, pumpkin, vanilla essence, and almond milk. Make sure everything is well combined.

3. Mix the two mixes and pour them into the baking dish.

4. Insert crisper basket in the unit. Select "AIR CRISP". set temperature to 350°F, and set time to 25 minutes. Select START/STOP to begin preheating.

5. When it shows "Add Food", place the baking dish in the "Crisper Basket" and cook for 25 minutes at 350 degrees F.

6. Take out the bread and set it aside to cool.

7. Slice and serve.

Serving Suggestions: Serve with maple syrup on the top.

Variation Tip: Coconut flour can be replaced with almond flour.

Nutritional Information per Serving:
Calories: 77 |Fat: 3.3g|Sat Fat: 1.3g|Carbohydrates: 8.1g|Fiber: 3.7g|Sugar: 0.9g|Protein: 4.1g

Grilled BBQ Turkey

Prep time: 5-10 min.
Cook time: 30 min.
Servings: 5-6

Ingredients

- ½ cup minced parsley
- ½ cup chopped green onions
- 4 garlic cloves, minced
- 1 cup Greek yogurt
- ½ cup lemon juice
- 1 tsp dried rosemary, crushed
- ⅓ cup canola oil
- 4 tbsp minced dill
- 1 tsp salt
- ½ tsp pepper
- 1-3 pounds turkey breast half, bone in

Preparation

1. In a mixing bowl, combine all the Ingredients except the turkey. Add and coat the turkey evenly. Refrigerate for 8 hours to marinate.
2. Take Ninja Foodi Grill, arrange it over your kitchen platform, and open the top lid.
3. Arrange the Grill Grate and close the top lid.
4. Press "GRILL" and select the "HIGH" grill function. Adjust the timer to 30 minutes and then press "START/STOP." Ninja Foodi will start pre-heating.
5. Ninja Foodi is preheated and ready to cook when it starts to beep. After you hear a beep, open the top lid.
6. Arrange the turkey over the grill grate.
7. Close the top lid and cook for 15 minutes. Now open the top lid, flip the turkey.
8. Close the top lid and cook for 15 more minutes. Cook until the food thermometer reaches 165°F.
9. Slice and serve.

Serving Suggestion: Serve with grill veggies.
Variation Tip: add red pepper flakes for spiciness.

Nutritional Information per Serving:
Calories: 426|Fat: 8.5g| Carbohydrates: 22g| Fiber: 3g| Sodium: 594mg| Protein: 38g

Sweet and Sour Chicken BBQ

Prep time: 10 minutes
Cook time: 40 minutes
Servings: 4

Ingredients

- 6 chicken drumsticks
- ¾ cup of sugar
- 1 cup of soy sauce
- 1 cup of water
- ¼ cup garlic, minced
- ¼ cup tomato paste
- ¾ cup onion, minced
- 1 cup white vinegar
- Salt and pepper, to taste

Preparation

1. Take a Ziploc bag and add all Ingredients into it.
2. Marinate for at least 2 hours in your refrigerator.
3. Insert the crisper basket, and close the hood.
4. Pre-heat Ninja Foodi by squeezing the "AIR CRISP" alternative at 390 degrees F for 40 minutes.
5. Place the grill pan accessory in the Grill.
6. Flip the chicken after every 10 minutes.
7. Take a saucepan and pour the marinade into it and heat over medium flame until sauce thickens.
8. Brush with the glaze.

Serving Suggestion: Serve warm and enjoy.
Variation Tip: use salt and pepper instead of BBQ sauce for variation.

Nutritional Information per Serving:
Calories: 460| Fat: 20 g| Carbohydrates: 26 g| Fiber: 3 g| Sodium: 126 mg| Protein: 28 g

The Tarragon Chicken Meal

Prep time: 10 minutes
Cook time: 5 minutes
Servings: 4

Ingredients

For Chicken
- 1 and ½ pounds chicken tenders
- Salt as needed
- 3 tbsp tarragon leaves, chopped
- 1 tsp lemon zest, grated
- 2 tbsp fresh lemon juice
- 2 tbsp extra virgin olive oil

For Sauce
- 2 tbsp fresh lemon juice
- 2 tbsp butter, salted
- ½ cup heavy whip cream

Preparation

1. Prepare your chicken by taking a baking dish and arranging the chicken over the dish in a single layer.
2. Season generously with salt and pepper.
3. Sprinkle chopped tarragon and lemon zest all around the tenders.
4. Drizzle lemon juice and olive oil on top.
5. Let them sit for 10 minutes.
6. Drain them well.
7. Insert Grill Grate in your Ninja Foodi Grill, select GRILL mode and set to HIGH temperature.
8. Set timer to 4 minutes.
9. Once you hear the beep, place chicken tenders in your grill grate.
10. Let it cook for 3-4 minutes until cooked completely.
11. Do in batches if needed.
12. Transfer the cooked chicken tenders to a platter.
13. For the sauce, take a small-sized saucepan.
14. Add cream, butter and lemon juice and bring to a boil.
15. Once thickened enough, pour the mix over chicken.
16. Serve and enjoy!

Serving Suggestion: Serve with pita bread.
Variation Tip: use chopped dill for garnish.
Nutritional Information per Serving:
Calories: 263|Fat: 18 g| Carbohydrates: 7 g|
Fiber: 1 g| Sodium: 363 mg| Protein: 19 g

Alfredo Chicken Apples

Prep time: 5-10 minutes
Cook time: 20 minutes
Servings: 4

Ingredients
- 1 large apple, wedged
- 1 tablespoon lemon juice
- 4 chicken breasts, halved
- 4 tsp chicken seasoning
- 4 slices provolone cheese
- ¼ cup blue cheese, crumbled
- ½ cup Alfredo sauce

Preparation

1. Take a bowl and add chicken, season it well.
2. Take another bowl and add in apple, lemon juice.
3. Pre-heat Ninja Foodi by pressing the "GRILL" option and setting it to "MEDIUM" and timer to 20 minutes.
4. Let it pre-heat until you hear a beep.
5. Arrange chicken over Grill Grate, lock lid and cook for 8 minutes, flip and cook for 8 minutes more.
6. Grill apple in the same manner for 2 minutes per side.

Serving Suggestion: Serve chicken with pepper, apple, blue cheese, and Alfredo sauce and Enjoy!
Variation Tip: use pears for variations.
Nutritional Information per Serving:
Calories: 247|Fat: 19 g| Carbohydrates: 29 g|
Fiber: 6 g |Sodium: 853 mg| Protein: 14 g

Hearty Chicken Zucchini Kabobs

Prep time: 10 minutes
Cook time: 15 minutes
Servings: 4

Ingredients

- 1-pound chicken breast, boneless, skinless and cut into cubes of 2 inches
- 2 tbsp Greek yogurt, plain
- 4 lemons juice
- 1 lemon zest
- ¼ cup extra-virgin olive oil
- 2 tbsp oregano
- 1 red onion, quartered
- 1 zucchini, sliced
- 4 garlic cloves, minced
- 1 tsp of sea salt
- ½ tsp ground black pepper

Preparation

1. Take a mixing bowl, add the Greek yogurt, lemon juice, oregano, garlic, zest, salt, and pepper, combine them well.
2. Add the chicken and coat well, refrigerate for 1-2 hours to marinate.
3. Arrange the grill grate and close the lid.
4. Pre-heat Ninja Foodi by pressing the "GRILL" option and setting it to "MEDIUM" and timer to 7 minutes.
5. Take the skewers, thread the chicken, zucchini and red onion and thread alternatively.
6. Let it pre-heat until you hear a beep.
7. Arrange the skewers over the grill grate lock lid and cook until the timer reads zero.
8. Baste the kebabs with a marinating mixture in between.
9. Take out your dish when it reaches 165 degrees F.
10. Serve warm and enjoy.

Serving Suggestion: Serve with ranch sauce.
Variation Tip: use tomatoes with zucchini.
Nutritional Information per Serving:
Calories: 277| Fat: 15 g| Carbohydrates: 10 g| Fiber: 2 g| Sodium: 146 mg

Delicious Maple Glazed Chicken

Prep time: 10 minutes
Cook time: 15 minutes
Servings: 4

Ingredients

- 2 pounds chicken wings, bone-in
- 1 tsp black pepper, ground
- ¼ cup teriyaki sauce
- 1 cup maple syrup
- ⅓ cup soy sauce
- 3 garlic cloves, minced
- 2 tsp garlic powder
- 2 tsp onion powder

Preparation

1. Take a mixing bowl, add garlic, soy sauce, black pepper, maple syrup, garlic powder, onion powder, and teriyaki sauce, combine well.
2. Add the chicken wings and combine well to coat.
3. Arrange the Grill Grate and close the lid.
4. Pre-heat Ninja Foodi by pressing the "GRILL" option and setting it to "MEDIUM" and timer to 10 minutes.
5. Let it pre-heat until you hear a beep.
6. Arrange the chicken wings over the grill grate lock lid and cook for 5 minutes.
7. Flip the chicken and close the lid, cook for 5 minutes more.
8. Serve warm and enjoy!

Serving Suggestion: Serve with chilled wine.
Variation Tip: add pepper flakes for more spice.
Nutritional Information Per Serving:
Calories: 543| Fat: 26 g| Carbohydrates: 46 g| Fiber: 4 g| Sodium: 648 mg | Protein: 42 g

Grilled Orange Chicken

Prep time: 5-10 minutes
Cook time: 10 minutes
Servings: 5-6

Ingredients

- 2 tsp ground coriander
- ½tsp garlic salt
- ¼ tsp ground black pepper
- 12 chicken wings
- 1 tablespoon canola oil

Sauce

- ¼ cup butter, melted
- 3 tbsp honey
- ½ cup orange juice
- ⅓ cup Sriracha chili sauce
- 2 tbsp lime juice
- ¼ cup chopped cilantro

Preparation

1. Coat chicken with oil and season with the spices; refrigerate for 2 hours to marinate.
2. Combine all the sauce Ingredients and set aside. Optionally, you can stir-cook the sauce mixture for 3-4 minutes in a saucepan.
3. Take Ninja Foodi Grill, organize it over your kitchen stage, and open the top cover.
4. Organize the barbecue mesh and close the top cover.
5. Click "GRILL" and choose the "MED" grill function. Adjust the timer to 10 minutes and afterward press "START/STOP." Ninja Foodi will begin pre-warming.
6. Ninja Foodi is preheated and prepared to cook when it begins to signal. After you hear a blare, open the top.
7. Organize chicken over the grill grate.
8. Close the top lid and cook for 5 minutes. Now open the top lid, flip the chicken.
9. Close the top lid and cook for 5 more minutes.

Serving Suggestion: Serve with fresh salad.
Variation Tip: add vinegar instead of lime juice.
Nutritional Information Per Serving:
Calories: 327| Fat: 14g| Carbohydrates: 19g|
Fiber: 1g| Sodium: 258mg| Protein: 25g

Baked Coconut Chicken

Prep time: 10 minutes
Cook time: 12 minutes
Servings: 4

Ingredients

- 2 large eggs
- 2 tsp garlic powder
- 1 tsp salt
- ½ tsp ground black pepper
- ¾ cup coconut aminos
- 1-pound chicken tenders
- Cooking spray as needed

Preparation

1. Pre-heat Ninja Foodi by squeezing the "AIR CRISP" alternative and setting it to "400 Degrees F" and timer to 12 minutes.
2. Take a large-sized baking sheet and spray it with cooking spray.
3. Take a wide dish and add garlic powder, eggs, pepper, and salt.
4. Whisk well until everything is combined.
5. Add the almond meal and coconut and mix well.
6. Take your chicken tenders and dip them in the egg followed by dipping in the coconut mix.
7. Shake off any excess.
8. Transfer them to your Ninja Foodi Grill and spray the tenders with a bit of oil.
9. Cook for 12-14 minutes until you have a nice golden-brown texture.

Serving Suggestion: Serve warm.
Variation Tip: use almond for crunch.
Nutritional Information Per Serving:
Calories: 180| Fat: 1 g| Carbohydrates: 3 g|
Fiber: 1 g| Sodium: 214 mg| Protein: 0 g

Spinach Turkey Burgers

Prep time: 15 minutes.
Cook time: 19 minutes.
Serves: 8
Ingredients:
- 1 tablespoon avocado oil
- 2 lbs. turkey ground
- 2 shallots, chopped
- 2 ½ cups spinach, chopped
- 3 garlic cloves, minced
- ⅔ cup feta cheese, crumbled
- ¾ teaspoon Greek seasoning
- ½ teaspoon salt
- ¼ teaspoon black pepper
- 8 hamburger buns, split

Preparation:
1. Start by sautéing shallots in a skillet for 2 minutes, then add garlic and spinach.
2. Cook for 45 seconds, then transfers to a suitable bowl.
3. Add all the seasoning, beef, and feta cheese to the bowl.
4. Mix well, then make 8 patties of ½ inch thickness.
5. Preheat the Ninja Foodi Grill on the "Grill Mode" at MEDIUM-temperature settings.
6. When the grill is preheated, open its hood and place the 2 patties in it.
7. Cover the grill's hood and grill for 8 minutes.
8. Flip the patties and continue grilling for another 8 minutes.
9. Grill the remaining patties in a similar way.
10. Serve the patties in between the buns with desired toppings.
11. Enjoy.
Serving Suggestion: Serve the burgers with roasted green beans and mashed potatoes.
Variation Tip: Add chopped kale instead of spinach to make the burgers.
Nutritional Information Per Serving:
Calories 529 | Fat 17g |Sodium 422mg | Carbs 55g | Fiber 0g | Sugar 1g | Protein 41g

Barbecued Turkey

Prep time: 15 minutes.
Cook time: 30 minutes.
Serves: 6
Ingredients:
- 1 cup Greek yogurt
- ½ cup lemon juice
- ⅓ cup canola oil
- ½ cup fresh parsley, minced
- 1 (3 lbs.) turkey breast half, bone-in
- ½ cup green onions, chopped
- 4 garlic cloves, minced
- 4 tablespoons dill, fresh minced
- 1 teaspoon dried rosemary, crushed
- 1 teaspoon salt
- ½ teaspoon black pepper

Preparation:
1. Take the first 10 ingredients in a bowl and mix well.
2. Mix turkey with this marinade in a suitable bowl for seasoning.
3. Cover it to marinate for 8 hours of marination.
4. Preheat the Ninja Foodi Grill on the "Grill Mode" at MEDIUM-temperature settings.
5. When the grill is preheated, open its hood and place the turkey in it.
6. Cover the grill's hood and grill for 15 minutes.
7. Flip the turkey and continue grilling for another 15 minutes until al dente.
8. Grill until the internal temperature reaches 165 degrees F.
9. Slice and serve.
Serving Suggestion: Serve the turkey with avocado guacamole.
Variation Tip: Add sweet paprika for a tangy taste.
Nutritional Information Per Serving:
Calories 440 | Fat 14g |Sodium 220mg | Carbs 22g | Fiber 0.2g | Sugar 1g | Protein 37g

Grilled Chicken Wings with Jaew

Prep time: 15 minutes.
Cook time: 30 minutes.
Serves: 4

Ingredients:
Jaew
- ½ cup fish sauce
- 3 tbsp. fresh lime juice
- 2 tbsp. granulated sugar
- 2 tsp. red Thai chile powder
- 1 ½ tsp. toasted sesame seeds

Wings
- ⅓ cup oyster sauce
- ¼ cup Thai seasoning sauce
- 2 tbsp. granulated sugar
- 2 tbsp. vegetable oil
- 1 ½ tsp. black pepper
- 30 chicken wing flats

Preparation:
1. Place the cooking pot in the Ninja Foodi Grill then set a grill grate inside.
2. Mix chile powder, sugar, lime juice, and fish sauce in a bowl.
3. Stir in sesame seeds, and mix well then keep 3 tbsp. marinade aside.
4. Mix the remaining marinade with the chicken in a large bowl.
5. Cover and refrigerate for 30 minutes for marination.
6. Mix the reserved marinade and remaining ingredients in a bowl.
7. Thread the chicken on the wooden skewers and brush the prepared glaze over them.
8. Select the "Grill" Mode, set the temperature to MED.
9. Press the START/STOP button to initiate preheating.
10. Once preheated, place the chicken in the Ninja Foodi Grill.
11. Cover the hood and cook for 10 to 15 minutes per side until golden brown and tender.
12. Serve warm.

Serving Suggestion: Serve the wings with yogurt sauce.
Variation Tip: Coat the chicken with parmesan before cooking.
Nutritional Information Per Serving:
Calories 344 | Fat 13g |Sodium 216mg | Carbs 7g | Fiber 3g | Sugar 4g | Protein 31g

Grilled Chicken with Banana Pepper Dip

Prep time: 15 minutes.
Cook time: 28 minutes.
Serves: 6

Ingredients:
- 3 tbsp. olive oil
- 2 medium banana peppers sliced
- 4 oz. feta cheese, crumbled
- 3 tsp. fresh lemon juice
- ½ tsp. kosher salt
- ¼ tsp. black pepper
- 1 oz. pita bread
- 1 (6-oz.) boneless chicken breast
- 4 grape tomatoes, halved
- 1 small Persian cucumber, halved
- 1 tbsp. red onion, chopped
- 5 pitted kalamata olives, halved
- 2 tsp. torn fresh mint

Preparation:
1. Sauté banana peppers with 1 tbsp. oil in a skillet for 6 minutes.
2. Allow them to cool then blend with 2 tbsp. lemon juice in a blender until smooth.
3. Stir in black pepper and salt then mix well.
4. Rub the chicken with black pepper, salt and oil.
5. Place the cooking pot in the Ninja Foodi Grill then set a grill grate inside.
6. Select the "Grill" Mode, set the temperature to MED.
7. Press the START/STOP button to initiate preheating.
8. Once preheated, place the chicken in the Ninja Foodi Grill.
9. Cover the hood and allow the grill to cook for 7 minutes per side.
10. Transfer the chicken to a plate and cook the pita for 4 minutes per side.
11. Mix tomatoes with other ingredients in a bowl.
12. Slice the chicken and serve with banana pepper dip, pita and tomato mixture.
13. Serve.

Serving Suggestion: Serve the chicken with cucumber salad.
Variation Tip: Add brussels sprouts to the meal.
Nutritional Information Per Serving:
Calories 348 | Fat 12g |Sodium 710mg | Carbs 24g | Fiber 5g | Sugar 3g | Protein 34g

Huli Huli Chicken Wings

Prep time: 15 minutes.
Cook time: 33 minutes.
Serves: 6

Ingredients:
- 1 cup unsweetened pineapple juice
- 1 cup chicken stock
- ½ cup soy sauce
- ½ cup packed light brown sugar
- ⅓ cup ketchup
- 2 tsp. grated peeled fresh ginger
- 1 ½ tsp. garlic, chopped
- 2 lbs. whole chicken wings
- ½ tsp. kosher salt
- 1 (3-lb.) fresh pineapple, peeled and cut into ½ -inch slices
- Sliced scallions

Preparation:
1. Mix pineapple juice, garlic, ginger, ketchup, brown sugar, soy sauce, and stock in a bowl
2. Keep 1 cup of this marinade aside and mix the remaining with chicken in a ziplock bag.
3. Seal the bag, and refrigerate for 3 hours for marination.
4. Remove the chicken from the marinade and season with salt.
5. Place the cooking pot in the Ninja Foodi Grill then set a grill grate inside.
6. Select the "Grill" Mode, set the temperature to MED.
7. .
8. Press the START/STOP button to initiate preheating.
9. Once preheated, place the chicken in the Ninja Foodi Grill.
10. Cover the hood and allow the grill to cook for 15 minutes.
11. Flip the chicken pieces and grill for another 10 minutes.
12. Grill the pineapple pieces for 4 minutes per side.
13. Pour the remaining marinade over the chicken and garnish with scallions.
14. Serve warm with grilled pineapple.
Serving Suggestion: Serve the chicken with fried rice.
Variation Tip: You can add dried herbs for seasoning as well.

Nutritional Information Per Serving:
Calories 373 | Fat 8g |Sodium 146mg | Carbs 28g | Fiber 5g | Sugar 1g | Protein 23g

Kewpie-Marinated Chicken

Prep time: 15 minutes.
Cook time: 25 minutes.
Serves: 6

Ingredients:
- 1 cup Kewpie mayonnaise
- 2 tsp. lime zest
- 1 ½ tbsp. ground cumin
- 1 ½ tbsp. hot paprika
- Kosher salt
- Black pepper
- Two 3-lb. whole chickens, cut into pieces
- olive oil, for brushing

Preparation:
1. Mix mayonnaise with 1 tsp. black pepper, 1 tbsp. salt, paprika, cumin and lime juice and zest.
2. Remove the chicken bones and flatten the meat with a mallet.
3. Cut slits over the chicken and place in a tray.
4. Spread and rub the prepared marinade over the chicken.
5. Cover and refrigerate for 2 hours.
6. Place the cooking pot in the Ninja Foodi Grill then set a grill grate inside.
7. Select the "Grill" Mode, set the temperature to MED.
8. Press the START/STOP button to initiate preheating.
9. Once preheated, place the chicken in the Ninja Foodi Grill.
10. Cover the hood and allow the grill to cook for 15 minutes. Flip the chicken pieces and grill again for 10 minutes.
11. Serve warm.
Serving Suggestion: Serve the chicken with yogurt dip and peas snaps.
Variation Tip: Add grilled zucchini to the recipe as well.
Nutritional Information Per Serving:
Calories 375 | Fat 16g |Sodium 255mg | Carbs 4.1g | Fiber 1.2g | Sugar 5g | Protein 24.1g

Grilled Chicken Thighs with Pickled Peaches

Prep time: 15 minutes.
Cook time: 22 minutes.
Serves: 4

Ingredients:
Peaches
- 6 medium peaches
- 1 ½ cups distilled white vinegar
- 1 cup sugar
- 1 stalk of lemongrass, sliced
- 1 (1-inch piece) ginger, peeled and sliced
- ½ teaspoon whole black peppercorns
- 5 allspice berries
- 2 whole cloves
- 1 (3-inch) cinnamon stick

Chicken
- 1 tablespoon sorghum syrup
- Kosher salt, to taste
- Black pepper, to taste
- 8 bone-in chicken thighs
- ½ cup 1 tablespoon olive oil
- 1 tablespoon red wine vinegar
- 2 garlic cloves, chopped
- ¼ cup parsley, basil, and tarragon chopped
- 4 cups arugula, thick stems discarded

Preparation:
1. Mix 8 cups water with 2 tbsp salt and sorghum syrup in a bowl
2. Add chicken to the sorghum water and cover to refrigerate overnight.
3. Remove the chicken to a bowl, then add garlic, herbs, 1 tsp pepper, vinegar, and ½ cup olive oil.
4. Preheat the Ninja Foodi Grill on the "Grill Mode" at MEDIUM-temperature settings.
5. When the grill is preheated, open its hood and place the chicken in it.
6. Cover the grill's hood and grill for 6 minutes per side.
7. Transfer the grilled chicken to a plate.
8. Add water to a saucepan and boil it.
9. Carve an X on top of the peaches and boil them in the water, then cook for 2 minutes.
10. Transfer the peaches to an ice bath, then peel the peaches.
11. Cut the peaches in half and remove the pit from the center.
12. Mix the rest of the ingredients for peaches and 1 ½ cups water in a saucepan.
13. Allow the glaze to cool, and toss in peaches.

14. Cover and refrigerate the peaches overnight.
15. Grill the peaches in the Ninja Foodi grill for 5 minutes per side.
16. Serve the chicken and peaches with arugula.
17. Enjoy.
Serving Suggestion: Serve the peach chicken with a fresh crouton salad.
Variation Tip: Add a drizzle of cheese on top of the chicken after grilling.
Nutritional Information Per Serving:
Calories 545 | Fat 7.9g |Sodium 581mg | Carbs 41g | Fiber 2.6g | Sugar 0.1g | Protein 42.5g

Chicken Kebabs with Currants

Prep time: 15 minutes.
Cook time: 16 minutes.
Serves: 6

Ingredients:
- 2 medium red bell peppers, cubed
- 1 cup dried currants
- 1 (14-ounce) jar sweet pickled red peppers, cubed
- ½ cup of the juices from pickles
- 2 tablespoons olive oil
- Kosher salt, to taste
- 3 pounds boneless chicken thighs, cut into 1-inch strips
- 3 pounds boneless chicken breasts, cut into strips

Preparation:
1. Toss chicken with olive oil, peppers, pickle juices, salt, and currants.
2. Cover and refrigerate the chicken for 30 minutes for marination.
3. Thread the marinated chicken on the wooden skewers.
4. Preheat the Ninja Foodi Grill on the "Grill Mode" at MEDIUM-temperature settings.
5. When the grill is preheated, open its hood and place the skewers in it.
6. Cover the grill's hood and grill for 8 minutes per side.
7. Serve warm.
Serving Suggestion: Serve the chicken kebabs with steaming white rice.
Variation Tip: Add 1 tablespoon lemon juice to the seasoning and marinate.
Nutritional Information Per Serving:
Calories 361 | Fat 16g |Sodium 189mg | Carbs 19.3g | Fiber 0.3g | Sugar 18.2g | Protein 33.3g

Piri Piri Chicken

Prep time: 15 minutes.
Cook time: 8 minutes.
Serves: 2
Ingredients:
- 1 small red bell pepper, chopped
- ½ cup cilantro leaves
- 1 small shallot, chopped
- 2 tablespoons red wine vinegar
- 2 tablespoons olive oil
- 1 tablespoon paprika
- 2 garlic cloves, crushed
- 2 Piri Piri chiles stemmed
- 1 ½ teaspoons dried oregano
- 1 tablespoon kosher salt
- 1 ¼ pounds chicken pieces
- Canola oil for brushing
- 1-pound Shishito peppers

Preparation:
1. Mix chicken piece with rest of the ingredients in a bowl.
2. Cover and refrigerate the chicken for 30 minutes for marination.
3. Preheat the Ninja Foodi Grill on the "Grill Mode" at MEDIUM-temperature settings.
4. When the grill is preheated, open its hood and place the chicken in it.
5. Cover the grill's hood and grill for 4 minutes per side.
6. Serve warm.

Serving Suggestion: Serve the chicken with roasted veggies on the side.
Variation Tip: Add sweet paprika for more taste.
Nutritional Information Per Serving:
Calories 334 | Fat 16g |Sodium 462mg | Carbs 31g | Fiber 0.4g | Sugar 3g | Protein 35.3g

Grilled Chicken with Grapes

Prep time: 15 minutes.
Cook time: 35 minutes.
Serves: 6
Ingredients:
- 1 cup whole buttermilk
- 1 cup water
- ½ cup yellow onion, sliced
- 2 tablespoons light brown sugar
- 1 ½ tablespoons hot sauce
- 1 tablespoon salt
- 1 teaspoon black pepper
- 3 garlic cloves, smashed
- 3 boneless, skin-on chicken breasts
- 6 boneless, skin-on chicken thighs
- 1-pound Bronx grapes, separated into small clusters

Preparation:
1. Mix chicken with the rest of the ingredients except the grapes.
2. Cover and marinate the chicken for 30 minutes in the refrigerator.
3. Preheat the Ninja Foodi Grill on the "Grill Mode" at MEDIUM-temperature settings.
4. When the grill is preheated, open its hood and place the chicken in it.
5. Cover the grill's hood and grill for 25 minutes.
6. Flip the chicken once cooked halfway through.
7. Grill the grapes for 5 minutes per side until slightly charred.
8. Serve chicken with grilled grapes.
9. Enjoy.

Serving Suggestion: Serve the chicken with tomato sauce and toasted bread slices.
Variation Tip: Add butter sauce on top of the chicken before cooking.
Nutritional Information Per Serving:
Calories 419 | Fat 13g |Sodium 432mg | Carbs 9.1g | Fiber 3g | Sugar 1g | Protein 33g

Grilled Chicken with Mustard Barbecue Sauce

Prep time: 15 minutes.
Cook time: 20 minutes.
Serves: 4
Ingredients:
- 2 tbsp. olive oil
- ¼ cup apple cider vinegar
- ¼ cup light brown sugar
- 2 tbsp. honey
- 2 tsp. Worcestershire sauce
- 1 tsp. garlic powder
- 1 tsp. paprika
- ¼ tsp. cayenne pepper
- ½ cup 2 tbsp. mustard
- 6 lb. bone-in chicken breasts
- Kosher salt
- 2 large sweet onions, sliced
- 1 (15-oz.) jar pickled green beans
- 2 lb. tomatoes, sliced into rounds

Preparation:
1. Mix the oil, vinegar, sugar, honey, Worcestershire sauce, garlic powder, paprika, cayenne, and ½ cup mustard in a bowl.
2. Rub the chicken with 2 tbsp. salt.
3. Place the cooking pot in the Ninja Foodi Grill then set a grill grate inside.
4. Select the "Grill" Mode, set the temperature to MED.
5. Press the START/STOP button to initiate preheating.
6. Once preheated, place the chicken in the Ninja Foodi Grill.
7. Cover the hood and cook for 10 minutes per side.
8. Meanwhile, mix rest of the tomato salad ingredients (mustard, onions, green beans and tomatoes) in a bowl.
9. Serve the grilled chicken with this salad.

10. Enjoy.
Serving Suggestion: Serve the chicken with garlic butter and sautéed broccoli.
Variation Tip: Drizzle paprika on top for more spice.
Nutritional Information Per Serving:
Calories 401 | Fat 7g | Sodium 269mg | Carbs 25g | Fiber 4g | Sugar 12g | Protein 26g

Peruvian Chicken Skewers

Prep time: 15 minutes.
Cook time: 10 minutes.
Serves: 4
Ingredients:
- ½ cup ají panca paste
- 5 tbsp. olive oil
- 3 tbsp. red wine vinegar
- 2 tbsp. gochujang
- 1 tbsp. tamari or soy sauce
- 1 ½ tsp. toasted cumin seeds
- ¼ tsp. dried Mexican oregano
- ⅛ tsp. black pepper
- 1 large garlic clove
- 1 ½ lbs. boneless chicken thighs, cut into cubes
- Huacatay Dipping Sauce

Preparation:
1. Mix chicken cubes with gochujang and other ingredients in a bowl.
2. Cover and refrigerate for 30 minutes then thread the chicken on the wooden skewers.
3. Place the cooking pot in the Ninja Foodi Grill then set a grill grate inside.
4. Select the "Grill" Mode, set the temperature to MED.
5. Press the START/STOP button to initiate preheating.
6. Once preheated, place the chicken in the Ninja Foodi Smart XL Grill.
7. Cover the hood and allow the grill to cook for 10 minutes, flipping halfway through.
8. Serve warm with dipping sauce.
Serving Suggestion: Serve the chicken with roasted cauliflower mash.
Variation Tip: Add some BBQ sauce to the seasoning.
Nutritional Information Per Serving:
Calories 329 | Fat 5g | Sodium 510mg | Carbs 17g | Fiber 5g | Sugar 4g | Protein 21g

Grilled Wild Duck Breast

Prep time: 15 minutes.
Cook time: 10 minutes.
Serves: 8

Ingredients:
- ¼ cup Worcestershire sauce
- 2 tbsp. olive oil
- ½ tsp. hot sauce
- 2 tbsp. garlic, minced
- ¼ tsp. black pepper
- 8 boned duck breast halves

Preparation:
1. Place duck breasts in a tray.
2. Mix oil and rest of the ingredients together and then pour over the duck.
3. Rub well and cover to refrigerate for 30 minutes.
4. Place the cooking pot in the Ninja Foodi Grill then set a grill grate inside.
5. Select the "Grill" Mode, set the temperature to MED.
6. Press the START/STOP button to initiate preheating.
7. Once preheated, place the chicken in the Ninja Foodi Grill.
8. Cover the hood and cook for 5 minutes per side.
9. Serve warm.

Serving Suggestion: Serve the duck with a kale salad on the side.
Variation Tip: Add lemon juice for a refreshing taste.
Nutritional Information Per Serving:
Calories 297 | Fat 25g |Sodium 122mg | Carbs 23g | Fiber 0.4g | Sugar 1g | Protein 43g

Spice-Rubbed Duck Breast

Prep time: 15 minutes.
Cook time: 24 minutes.
Serves: 4

Ingredients:
- 2 cups orange juice
- 1 pint blackberries
- 1 tbsp. dry mustard
- 1 tbsp. sweet paprika
- 1 tsp. ground chile de arbol
- ½ tsp. ground cinnamon
- ½ tsp. five-spice powder
- ½ tsp. ground coriander
- 4 duck breasts
- Kosher salt
- Freshly ground black pepper
- Olive oil

Preparation:
1. Boil orange juice and black berries in a saucepan and cook for 10 minutes stirring it occasionally.
2. Stir in the rest of the spices to this sauce, mix well and allow it to cool.
3. Place duck breasts in a tray then pour the sauce over the duck breasts.
4. Rub well and cover and refrigerate for 30 minutes.
5. Place the cooking pot in the Ninja Foodi Grill then set a grill grate inside.
6. Select the "Grill" Mode, set the temperature to MED.
7. Press the START/STOP button to initiate preheating.
8. Once preheated, place the chicken in the Ninja Foodi Grill.
9. Cover the hood and cook for 7 minutes per side.
10. Serve warm.

Serving Suggestion: Serve the duck with fresh kale salad.
Variation Tip: Add shredded cheese to the duck.
Nutritional Information Per Serving:
Calories 440 | Fat 5g |Sodium 244mg | Carbs 16g | Fiber 1g | Sugar 1g | Protein 27g

Chicken Breasts with Pineapple Relish

Prep time: 15 minutes.
Cook time: 15 minutes.
Serves: 4

Ingredients:
Marinade
- 1 ripe pineapple, peeled but left whole

- 1 jalapeño chile
- ½ red onion
- ½ cup vinegar
- 1 tbsp. roasted garlic
- 1 tbsp. salt
- 4 boneless chicken breasts

Grilled Pineapple Relish
- ½ peeled pineapple, chopped
- Oil, for coating
- Honey, for coating
- Salt, for seasoning
- 1 jalapeño chile
- ½ red onion, peeled and halved
- ¼ cup vinegar
- ½ cup cilantro leaves, chopped

Preparation:
1. Blend all the marinade ingredients in a blender and pour over the chicken in a bowl.
2. Mix well, cover and refrigerate for 1 hour.
3. Meanwhile, mix the remaining relish ingredients in a bowl and keep it aside.
4. Place the cooking pot in the Ninja Foodi Grill then set a grill grate inside.
5. Select the "Grill" Mode, set the temperature to MED.
6. Press the START/STOP button to initiate preheating.
7. Once preheated, place the chicken in the Ninja Foodi Grill.
8. Cover the hood and cook for 10 minutes. Flip the chicken and grill again for 5 minutes.
9. Serve the chicken with the relish.

Serving Suggestion: Serve the chicken with parsley on top.
Variation Tip: Coat the chicken with lemon juice for some zest.
Nutritional Information Per Serving:
Calories 418 | Fat 22g |Sodium 350mg | Carbs 22g | Fiber 0.7g | Sugar 1g | Protein 24.3g

Chicken Thigh Yakitori

Prep time: 15 minutes.
Cook time: 10 minutes.
Serves: 4

Ingredients:
- ⅓ cup mild tare sauce
- 3 tbsp. tamari
- 1 ½ tbsp. wasabi paste
- 4 skinless, boneless chicken thighs
- 3 scallions, cut into 1-inch lengths
- Olive oil
- Salt, to taste

Preparation:

1. Mix wasabi with tamari and tare sauce in a bowl.
2. Toss in chicken pieces and mix well to coat.
3. Thread these chicken pieces and scallions over the wooden skewers then drizzle oil and salt.
4. Place the cooking pot in the Ninja Foodi Grill then set a grill grate inside.
5. Select the "Grill" Mode, set the temperature to MED.
6. Press the START/STOP button to initiate preheating.
7. Once preheated, place the chicken in the Ninja Foodi Grill.
8. Cover the hood and allow the grill to cook for 5 minutes per side.
9. Serve warm.

Serving Suggestion: Serve the grilled chicken with cucumber dip.
Variation Tip: Drizzle dried herbs on top and press before grilling.
Nutritional Information Per Serving:
Calories 357 | Fat 12g |Sodium 48mg | Carbs 16g | Fiber 2g | Sugar 0g | Protein 24g

Crispy Cajun Chicken

Prep time: 10 minutes
Cook time: 25 minutes
Serves: 2

Ingredients:
- 2 chicken breasts
- 1 teaspoon Cajun seasoning
- 2 tablespoon mayonnaise
- ¾ cup breadcrumbs
- 1 teaspoon garlic powder
- 1 teaspoon paprika
- Pepper
- Salt

Directions:
1. Place the cooking pot in the Ninja Foodi Grill Main Unit.
2. In a shallow dish, mix breadcrumbs, paprika, garlic powder, Cajun seasoning, pepper and salt.
3. Brush chicken with mayo and coat with breadcrumb mixture.
4. Place coated chicken into the baking dish.
5. Press Bake mode, set the temperature to 400°F, and set time to 25 minutes. Press Start.
6. Once a unit is preheated then place the baking dish in the cooking pot.
7. Cover with lid and cook for 25 minutes.

Serving Suggestion: Serve warm.
Variation Tip: None
Nutritional Information per Serving:
Calories 503 | Fat 18g |Sodium 630mg | Carbs 34.3g | Fiber 2.4g | Sugar 3.9g | Protein 48.2g

Grill Pesto Chicken Breast

Prep time: 10 minutes
Cook time: 30 minutes
Serves: 4
Ingredients:
- 4 chicken breasts, boneless & skinless
- 8 ounces ofMozzarella cheese, sliced
- 1 tablespoon garlic, minced
- 2 tomatoes, sliced
- ½ cup pesto
- 2 tablespoons fresh basil
- Pepper
- Salt

Directions:
1. Place the cooking pot in the Ninja Foodi Grill Main Unit.
2. Place chicken into the baking dish and sprinkle with garlic and basil.
3. Pour pesto over chicken. Arrange tomato slices and cheese on top of the chicken.
4. Press Bake mode, set the temperature to 400°F, and set time to 30 minutes. Press Start.
5. Once a unit is preheated then place the baking dish in the cooking pot.
6. Cover with lid and cook for 30 minutes.
Serving Suggestion: Serve warm with plain rice.
Variation Tip: Add chili flakes for more flavor.
Nutritional Information per Serving:
Calories 587 | Fat 34g |Sodium 698mg | Carbs 7.1g | Fiber 1.3g | Sugar 3.6g | Protein 62g

Balsamic Chicken

Prep time: 10 minutes
Cook time: 25 minutes
Serves: 4
Ingredients:
- 4 chicken breasts, boneless & skinless

- ½ cup Balsamic vinegar
- 2 tablespoons soy sauce
- ¼ cup olive oil
- 2 teaspoons dried oregano
- 1 teaspoon garlic, minced
- Pepper
- Salt

Directions:
1. Place the cooking pot in the Ninja Foodi Grill Main Unit.
2. Place chicken into the baking dish.
3. Mix together remaining ingredients and pour over chicken.
4. Press Bake mode, set the temperature to 400°F, and set time to 25 minutes. Press Start.
5. Once a unit is preheated then place the baking dish in the cooking pot.
6. Cover with lid and cook for 25 minutes.
Serving Suggestion: Serve warm.
Variation Tip: None
Nutritional Information per Serving:
Calories 399 | Fat 23.5g |Sodium 617mg | Carbs 1.6g | Fiber 0.4g | Sugar 0.3g | Protein 42.9g

Marinated Grill Chicken Breast

Prep time: 10 minutes
Cook time: 10 minutes
Serves: 4
Ingredients:
- 4 chicken breasts, boneless & skinless
For marinade:
- ½ cup orange juice
- 1 tsp garlic, minced
- 3 tablespoons olive oil
- ½ teaspoon allspice
- ¾ teaspoon ground nutmeg

Directions:
1. Place the cooking pot in the Ninja Foodi Grill Main Unit then place the grill plate in the pot.
2. Add chicken and marinade ingredients into the zip-lock bag. Seal bag and place in the refrigerator for two hours.
3. Press Grill mode, set the temperature to HIGH, and set time to ten minutes. Press Start.
4. Once a unit is preheated then place marinated chicken on the grill plate.
5. Cover with lid and cook for 10 minutes.
Serving Suggestion: Serve warm.
Variation Tip: Add fresh choppedparsley once cooked.
Nutritional Information per Serving:
Calories 385 | Fat 21.6g |Sodium 126mg | Carbs 3.8g | Fiber 0.2g | Sugar 2.7g | Protein 42.5g

Greek Chicken

Prep time: 10 minutes
Cook time: 20 minutes
Serves: 4
Ingredients:
- 4 chicken breast, boneless and halves
- 3 tablespoons olive oil
- 3 tablespoons capers, rinsed and drained
- 10 olives, pitted and halved
- 2 cups cherry tomatoes
- Pepper
- Salt

Directions:
1. Place the cooking pot in the Ninja Foodi Grill Main Unit.
2. In a bowl, mix tomatoes, capers, olives and oil. Set aside.
3. Season chicken with pepper and salt.
4. Place chicken in the baking dish. Top with tomato mixture.
5. Press Bake mode, set the temperature to 400°F, and set time to 20 minutes. Press Start.
6. Once a unit is preheated then place the baking dish in the cooking pot.
7. Cover with lid and cook for 20 minutes.
Serving Suggestion: Serve warm.
Variation Tip: Add ¼ teaspoon of Italian seasonings.
Nutritional Information per Serving:
Calories 156 | Fat 12.6g |Sodium 345mg | Carbs 4.5g | Fiber 1.7g | Sugar 2.4g | Protein 7.9g

Chicken Cheese Patties

Prep time: 10 minutes
Cook time: 25 minutes
Serves: 4
Ingredients:

- 1 egg
- 1 pound ground chicken
- ⅛ teaspoon red pepper flakes
- 2 garlic cloves, minced
- ½ cup onion, minced
- ¾ cup breadcrumbs
- 1 cup Cheddar cheese, shredded
- 1 cup carrot, grated
- 1 cup cauliflower, grated
- Pepper
- Salt

Directions:
1. Place the cooking pot in the Ninja Foodi Grill Main Unit.
2. Add all ingredients into the bowl and mix until well combined.
3. Make patties from the meat mixture and place in the baking dish.
4. Press Bake mode, set the temperature to 400°F, and set time to 25 minutes. Press Start.
5. Once a unit is preheated then place the baking dish in the cooking pot.
6. Cover with lid and cook for 25 minutes.
Serving Suggestion: Serve warm.
Variation Tip: Add your choice of seasonings.
Nutritional Information per Serving:
Calories 451 | Fat 20g |Sodium 503mg | Carbs 20.9g | Fiber 2.6g | Sugar 4.1g | Protein 44.9g

Mexican Chicken

Prep time: 10 minutes
Cook time: 30 minutes
Serves: 6
Ingredients:
- 4 chicken breasts, skinless & boneless
- 1 ¾ cups Cheddar cheese, shredded
- 1 teaspoontaco seasoning
- 12 ouncesof salsa
- ¼ teaspoon ground cumin
- ¼ teaspoon garlic powder
- Pepper
- Salt

Directions:
1. Place the cooking pot in the Ninja Foodi Grill Main Unit.
2. Place chicken into the baking dish and sprinkle with cumin, garlic powder, pepper and salt.
3. Pour salsa over chicken. Sprinkle cheese on top of chicken.
4. Press Bake mode, set the temperature to 375°F, and set time to 30 minutes. Press Start.
5. Once a unit is preheated then place the baking dish in the cooking pot.

6. Cover with lid and cook for 30 minutes.
Serving Suggestion: Serve warm.
Variation Tip: None
Nutritional Information per Serving:
Calories 334 | Fat 18.2g |Sodium 656mg | Carbs 4.1g | Fiber 0.9g | Sugar 1.9g | Protein 37.3g

Daisy Fresh Maple Chicken

Prep time: 10 minutes
Cook time: 15 minutes
Servings: 4
Ingredients
- 2 tsp onion powder
- 2 tsp garlic powder
- 3 garlic cloves, minced
- ⅓ cup soy sauce
- 1 cup maple syrup
- ¼ cup teriyaki sauce
- 1 tsp black pepper
- 2 pounds chicken wings, bone-in

Preparation
1. Take a medium-sized bowl and add soy sauce, garlic, pepper, maple syrup, garlic powder, onion powder, teriyaki sauce and mix well
2. Add the chicken wings to the mixture and coat it gently
3. Preheat your Ninja Foodi Grill at GRILL mode, setting the temperature to MEDIUM heat and timer to 10 minutes
4. Once you hear a beep, arrange your prepared wings in the grill grate
5. Cook for 5 minutes, flip and cook for 5 minutes more until the internal temperature reaches 165 degrees F
Serving Suggestion: Serve with chilled red wine.
Variation Tip: sprinkle chopped dill for freshness.
Nutritional Information per Serving:
Calories: 543| Fat: 26 g| Carbohydrates: 46 g| Fiber: 4 g| Sodium: 648 mg| Protein: 42 g

Chicken Chili and Beans

Prep time: 10 minutes
Cook time: 15 minutes
Servings: 4
Ingredients
- 1 and ¼ pounds chicken breast, cut into pieces
- 1 can corn
- ¼ tsp garlic powder
- 1 can black beans, drained and rinsed
- 1 tablespoon oil
- 2 tbsp chili powder
- 1 bell pepper, chopped
- ¼ tsp garlic powder
- ¼ tsp salt

Preparation
1. Pre-heat Ninja Foodi by squeezing the "AIR CRISP" alternative and setting it to "360 Degrees F" and timer to 15 minutes.
2. Place all the Ingredients in your Ninja Foodi Grill cooking basket/alternatively, you may use a dish to mix the Ingredients and then put the dish in the cooking basket.
3. Stir to mix well.
4. Cook for 15 minutes.
5. Serve and enjoy!
Serving Suggestion: Serve warm and enjoy.
Variation Tip: add mushroom for freshness.
Nutritional Information per Serving:
Calories: 220| Fat: 4 g| Carbohydrates: 24 g| Fiber: 2 g| Sodium: 856 mg | Protein: 20 g

Grilled Duck Breast

Prep time: 15 minutes.
Cook time: 10 minutes.
Serves: 4
Ingredients:
* 4 large duck or small goose breasts, sliced
* Salt, to taste
* Olive or vegetable oil
* Black pepper, to taste
Preparation:
1. Season the duck breasts with black pepper, salt and oil.
2. Place the cooking pot in the Ninja Foodi Grill then set a grill grate inside.
3.
4. Select the "Grill" Mode, set the temperature to MED.
5. Press the START/STOP button to initiate preheating.
6. Once preheated, place the chicken in the Ninja Foodi Grill.
7. Cover the hood and cook for 5 minutes per side.
8. Serve warm.
Serving Suggestion: Serve the duck with keto bread.
Variation Tip: Add a pinch of sugar to season the duck mildly sweet.
Nutritional Information Per Serving:
Calories 278 | Fat 4g |Sodium 232mg | Carbs 14g | Fiber 1g | Sugar 0g | Protein 21g

Creamy Chicken Breasts

Prep time: 10 minutes
Cook time: 55 minutes
Serves: 4

Ingredients:
* 4 chicken breasts
* ¾ cup Parmesan cheese, grated
* 1 cup sour cream
* 1 cup Mozzarella cheese, shredded
* 1 teaspoon garlic powder
* 1 teaspoon dried basil
* 1 teaspoon dried oregano
* Pepper
* Salt
Directions:
1. Place the cooking pot in the Ninja Foodi Grill Main Unit.
2. Season chicken with pepper and salt and place into the baking dish.
3. Mix together sour cream, Parmesan cheese, Mozzarella cheese, oregano, basil, garlic powder and salt and pour over chicken.
4. Press Bake mode, set the temperature to 375°F, and set time to 55 minutes. Press Start.
5. Once a unit is preheated then place the baking dish in the cooking pot.
6. Cover with lid and cook for 55 minutes.
7. Serve and enjoy.
Serving Suggestion: Serve warm.
Variation Tip: Add ¼ teaspoon of Italian seasonings.
Nutritional Information per Serving:
Calories 574 | Fat 33.2g |Sodium 838mg | Carbs 3.5g | Fiber 0.2g | Sugar 0.3g | Protein 58.3g

Classic BBQ Chicken Delight

Prep time: 5-10 minutes
Cook time: 12 minutes
Servings: 4
Ingredients:
* ⅓ cup spice seasoning
* ½ tablespoon Worcestershire sauce
* 1 tsp dried onion, chopped
* 1 tablespoon bourbon
* 1 tablespoon brown sugar
* ½ cup ketchup
* 1 pinch salt
* 2 tsp BBQ seasoning
* 6 chicken drumsticks
Preparation:

1. Take your saucepan and add listed Ingredients except for drumsticks, stir cook for 8-10 minutes
2. Keep it on the side and let them cool
3. Pre-heat your Ninja Foodi Grill with GRILL mode, set the temperature to MEDIUM heat and timer to 12 minutes
4. Once the beep sound is heard, arrange your drumsticks over the grill grate and brush with remaining sauce
5. Cook for 6 minutes, flip with some more sauce and grill for 6 minutes more
6. Enjoy once done!

Serving Suggestion: Serve with sauce and enjoy.

Variation Tip: use pepper flakes for spiciness.

Nutritional Information per Serving:

Calories: 300| Fat: 8 g| Carbohydrates: 10 g | Fiber: 1.5 g |Sodium: 319 mg| Protein: 12.5 g

BBQ Chicken Drumstick

Prep time: 5-10 minutes
Cook time: 12 minutes
Servings: 5

Ingredients
- ⅓ cup spice seasoning
- ½ tablespoon Worcestershire sauce
- 1 tsp dried onion, chopped
- 1 tablespoon bourbon
- 1 tablespoon brown sugar
- ½ cup ketchup
- 1 pinch salt
- 2 tsp seasoned BBQ
- 6 chicken drumsticks

Preparation
1. Take a deep pan and add all Ingredients except for drumsticks, stir the mixture well.
2. Place it over medium heat, and stir cook for 8-10 minutes.
3. Keep the mix on the side.
4. Pre-heat your Ninja Foodi Grill to "MEDIUM" mode and set the timer to 12 minutes.
5. Once you hear beep, arrange the drumsticks over grill grate and brush half of your prepared sauce.

6. Cook for 6 minutes, flip and brush more sauce, cook for 6 minutes more.

Serving Suggestion: Serve and enjoy once done with any remaining sauce.

Variation Tip: use turkey drumsticks for taste.

Nutritional Information per Serving:

Calories: 342|Fat: 9 g| Carbohydrates: 10 g| Fiber: 2 g| Sodium: 319 mg| Protein: 12 g

Montreal Chicken Sandwiches

Prep time: 15 minutes.
Cook time: 12 minutes.
Serves: 4

Ingredients:
- ¼ cup mayonnaise
- 1 tablespoon Dijon mustard
- 1 tablespoon honey
- 4 chicken breasts, halves
- ½ teaspoon Montreal seasoning
- 4 slices Swiss cheese
- 4 hamburger buns, split
- 2 bacon strips, cooked and crumbled
- Lettuce leaves and tomato slices, optional

Preparation:
1. First, lb. the chicken with a mallet into ½ inch thickness.
2. Now season it with steak seasoning and rub it well.
3. Preheat the Ninja Foodi Grill on the "Grill Mode" at MEDIUM-temperature settings.
4. When the grill is preheated, open its hood and place the chicken pieces in it.
5. Cover the grill's hood and grill for 6 minutes.
6. Flip the chicken and continue grilling for another 6 minutes.
7. Cook the remaining chicken in a similar way.
8. Mix mayonnaise with honey and mustard in a bowl
9. Place the one chicken piece on top of each half of the bun.
10. Top it with a mayo mixture, 1 cheese slice, and other toppings.
11. Place the other bun halve on top.
12. Serve.

Serving Suggestion: Serve the sandwiches with roasted veggies.

Variation Tip: Replace chicken with the turkey meat to make these sandwiches

Nutritional Information Per Serving:

Calories 284 | Fat 25g |Sodium 460mg | Carbs 36g | Fiber 0.4g | Sugar 2g | Protein 26g

Tomato Turkey Burgers

Prep time: 15 minutes.
Cook time: 14 minutes.
Serves: 6

Ingredients:
- 1 large red onion, chopped
- 6 ciabatta rolls, sliced in half
- 1 cup (4 oz.) feta cheese
- ⅔ cup sun-dried tomatoes, chopped
- ¼ teaspoon salt
- ¼ teaspoon black pepper
- 2 lbs. lean ground turkey

Preparation:
1. Take all the ingredients for burgers in a bowl except the ciabatta rolls.
2. Mix well and make six patties out of this turkey mixture.
3. Preheat the Ninja Foodi Grill on the "Grill Mode" at MEDIUM-temperature settings.
4. When the grill is preheated, open its hood and place 2 patties in it.
5. Cover the grill's hood and grill for 7 minutes.
6. Flip the patties and continue grilling for another 7 minutes.
7. Grill the remaining patties in a similar way.
8. Serve with ciabatta rolls.

Serving Suggestion: Serve the turkey meatballs with toasted bread slices.
Variation Tip: Add canned corn kernels to the burgers.
Nutritional Information Per Serving:
Calories 301 | Fat 16g |Sodium 412mg | Carbs 32g | Fiber 0.2g | Sugar 1g | Protein 28.2g

Chicken and Tomatoes

Prep time: 15 minutes.
Cook time: 10 minutes.
Serves: 4

Ingredients:

- 2 tablespoons olive oil
- 1 garlic clove, minced
- ½ teaspoon salt
- ¼ cup fresh basil leaves
- 8 plum tomatoes
- ¾ cup vinegar
- 4 chicken breast, boneless skinless

Preparation:
1. Take the first five ingredients together in a blender jug.
2. Blend them well, then add four tomatoes to blend again.
3. Take chicken in a suitable bowl and pour ⅔ cup of the prepared marinade.
4. Mix well and refrigerate the chicken for 1 hour.
5. Preheat the Ninja Foodi Grill on the "Grill Mode" at MEDIUM-temperature settings.
6. When the grill is preheated, open its hood and place the chicken pieces in it.
7. Cover the grill's hood and grill for 5 minutes.
8. Flip the grilled chicken and continue grilling until it is al dente.
9. Cook the remaining chicken in a similar way.
10. Serve.

Serving Suggestion: Serve the chicken and tomatoes with a kale salad on the side.
Variation Tip: Add lemon juice for a refreshing taste.
Nutritional Information Per Serving:
Calories 335 | Fat 25g |Sodium 122mg | Carbs 13g | Fiber 0.4g | Sugar 1g | Protein 33g

Sriracha Wings

Prep time: 15 minutes.
Cook time: 29 minutes.
Serves: 6

Ingredients:
- 12 chicken wings
- 1 tablespoon canola oil
- 2 teaspoons ground coriander
- ½ teaspoon garlic salt
- ¼ teaspoon black pepper

Glaze
- ½ cup orange juice
- ⅓ cup Sriracha chili sauce
- ¼ cup butter, cubed
- 3 tablespoons honey
- 2 tablespoons lime juice
- ¼ cup fresh cilantro, chopped

Preparation:
1. Season the wings with all their seasoning in a suitable bowl.
2. Mix well, then cover to refrigerate for 2 hours of marination.

3. Meanwhile, prepare the sauce by cooking its ingredients in a saucepan for 4 minutes.
4. Preheat the Ninja Foodi Grill on the "Grill Mode" at MEDIUM-temperature settings.
5. When the grill is preheated, open its hood and place the chicken wings in it.
6. Cover the grill's hood and grill for 15 minutes.
7. Flip the grilled wings and continue cooking for another 10 minutes.
8. Drizzle the prepared sauce over the wings in a bowl.
9. Toss well and serve.
Serving Suggestion: Serve the wings with fresh cucumber and couscous salad.
Variation Tip: Toss the wings, the pork rinds, and the bacon serving.
Nutritional Information Per Serving:
Calories 352 | Fat 2.4g |Sodium 216mg | Carbs 16g | Fiber 2.3g | Sugar 1.2g | Protein 27g

Bourbon Drumsticks

Prep time: 15 minutes.
Cook time: 40 minutes.
Serves: 6
Ingredients:
- 1 cup ketchup
- 2 tablespoons brown sugar
- 12 chicken drumsticks
- 2 tablespoons bourbon
- 4 teaspoons barbecue seasoning
- 1 tablespoon Worcestershire sauce
- ⅔ cup Dr. Pepper spice
- 2 teaspoons dried minced onion
- ⅛ teaspoon salt
- ¼ teaspoon celery salt, optional
Preparation:
1. Take the first eight ingredients in a saucepan.
2. Stir cook for 10 minutes on a simmer until the sauce thickens.
3. Preheat the Ninja Foodi Grill on the "Grill Mode" at MEDIUM-temperature settings.
4. Place 6 drumsticks in the Ninja Foodi grill and brush it with the sauce.
5. Cover the grill's hood and grill for 10 minutes.
6. Flip the grilled chicken and baste it with the remaining sauce.
7. Continue grilling for another 10 minutes until al dente.
8. Cook the remaining drumsticks in a similar way.
9. Garnish with remaining sauce on top.
10. Serve.

Serving Suggestion: Serve the drumsticks with fresh herbs on top and a bowl of steamed rice.
Variation Tip: Use honey or maple syrup for the marinade.
Nutritional Information Per Serving:
Calories 388 | Fat 8g |Sodium 611mg | Carbs 8g | Fiber 0g | Sugar 4g | Protein 13g

Chicken with Grilled Apples

Prep time: 15 minutes.
Cook time: 20 minutes.
Serves: 4
Ingredients:
- 4 chicken breasts, halved
- 4 teaspoons chicken seasoning
- 1 large apple, wedged
- 1 tablespoon lemon juice
- 4 slices provolone cheese
- ½ cup Alfredo sauce
- ¼ cup blue cheese, crumbled
Preparation:
1. Take chicken in a bowl and season it with chicken seasoning.
2. Toss apple with lemon juice in another small bowl.
3. Preheat the Ninja Foodi Grill on the "Grill Mode" at MEDIUM-temperature settings.
4. When the grill is preheated, open its hood and place the chicken in it.
5. Cover the grill's hood and grill for 8 minutes.
6. Flip the grilled chicken and continue cooking for another 8 minutes.
7. Now grill the apple in the same grill for 2 minutes per side.
8. Serve the chicken with apple, blue cheese, and alfredo sauce.
9. Enjoy.
Serving Suggestion: Serve the chicken with apples with white rice or vegetable chow Mein.
Variation Tip: Wrap the chicken with bacon before grilling for more taste.
Nutritional Information Per Serving:
Calories 231 | Fat 20.1g |Sodium 364mg | Carbs 30g | Fiber 1g | Sugar 1.4g | Protein 15g

Turkey Meatballs

Prep time: 10 minutes
Cook time: 20 minutes
Serves: 4
Ingredients:
- 1 egg, lightly beaten
- 1 pound ground turkey
- ¼ cup basil, chopped
- 1 tablespoon lemongrass, chopped
- 1 ½ tablespoon fish sauce
- 1 teaspoon garlic, minced
- ½ cup almond flour
- Pepper
- Salt

Directions:
1. Place the cooking pot in the Ninja Foodi Grill Main Unit then place the Ninja Foodi Crisper Basket in the pot.
2. Add all ingredients into a bowl and mix until well combined.
3. Make balls from the meat mixture and place into the Ninja Foodi Crisper Basket.
4. Press Air Crisp mode, set the temperature to 380°F, and set time to 20 minutes.
5. Cover with lid and press Start.
Serving Suggestion: Allow to cool completely then serve.
Variation Tip: Add some chili flakes for more flavor.
Nutritional Information per Serving:
Calories 327 | Fat 20.6g |Sodium 697mg | Carbs 5.1g | Fiber 1.7g | Sugar 1.6g | Protein 36g

Garlic Butter Chicken Wings

Prep time: 10 minutes
Cook time: 20 minutes
Serves: 2
Ingredients:
- 1 pound chicken wings
- 2 tablespoons butter, melted
- 1 ½ tablespoon ranch seasoning
- 1 tablespoon garlic, minced
- Pepper
- Salt

Directions:
1. Place the cooking pot in the Ninja Foodi Grill Main Unit then place the Ninja Foodi Crisper Basket in the pot.
2. In a bowl, toss chicken wings with butter, garlic, ranch seasoning, pepper and salt. Cover and place in the refrigerator for one hour.
3. Add chicken wings in the Ninja Foodi Crisper Basket.
4. Press Air Crisp mode, set the temperature to 360°F, and set time to 20 minutes.
5. Cover with lid and press Start.
Serving Suggestion: Allow to cool completely then serve.
Variation Tip: Once cooked then sprinkle some grated Parmesan cheese.
Nutritional Information per Serving:
Calories 539 | Fat 28.4g |Sodium 355mg | Carbs 1.4g | Fiber 0.1g | Sugar 0.1g | Protein 66g

Tasty Chicken Drumsticks

Prep time: 10 minutes
Cook time: 25 minutes
Serves: 6
Ingredients:
- 6 chicken drumsticks
- ½ teaspoon ground cumin
- ½ teaspoon garlic powder
- 2 tablespoon olive oil
- ¾ teaspoon paprika
- Pepper
- Salt

Directions:
1. Place the cooking pot in the Ninja Foodi Grill Main Unit then place the Ninja Foodi Crisper Basket in the pot.
2. In a bowl, toss chicken drumsticks with oil, paprika, garlic powder, cumin, pepper and salt.
3. Add chicken drumsticks in the Ninja Foodi Crisper Basket.
4. Press Air Crisp mode, set the temperature to 400°F, and set time to 25 minutes.
5. Cover with lid and press Start.
Serving Suggestion: Serve warm.
Variation Tip: Add your choice of seasonings.
Nutritional Information per Serving:
Calories 120 | Fat 7.4g |Sodium 64mg | Carbs 0.4g | Fiber 0.2g | Sugar 0.1g | Protein 12.8g

Thai Grill Chicken

Prep time: 10 minutes
Cook time: 10 minutes
Serves: 4
Ingredients:
- 4 chicken breasts, boneless & skinless

For marinade:
- 1 ½ tablespoon Thai red curry
- ½ cup coconut milk
- 1 teaspoon brown sugar
- 1 ½ tablespoon fish sauce

Directions:
1. Place the cooking pot in the Ninja Foodi Grill Main Unit then place the grill plate in the pot.
2. Add chicken and marinade ingredients into the zip-lock bag. Seal bag and place in the refrigerator for four hours.
3. Press Grill mode, set the temperature to HIGH, and set time to 10 minutes. Press Start.
4. Once a unit is preheated then place marinated chicken on the grill plate.
5. Cover with lid and cook for 10 minutes.
Serving Suggestion: Serve warm and enjoy.
Variation Tip: None
Nutritional Information per Serving:
Calories 352 | Fat 18g |Sodium 651mg | Carbs 2.7g | Fiber 0.7g | Sugar 2g | Protein 43.3g

Juicy Chicken Tenders

Prep time: 10 minutes
Cook time: 20 minutes
Serves: 4
Ingredients:
- 1 pound chicken tenders
- 2 tablespoons fresh tarragon, chopped
- ½ cup whole grain mustard

- 1 teaspoon garlic, minced
- ½ ounces of fresh lemon juice
- ½ teaspoon paprika
- Pepper
- Salt

Directions:
1. Place the cooking pot in the Ninja Foodi Grill Main Unit.
2. Add all ingredients except chicken to the bowl and mix well.
3. Add chicken tenders to the bowl and mix until well coated.
4. Transfer chicken to a baking dish.
5. Press Bake mode, set the temperature to 400°F, and set time to 20 minutes. Press Start.
6. Once a unit is preheated then place the baking dish in the cooking pot.
7. Cover with lid and cook for 20 minutes.
Serving Suggestion: Serve warm.
Variation Tip: Add your choice of seasonings.
Nutritional Information per Serving:
Calories 241 | Fat 9.5g |Sodium 273mg | Carbs 2.9g | Fiber 0.2g | Sugar 0.1g | Protein 33.1g

Grilled Chicken Breasts with Grapefruit Glaze

Prep time: 15 minutes.
Cook time: 23 minutes.
Serves: 4

Ingredients:
- 2 garlic cloves, minced
- 1 teaspoon grapefruit zest
- ½ cup grapefruit juice
- 1 tablespoon cooking oil
- 2 tablespoons honey
- ½ teaspoon salt
- ¼ teaspoon black pepper
- 4 bone-in chicken breasts

Preparation:
1. Mix garlic, black pepper, salt, honey, oil, grapefruit juice, and zest in a small saucepan.
2. Cook the grapefruit mixture for 5-7 minutes until it thickens.
3. Preheat the Ninja Foodi Grill on the "Grill Mode" at MEDIUM-temperature settings.

4. When the grill is preheated, open its hood and place the chicken in it.
5. Cover the grill's hood and grill for 8 minutes per side.
6. Pour this glaze over the chicken breasts.
7. Slice and serve warm.
Serving Suggestion: Serve the chicken breasts with warmed pita bread.
Variation Tip: Add maple syrup instead of honey.
Nutritional Information Per Serving:
Calories 380 | Fat 8g |Sodium 339mg | Carbs 33g | Fiber 1g | Sugar 2g | Protein 21g

Juicy Greek Turkey Meatballs

Prep time: 10 minutes
Cook time: 25 minutes
Serves: 6
Ingredients:
- 2 eggs
- 2 pounds of ground turkey
- 1 teaspoon fresh mint, chopped
- ½ cup parsley, chopped
- ½ cup onion, minced
- ½ cup breadcrumbs
- 1 teaspoon cumin
- 1 teaspoon oregano
- 1 tablespoon garlic, minced
- ½ teaspoon pepper
- Pepper
- Salt
Directions:
1. Place the cooking pot in the Ninja Foodi Grill Main Unit.
2. Add all ingredients into the bowl and mix until well combined.
3. Make small balls from the meat mixture and place into the baking dish.
4. Press Bake mode, set the temperature to 375°F, and set time to 25 minutes. Press Start.
5. Once a unit is preheated then place the baking dish in the cooking pot.
6. Cover with lid and cook for 25 minutes.
Serving Suggestion: Serve warm.
Variation Tip: Add one tablespoon of fresh chopped basil.
Nutritional Information per Serving:
Calories 362 | Fat 18.7g |Sodium 280mg | Carbs 8.7g | Fiber 1.1g | Sugar 1.2g | Protein 44.9g

Balinese Grilled Chicken

Prep time: 15 minutes.
Cook time: 10 minutes.
Serves: 6
Ingredients:
- 3 tbsp. coconut oil
- 5 garlic cloves, smashed
- 2 tbsp. fresh makrut lime juice
- 1 tbsp. peeled fresh turmeric root, chopped
- 1 tbsp. peeled fresh ginger, chopped
- 1 tbsp. kosher salt
- 1 tsp. tamarind paste
- 1 tsp. ground coriander
- 3 lbs. chicken pieces
Preparation:
1. Place the cooking pot in the Ninja Foodi Grill then set a grill grate inside.
2. Blend coconut oil and all other ingredients except chicken in a food processor.
3. Leave this mixture for 20 minutes then add the chicken and mix well.
4. Cover and marinate the chicken for 1 hour in the refrigerator.
5. Select the "Grill" Mode, set the temperature to MED.
6. Press the START/STOP button to initiate preheating.
7. Once preheated, place the chicken in the Ninja Foodi Grill.
8. Cover the hood and allow the grill to cook for 5 minutes per side.
9. Serve warm.
Serving Suggestion: Serve the chicken with mayonnaise dip.
Variation Tip: Add shredded cheese on top.
Nutritional Information Per Serving:
Calories 380 | Fat 19g |Sodium 318mg | Carbs 9g | Fiber 5g | Sugar 3g | Protein 26g

Ninja Foodi Lemon Turkey Legs

Prep time: 10 minutes
Cook time: 30 minutes
Serves: 4

Ingredients:
- 4 turkey legs
- 4 garlic cloves, minced
- 2 teaspoons fresh lime zest, finely grated
- 2 tablespoons fresh lime juice
- 2 tablespoons fresh rosemary, minced
- 4 tablespoons olive oil
- Salt and black pepper, to taste

Preparation:
1. Toss the turkey legs with the remaining ingredients and chill for about 8 hours.
2. Insert crisper basket in the unit. Select AIR CRISP, set temperature to 350°F, and set time to 30 minutes. Select START/STOP to begin preheating
3. When it shows "Add Food", place the turkey legs and cook for half an hour at 350 degrees F.
4. Flip halfway through and take out when cooked completely.
5. Serve and enjoy!

Serving Suggestions: Serve with ranch sauce.
Variation Tip: Canola oil can also be used.
Nutritional Information per Serving:
Calories: 284 |Fat: 21.3g|Sat Fat: 4.3g|Carbohydrates: 4.1g|Fiber: 1g|Sugar: 0.4g|Protein: 20.2g

Ninja Foodi Glazed Duck Breasts

Prep time: 10 minutes
Cook time: 20 minutes
Serves: 4

Ingredients:
- 2 duck breasts
- 2 teaspoons honey
- 2 tablespoon mustard seeds

- 2 teaspoons vinegar
- Salt and black pepper, to taste

Preparation:
1. In a mixing dish, combine the honey, mustard seeds, vinegar, salt, and pepper. Set aside after thoroughly mixing.
2. Insert crisper basket in the unit. Select AIR CRISP, set temperature to 365°F, and set time to 20 minutes. Select START/STOP to begin preheating
3. After 15 minutes, add the honey mixture and simmer for another 5 minutes.
4. Remove the dish from the oven and serve immediately.

Serving Suggestions: Top with sesame seeds before serving.
Variation Tip: Honey can be replaced with maple syrup.
Nutritional Information per Serving:
Calories: 141 |Fat: 4.8g|Sat Fat: 0.1g|Carbohydrates: 4.9g|Fiber: 0.8g|Sugar: 3.3g|Protein: 19g

Grilled Red Curry Chicken

Prep time: 15 minutes.
Cook time: 30 minutes.
Serves: 6

Ingredients:
- 1 (3-pounds) chicken wings, tips removed
- ¼ cup unsweetened coconut milk
- 2 tablespoons red curry paste
- 1 teaspoon dark brown sugar
- Salt and freshly ground pepper, to taste

Preparation:
1. Mix coconut milk with red curry paste, brown sugar, black pepper, salt in a bowl.
2. Toss in chicken wings and mix well.
3. Cover and marinate the wings for 1 hour in the refrigerator.

4. Preheat the Ninja Foodi Grill on the "Grill Mode" at MEDIUM-temperature settings.
5. When the grill is preheated, open its hood and place the wings in it.
6. Cover the grill's hood and grill for 10 minutes.
7. Flip the wings and grill for 20 minutes.
8. Serve warm.
Serving Suggestion: Serve the curry chicken with a warmed tortilla.
Variation Tip: Add dried herbs to the seasoning.
Nutritional Information Per Serving:
Calories 405 | Fat 20g |Sodium 941mg | Carbs 26.1g | Fiber 0.9g | Sugar 0.9g | Protein 45.2g

Ninja Foodi Spicy Turkey Breasts

Prep time: 15 minutes
Cook time: 35 minutes
Serves: 6
Ingredients:
- 2 turkey breasts
- 2 tablespoons olive oil
- 1 teaspoon garlic powder
- 2 teaspoons red chili powder
- 1 teaspoon red chili flakes
- 1 teaspoon onion powder
- 1 teaspoon cayenne pepper
- Salt and black pepper, to taste

Preparation:
1. Combine the turkey breasts, olive oil, salt, and all of the spices in a mixing bowl. Set aside.
2. Insert crisper basket in the unit. Select AIR CRISP, set temperature to 360°F, and set time to 35 minutes. Select START/STOP to begin preheating
3. When it shows "Add Food", place the turkey breasts in it and cook for 35 minutes at 360 degrees F.
4. Dish out and serve hot.
Serving Suggestions: Top with thyme before serving.
Variation Tip: You can also add some herbs to enhance taste.
Nutritional Information per Serving:
Calories: 62 |Fat: 5.1g|Sat Fat: 0.8g|Carbohydrates: 1.9g|Fiber: 0.5g|Sugar: 0.8g|Protein: 2.7g

Ninja Foodi Roasted Chicken

Prep time: 10 minutes
Cook time: 1 hour
Serves: 1
Ingredients:
- 1 pound whole chicken
- 2 tablespoons dried rosemary
- Salt and black pepper, to taste
Preparation:
1. Insert crisper basket in the unit. Select AIR CRISP, set temperature to 390°F, and set time to 60 minutes. Select START/STOP to begin preheating
2. Season the chicken with salt, pepper, and rosemary in the meantime. Set aside
3. Place chicken in "Crisper Basket" and cook for 1 hour at 390 degrees F when the Ninja Foodi Grill says "Add Food."
4. Remove from the oven and serve immediately.
Serving Suggestions: Top with chopped cilantro before serving.
Variation Tip: You can add melted butter for better taste.
Nutritional Information per Serving:
Calories: 884 |Fat: 34.6g|Sat Fat: 9.7g|Carbohydrates: 4.3g|Fiber: 2.8g|Sugar: 0g|Protein: 131.6g

Ninja Foodi Barbeque Chicken Breasts

Prep time: 5 minutes
Cook time: 22 minutes
Serves: 2
Ingredients:
- 2 chicken breasts, skinless and boneless

- ½ cup barbeque sauce
- 1 tablespoon olive oil
- Salt and black pepper, to taste

Preparation:
1. Season the chicken breasts with salt and pepper, as well as half a tablespoon of olive oil. Set aside
2. Insert grill grate in the unit and close hood. Select GRILL, set temperature to MEDIUM, and set time to 22 minutes. Select START/STOP to begin preheating.
3. When "Add Food" appears, add the chicken breasts and simmer for 10 minutes.
4. Turn the chicken breasts over and brush with the remaining olive oil and barbeque sauce.
5. Remove from the oven after 12 minutes of cooking.
6. Finally, serve and enjoy!

Serving Suggestions: Serve with lime wedges.
Variation Tip: Olive oil can be replaced with corn oil.
Nutritional Information per Serving:
Calories: 420 |Fat: 17.6g|Sat Fat: 3.9g|Carbohydrates: 22.7g|Fiber: 0.4g|Sugar: 16.3g|Protein: 40.5g

Ninja Foodi Marinated Chicken Thighs

Prep time: 15 minutes
Cook time: 30 minutes
Serves: 2
Ingredients:
- 2 chicken thighs
- ¼ cup Italian salad dressing
- ½ teaspoon garlic powder
- ½ teaspoon onion powder
- Salt and black pepper, to taste

Preparation:
1. Sprinkle salt and pepper on the chicken thighs. Set aside.
2. In a mixing dish, combine the Italian salad dressing and the thighs. Toss well to coat.
3. Wrap the bowl in foil and place it in the refrigerator overnight.
4. Take the chicken breasts out of the pan and season them with onion and garlic powder.
5. Insert crisper basket in the unit. Select AIR CRISP, set temperature to 360°F, and set time to 30 minutes. Select START/STOP to begin preheating. Press START/STOP to begin preheating.

6. When it shows "Add Food", place the chicken breasts in "Crisper Basket" and cook for half an hour at 360 degrees F.
7. Flip halfway through and dish out.
8. Serve and enjoy!

Serving Suggestions: Top with chopped cilantro before serving.
Variation Tip: You can omit onion powder.
Nutritional Information per Serving:
Calories: 356 |Fat: 18.7g|Sat Fat: 4.2|Carbohydrates: 4.1g|Fiber: 0.1g|Sugar: 2.8g|Protein: 40.8g

Ninja Foodi Herbed Turkey Breasts

Prep time: 15 minutes
Cook time: 35 minutes
Serves: 6
Ingredients:
- 2 teaspoons dried thyme
- 1 teaspoon dried sage
- 2 tablespoons olive oil
- 2 teaspoons dried rosemary
- 1 teaspoon brown sugar
- 1 teaspoon paprika
- 2 turkey breasts
- Salt and black pepper, to taste

Preparation:
1. Combine the turkey breasts, herbs, olive oil, salt, pepper, and brown sugar in a mixing bowl. Toss well to coat.
2. Insert crisper basket in the unit. Select AIR CRISP, set temperature to 360°F, and set time to 35 minutes. Select START/STOP to begin preheating
3. When it shows "Add Food", place the turkey breasts in "Crisper Basket" and cook for 35 minutes at 360 degrees F.
4. Flip halfway through and take out.
5. Serve and enjoy!

Serving Suggestions: Serve with lime wedges.
Variation Tip: Olive oil can be replaced with corn oil.
Nutritional Information per Serving:
Calories: 60 |Fat: 5.1g|Sat Fat: 0.8g|Carbohydrates: 1.8g|Fiber: 0.5g|Sugar: 1g|Protein: 2.6g

Ninja Foodi Southern Chicken

Prep time: 15 minutes
Cook time: 20 minutes
Serves: 3

Ingredients:
- 2 pounds whole chicken, sliced
- 1 egg, beaten
- ½ teaspoon paprika
- ½ teaspoon garlic salt
- ½ tablespoon fresh parsley, chopped
- 1 cup bread crumbs
- ¼ teaspoon ground cumin
- Salt and pepper, to taste

Preparation:
1. In a separate bowl, whisk together the egg and all other ingredients except the chicken.
2. 2. Dip the chicken pieces in the egg mixture first, then in the bread crumbs. Set aside.
3. Insert crisper basket in the unit. Select AIR CRISP, set temperature to 350°F, and set time to 20 minutes. Select START/STOP to begin preheating
4. . When it shows "Add Food," add the chicken pieces and cook for 20 minutes.
5. Remove the dish from the oven and serve.

Serving Suggestions: Top with butter before serving.
Variation Tip: You can omit garlic salt.
Nutritional Information per Serving:
Calories: 741 |Fat: 25.9g|Sat Fat: 7.1g|Carbohydrates: 26.7g|Fiber: 1.9g|Sugar: 2.5g|Protein: 94.3g

Ninja Foodi Duck Legs with Honey Sauce

Prep time: 10 minutes
Cook time: 20 minutes
Serves: 2

Ingredients:
- 2 duck legs
- 2 teaspoons honey
- 1 teaspoon vinegar
- 1 teaspoon sesame seeds
- 1 teaspoon mustard seeds
- Salt and pepper, to taste

Preparation:
1. In a mixing dish, combine the honey, vinegar, sesame seeds, and mustard seeds. Set aside after thoroughly mixing.
2. Insert crisper basket in the unit. Select AIR CRISP, set temperature to 360°F, and set time to 20 minutes. Select START/STOP to begin preheating
3. Season duck legs with salt and pepper then set them in the "Crisper Basket" when the Ninja Foodi Grill prompts you to "Add Food."
5. Cook for 15 minutes at 360°F and baste the legs with honey sauce.
6. Cook for 5 more minutes and take out when cooked completely.
7. Finally, serve and enjoy!

Serving Suggestions: Top with chopped mint leaves before serving.
Variation Tip: You can add water to make a thin honey sauce.
Nutritional Information per Serving:
Calories: 172 |Fat: 5.7g|Sat Fat: 1.1g|Carbohydrates: 6.8g|Fiber: 0.4g|Sugar: 5.9g|Protein: 22.5g

Ninja Foodi Butter Turkey Legs

Prep time: 5 minutes
Cook time: 30 minutes
Serves: 2

Ingredients:
- 2 turkey legs
- 2 garlic cloves, minced
- 2 tablespoons fresh rosemary, minced
- 2 tablespoons almond oil
- 4 tablespoons melted butter
- Salt and black pepper, to taste

Preparation:
1. Toss the turkey legs with the remaining ingredients and chill for about 6 hours.

2. Insert crisper basket in the unit. Select AIR CRISP, set temperature to 350°F, and set time to 30 minutes. Select START/STOP to begin preheating.
3. Place the turkey legs in it when it Shows "Add Food" and cook for 30 minutes at 350 degrees F.
8. Remove halfway through and flip.
9. Serve immediately and enjoy!
Serving Suggestions: Serve with chopped mint leaves on the top.
Variation Tip: You can add more butter if you want.
Nutritional Information per Serving:
Calories: 487 |Fat: 44.1g|Sat Fat: 18.1g|Carbohydrates: 3.2g|Fiber: 1.5g|Sugar: 0.1g|Protein: 20.4g

Ninja Foodi Herbed Chicken Thighs

Prep time: 5 minutes
Cook time: 18 minutes
Serves: 3
Ingredients:
- 1 teaspoon garlic powder
- 3 chicken thighs
- ¼ teaspoon dried sage
- ½ teaspoon spike seasoning
- ¼ teaspoon onion powder
- 2 tablespoons olive oil
- 1 teaspoon lemon juice
- ½ teaspoon dried basil
- ¼ teaspoon dried oregano
- Salt and black pepper, to taste

Preparation:
1. Combine all of the ingredients in a large mixing bowl and Set aside for 6 hours.
2. In the meantime, in a Ninja Foodi Grill, press the "ROAST" button and set the time to 18 minutes. Set temperature 350 degrees F
3. To begin preheating, press START/STOP.
4. When it says "Add Food," add the chicken thighs and cook thoroughly.
5. Turn halfway through and serve.
6. Finally, serve and enjoy!
Serving Suggestions: Top with mint leaves before serving.
Variation Tip: You can also add spices to enhance taste.
Nutritional Information per Serving:
Calories: 351 |Fat: 19.7g|Sat Fat:

4.2g|Carbohydrates: 1g|Fiber: 0.2g|Sugar: 0.4g|Protein: 40.7g

Ninja Foodi Lemon Pepper Chicken Breasts

Prep time: 10 minutes
Cook time: 20 minutes
Serves: 8
Ingredients:
- 2 tablespoons lemon pepper
- 3 tablespoons garlic powder
- 8 chicken breasts, boneless and skinless
- Salt, to taste

Preparation:
1. Combine the chicken breasts, lemon pepper, salt, and garlic powder in a mixing bowl. Set aside.
2. Insert grill grate in the unit and close hood. Select GRILL, set temperature to MEDIUM, and set time to 20 minutes. Select START/STOP to begin preheating.
3. When the Ninja Foodi Grill Shown "Add Food," put the chicken breasts in, and cook until done.
4. Turn halfway through and serve when cooked completely.
5. Finally, serve and enjoy!
Serving Suggestions: Serve with rice.
Variation Tip: You can also add lemon juice to enhance taste.
Nutritional Information per Serving:
Calories: 281 |Fat: 10.4g|Sat Fat: 2.9g|Carbohydrates: 3.3g|Fiber: 0.7g|Sugar: 0.8g|Protein: 41.2g

Ninja Foodi Crispy Chicken Thighs

Prep time: 5 minutes
Cook time: 18 minutes
Serves: 2
Ingredients:
- 2 chicken thighs

- 2 teaspoons garlic powder
- Salt and black pepper, to taste

Preparation:

1. Season the chicken thighs with salt, pepper, and garlic powder before cooking. Set aside.
2. Insert crisper basket in the unit. Select AIR CRISP, set temperature to 400°F, and set time to 18 minutes. Select START/STOP to begin preheating.
3. When it shows "Add Food", place chicken thighs in it and cook for 18 minutes, flipping halfway through.
4. Remove the dish from the unit and serve immediately.

Serving Suggestions: Serve with melted butter on the top.

Variation Tip: You can add onion powder to enhance taste.

Nutritional Information per Serving:
Calories: 275 |Fat: 10.4g|Sat Fat: 2.9g|Carbohydrates: 2.1g|Fiber: 0.3g|Sugar: 0.7g|Protein: 41g

Ninja Foodi Sesame Chicken Breasts

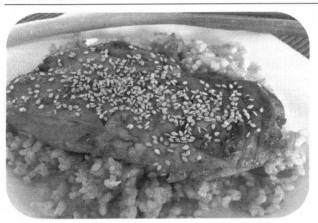

Prep time: 10 minutes
Cook time: 20 minutes
Serves: 4

Ingredients:

- 4 tablespoons sesame oil
- ½ teaspoon cayenne pepper
- 2 tablespoons sweet paprika
- 4 chicken breasts
- 2 tablespoons onion powder
- 2 tablespoons garlic powder
- 2 teaspoons sesame seeds
- Salt and black pepper, to taste

Preparation:

1. Toss the chicken breasts with the remaining ingredients and put them aside.
2. In the meantime, preheat the Ninja Foodi Grill to 380 degrees F and press the "BAKE" button. Make the timer go to 20 minutes.
3. To begin preheating, press START/STOP.
4. Place the chicken breasts in the pan when it says "Add Food" and cook for 20 minutes.
5. Remove the dish from the unit and serve immediately.

Serving Suggestions: Top with chopped mint leaves before serving.

Variation Tip: You can squeeze lemon on chicken breasts to enhance taste.

Nutritional Information per Serving:
Calories: 432 |Fat: 25.3g|Sat Fat: 5g|Carbohydrates: 8.3g|Fiber: 2.2g|Sugar: 2.6g|Protein: 42.4g

Delicious Pot Roast

Prep time: 10 minutes.
Cook time: 6 hours.
Serves: 6

Ingredients
Seasoning Blend
- 2 tsp thyme leaves dried
- 2 tsp sea salt
- 1 tsp black pepper
- 1 tsp garlic powder
- 1 tsp onion powder
- ½ tsp red pepper flakes

Pot Roast Ingredients
- 1-2 Tbsp avocado oil
- 3-41 bs Chuck Roast
- 1 onion
- 4 cups beef stock divided
- ¼ cup flour
- 6 carrots
- 6 small potatoes

Preparation
1. Add the oil to the inner pan of the indoor Grill and preheat on "GRILL" function and set the temperature to "HI" for 10 minutes..
2. Combine the seasoning in a bowl and rub onto both sides of the chuck roast. When the grill has preheated, place the roast on the bottom of the inner pan. Close the lid and grill on high for 5 minutes.
3. Flip and grill another 5 minutes.
4. Cut your onion into chunks and add to the pan. Pour in 2 cups of beef stock and select the ROAST function on 250°F/121°C and set the time for 3 hours.
5. After the 3 hours, remove the meat and make the gravy by combining the remaining beef stock and flour with some of the liquid in the pan into a large glass Mason jar with a lid and shake until well combined.
6. Pour into the pan. Put the roast in along with the vegetables and set the grill to the ROAST setting on 250°F/121°C for another 3 hours.

7. The total cook time will depend on your roast, so start checking it after the 1st hour and give it a flip.
Serving Suggestion: Serve with the vegetables.
Variation Tip: For keto version uses ½ cup of coconut flour for gravy.
Nutritional Information Per Serving:
Calories 658 | Carbohydrates 44g | Protein 52g | Fat 31g | Sodium 156mg| Fiber 6g

Chipotle-Raspberry Pork Chops

Prep time: 10 minutes
Cook time: 10 minutes
Servings: 4

Ingredients
- ½ cup seedless raspberry
- 4 bone-in pork loin chops (7 ounces each)
- 1 chipotle pepper in adobo sauce, finely chopped
- ½ tsp salt

Preparation
1. .
2. In a saucepan, cook and stir and chipotle pepper over medium heat until heated through. Reserve ¼ cup for serving. Sprinkle pork with salt; brush with remaining raspberry sauce.
3. Lightly grease a grill or broiler pan rack. Select the GRILL mode, set the temperature to MAX heat and time to 10 minutes. Select the option START/STOP to begin cooking, flipping occasionally for even cooking.
Serving Suggestion: Serve with raspberry sauce.
Variation Tip: for spice add pepper to your taste.
Nutritional Information Per Serving:
Calories 412 | Carbohydrates 64.3g | Protein 16.1g | Fat 10.1g | Sodium 895mg| Fiber 2g

Steak Pineapple Mania

Prep time: 5-10 minutes
Cook time: 8 minutes
Servings: 4-5

Ingredients

- ½ medium pineapple, cored and diced
- 1 jalapeño pepper, seeded, stemmed, and diced
- 1 medium red onion, diced
- 4 (6-8-ounce) filet mignon steaks
- 1 tablespoon canola oil
- Sea salt and ground black pepper to taste
- 1 tablespoon lime juice
- ¼ cup chopped cilantro leaves
- Chili powder and ground coriander to taste

Preparation

1. Rub the fillets with the oil evenly, and then season with the salt and black pepper.
2. Take Ninja Foodi Grill, arrange it over your kitchen platform, and open the top lid.
3. Arrange the Grill Grate and close the top lid.
4. Press "GRILL" and select the "HIGH" grill function. Adjust the timer to 8 minutes and then press "START/STOP." Ninja Foodi will start preheating.
5. Ninja Foodi is preheated and ready to cook when it starts to beep. After you hear a beep, open the top lid.
6. Arrange the fillets over the Grill Grate. Close the top lid and cook for 4 minutes. Now open the top lid, flip the fillets.
7. Close the top lid and cook for 4 more minutes. Cook until the food thermometer reaches 130°F.
8. In a mixing bowl, add the pineapple, onion, and jalapeño. Combine well. Add the lime juice, cilantro, chili powder, and coriander. Combine again.

Serving Suggestion: Serve the fillets warm with the pineapple mixture on top.

Variation Tip: Add chilies for spicy taste.

Nutritional Information Per Serving:
Calories: 536| Fat: 22.5g|Carbohydrates: 21g| Fiber: 4g|Sodium: 286mg|Protein: 58g

Bourbon Pork Chops

Prep time: 5-10 minutes
Cook time: 20 minutes
Servings: 4

Ingredients

- 4 boneless pork chops
- Ocean salt and ground dark pepper to taste
- ¼ cup apple cider vinegar
- ¼ cup soy sauce
- 3 tbsp Worcestershire sauce
- 2 cups ketchup
- ¾ cup bourbon
- 1 cup packed brown sugar
- ½ tablespoon dry mustard powder

Preparation

1. Take Ninja Foodi Grill, orchestrate it over your kitchen stage, and open the top cover. Orchestrate the flame broil mesh and close the top cover.
2. Click "GRILL" and choose the "MEDIUM" grill function.Press START/STOP to begin preheating.
3. Ninja Foodi is preheated and prepared to cook when it begins to signal. After you hear a signal, open the top.
4. Arrange the pork chops over the grill grate.
5. Close the top lid and cook for 8 minutes. Now open the top lid, flip the pork chops.
6. Close the top lid and cook for 8 more minutes. Check the pork chops for doneness, cook for 2 more minutes if required.
7. In a saucepan, heat the soy sauce, sugar, ketchup, bourbon, vinegar, Worcestershire sauce, and mustard powder; stir-cook until boils.
8. Reduce heat and simmer for 20 minutes to thicken the sauce.
9. Coat the pork chops with salt and ground black pepper.

Serving Suggestion: Serve warm with the prepared sauce.

Variation Tip: use beef for variation.

Nutritional Information per Serving:
Calories: 346| Fat: 13.5g| Carbohydrates: 27g| Fiber: 0.5g|Sodium: 1324mg|Protein: 27g

Grilled Beef Burgers

Prep time: 5-10 minutes
Cook time: 10 minutes
Servings: 4

Ingredients

- 4 pounces cream cheese
- 4 slices bacon, cooked and crumbled
- 2 seeded jalapeño peppers, stemmed, and minced
- ½ cup shredded Cheddar cheese
- ½ tsp chili powder
- ¼ tsp paprika
- ¼ tsp ground black pepper
- 2 pounds ground beef
- 4 hamburger buns
- 4 slices pepper Jack cheese
- Optional - Lettuce, sliced tomato, and sliced red onion

Preparation

1. In a mixing bowl, combine the peppers, Cheddar cheese, cream cheese, and bacon until well combined.
2. Prepare the ground beef into 8 patties. Add the cheese mixture onto four of the patties; arrange a second patty on top of each to prepare four burgers. Press gently.
3. In another bowl, combine the chili powder, paprika, and pepper. Sprinkle the mixture onto the sides of the burgers.
4. Take Ninja Foodi Grill, organize it over your kitchen stage, and open the top cover.
5. Organize the flame broil mesh and close the top cover.
6. Press " ROAST" function at the 350 degrees F for 5 minutes and afterward press "START/STOP." Ninja Foodi will begin pre-warming.
7. Ninja Foodi is preheated and prepared to cook when it begins to blare. After you hear a blare, open the top. Arrange the burgers over the grill grate.

8. Close the top lid and allow it to cook until the timer reads zero. Cook for 3-4 more minutes, if needed.
9. Cook until the food thermometer reaches 145°F. Serve warm.

Serving Suggestion: Serve warm with buns.

Variation Tip: Add your choice of toppings: pepper Jack cheese, lettuce, tomato, and red onion.

Nutritional Information Per Serving:
Calories: 783| Fat: 38g| Carbohydrates: 25g| Fiber: 3g| Sodium: 1259mg| Protein: 57.5g

Steak with Salsa Verde

Prep time: 15 minutes.
Cook time: 18 minutes.
Serves: 2

Ingredients:

- ¼ teaspoon salt
- ¼ teaspoon black pepper
- 1 cup salsa Verde
- ½ cup fresh cilantro leaves
- 1 ripe avocado, diced
- 1 beef flank steak, diced
- 1 medium tomato, seeded and diced

Preparation:

1. First, rub the steak with salt and pepper to season well.
2. Preheat the Ninja Foodi Grill on the "Grill Mode" at MAX-temperature settings.
3. When the grill is preheated, open its hood and place the steak in it.
4. Cover the grill's hood and grill for 9 minutes.
5. Flip and grill for another 9 minutes until al dente.
6. During this time, blend salsa with cilantro in a blender jug.
7. Slice the steak and serve it with salsa, tomato, and avocado.

Serving Suggestion: Serve the steak with sweet potato casserole.

Variation Tip: Add cheese on top of the steak and then bake after grilling.

Nutritional Information Per Serving:
Calories 425 | Fat 15g |Sodium 345mg | Carbs 12.3g | Fiber 1.4g | Sugar 3g | Protein 23.3g

Spinach Salad with Steak & Blueberries

Prep time: 30 minutes
Cook time: 30 minutes
Servings: 4

Ingredients
- 1 cup fresh blueberries, divided
- ½ cup chopped walnuts, toasted
- 1 tsp sugar
- ½ tsp salt, divided
- 3 tbsp fruity vinegar, such as raspberry vinegar
- 1 tablespoon minced shallot
- 3 tbsp walnut oil or canola oil
- 8 cups baby spinach
- 1 pound sirloin steak
- ½ tsp freshly ground pepper
- ¼ cup crumbled feta cheese

Preparation
1. Preheat the grill for eight minutes.
2. Pulse quarter cup blueberries, quarter cup walnuts, vinegar, shallots, ¼ tsp salt, and sugar in a food processor to form a paste. With the running motor, add oil until incorporated. Then transfer the dressing to a big bowl.
3. Sprinkle the steak with pepper and the left quarter with tsp salt.
4. Insert Grill Grate in the unit, select the GRILL mode, set the temperature to MAX heat, and close the hood. Cook the steak for 15 minutes, flipping every 5 minutes for even cooking.
5. Add the spinach to a bowl with the dressing and toss to coat. Divide the spinach among four plates. Slice the steak thinly, crosswise.

Serving Suggestion: Serve top spinach with the feta, steak, and remaining blueberries and walnuts.

Variation Tip: use fresh berries of your choice.

Nutritional Information per Serving:
Calories 412 | Carbohydrates 64.3g | Protein 16.1g | Fat 10.1g | Sodium 895mg| Fiber 2g

Grilled Pork Tenderloin Marinated in Spicy Soy Sauce

Prep time: 20 minutes
Cook time: 140 minutes
Servings: 6

Ingredients
- ¼ cup reduced-sodium soy sauce
- 1 tablespoon finely grated fresh ginger
- 2 tbsp sugar
- 1 large garlic clove, minced
- 1 fresh red Thai chile, minced
- 1 tablespoon toasted sesame oil
- 1½ pounds pork tenderloin, trimmed of fat and cut into 1-inch-thick medallions

Preparation
1. Select GRILL mode, set the temperature to MEDIUM heat and time to 8 minutes.
2. Whisk the soy sauce and sugar in a medium bowl until the sugar is dissolved. Stir in ginger, garlic, chili, and oil.
3. Place the pork in a plastic bag. Add the marinade and then seal the bag, squeezing out the air. Turn the bag for coating the medallions. Refrigerate for two hours, turning bag once to redistribute the marinade.
4. Insert grill grate in the unit and close the hood. Remove the pork. Select the option START/STOP to begin cooking. Cook pork until desire tenderness or until meat reaches to 160°F internal temperature.

Serving Suggestion: Serve hot with cold wine.

Variation Tip: use cayenne Chile pepper for spice.

Nutritional Information Per Serving:
Calories 155.5 | Carbohydrates 24.8g | Protein 3g | Fat 5.4g | Sodium 193.7mg| Fiber 1 g

Lettuce Cheese Steak

Prep time: 5-10 minutes
Cook time: 16 minutes
Servings: 5-6

Ingredients

- 4 (8-ounce) skirt steaks
- 6 cups romaine lettuce, chopped
- ¾ cup cherry tomatoes halved
- ¼ cup blue cheese, crumbled
- Ocean salt and Ground Black Pepper
- 2 avocados, peeled and sliced
- 1 cup croutons
- 1 cup blue cheese dressing

Preparation

1. Coat steaks with black pepper and salt.
2. Take Ninja Foodi Grill, mastermind it over your kitchen stage, and open the top. Organize the barbecue mesh and close the top.
3. Click "GRILL" and choose the "HIGH" function. Change the clock to 8 minutes and afterward press "START/STOP." Ninja Foodi Grill will begin pre-warming.
4. Ninja Foodi is preheated and prepared to cook when it begins to blare. After you hear a blare, open the top cover.
5. Fix finely the 2 steaks on the barbeque mesh.
6. Close the top cover and cook for 4 minutes. Presently open the top cover, flip the steaks.
7. Close the top cover and cook for 4 additional minutes. Cook until the food thermometer comes to 150°F. Cook for 3-4 more minutes if needed. Grill the remaining steaks.
8. In a mixing bowl, add the lettuce, tomatoes, blue cheese, and croutons. Combine the Ingredients to mix well with each other.

Serving Suggestion: Serve the steaks warm with the salad mixture, blue cheese dressing, and avocado slices on top.

Variation Tip: use your favorite steak

Nutritional Information per Serving:
Calories: 576|, Fat: 21g| Carbohydrates: 23g| Fiber: 6.5g|Sodium: 957mg|Protein: 53.5g

Turmeric Pork Chops with Green Onion Rice

Prep time: 15 minutes
Cook time: 15 minutes
Servings: 4

Ingredients

- 4 (6-oz.) bone-in pork chops
- ½ tsp kosher salt, divided
- ½ tsp black pepper, divided
- 3 tbsp olive oil, divided
- 1 large garlic clove, halved
- ½ tsp ground turmeric
- 1 tablespoon fish sauce
- 2 tsp oyster sauce
- 1 tsp tomato paste
- 1 bunch green onions
- 2 (8.8-oz.) packages precooked brown rice
- ¼ cup fresh cilantro leaves
- 1 lime, cut into 4 wedges

Preparation

1. Select the "GRILL" function to "HI" temperature setting.Heat the grill for 8 minutes before use. Rub pork with cut sides of garlic; discard garlic. Sprinkle pork with turmeric, ¼ tsp salt, and ¼ tsp pepper. Combine 2 tsp oil, fish sauce, oyster sauce, and tomato paste.
2. Brush both sides of pork with half of the oil mixture. Grill pork for 4 minutes on each side or until the desired degree of doneness. Transfer to a plate; brush both sides of pork with the remaining oil mixture. Keep warm.
3. Add onions to grill. Over MEDIUM heat, grill for 2 minutes. Coarsely chop onions.
4. Heat rice according to package Preparation. Combine green onions, rice, remaining one tablespoon oil, ¼ tsp salt, and ¼ tsp pepper.

Serving Suggestion: Serve rice with pork. Sprinkle with cilantro; serve with lime wedges.

Variation Tip: can be eat without rice and taste will be marvelous.

Nutritional Information Per Serving:
Calories 412 | Carbohydrates 64.3g | Protein 16.1g | Fat 10.1g | Sodium 895mg| Fiber 2g

Avocado Salsa Steak

Prep time: 5-10 minutes
Cook time: 18 minutes
Servings: 4

Ingredients

- 1 cup cilantro leaves
- 2 ripe avocados, diced
- 2 cups salsa Verde
- 2 beef flank steak, diced
- ½ tsp salt
- ½ tsp pepper
- 2 medium tomatoes, seeded and diced

Preparation

1. Rub the beef steak with salt and black pepper to season well.
2. Take Ninja Foodi Grill, orchestrate it over your kitchen stage, and open the top cover.
3. Orchestrate the flame broil mesh and close the top cover.
4. Press "GRILL" and select the "MEDIUM" temperature setting. Alter the clock to 18 minutes and afterward press "START/STOP." Ninja Foodi will begin pre-warming.
5. Ninja Foodi is preheated and prepared to cook when it begins to signal. After you hear a blare, open the top. Arrange the diced steak over the grill grate.
6. Close the top lid and cook for 9 minutes. Now open the top lid, flip the diced steak.
7. Close the top lid and cook for 9 more minutes.
8. In a blender, blend the salsa and cilantro.

Serving Suggestion: Serve the grilled steak with the blended salsa, tomato, and avocado.

Variation Tip: for spicier steak use cayenne pepper.

Nutritional Information Per Serving:

Calories: 523| Fat: 31.5g|Carbohydrates: 38.5g| Fiber: 2g| Sodium: 301mg| Protein: 41.5g

Sausage and Pepper Grinders

Prep time: 15 minutes
Cook time: 26 minutes
Servings: 6

Ingredients

- 2 bell peppers, cut in quarters, seeds and ribs removed
- Kosher salt, as desired
- Ground black pepper, as desired
- 1 white onion, peeled, sliced in 1-inch rings
- 2 tbsp canola oil, divided
- 6 raw sausages (4 ounces each)
- 6 hot dog buns
- Condiments, as desired

Preparation

1. Select the "GRILL" function and adjust temperature to "LO" and preheat the Ninja Foodi Smart XL Grill for 8 minutes.
2. Insert grill grate in the unit and close the hood.
3. When the unit starts beeping to signal that it has preheated, place steaks on the grill grate. Close hood and cook for 12 minutes.
4. After 12 minutes, transfer the peppers and onions to a medium mixing bowl. Place the sausages on the grill grate; close the hood and cook for 6 minutes.
5. After 6 minutes, flip the sausages. Close the hood and cook for 6 extra minutes.
6. Meanwhile, gently tear up the grilled onions into individual rings and mix them well with the peppers.
7. After 6 minutes, remove the sausages from the Grill Grate. Place the buns, cut-side them down, over the grill grate. Close the hood and cook for 2 remaining minutes.
8. When cooking is done, spread any desired condiments on the buns, then place the sausages in buns.

Serving Suggestion: Serve topped each with onions peppers.

Variation Tip: use your preferred condiments.

Nutritional Information Per Serving:

Calories 155.5 | Carbohydrates 24.8g | Protein 3g | Fat 5.4g | Sodium 193.7mg| Fiber 1g

Korean Chili Pork

Prep time: 5-10 minutes
Cook time: 8 minutes
Servings: 4

Ingredients
- 2 pounds pork, cut into ⅛-inch slices
- 5 minced garlic cloves
- 3 tbsp minced green onion
- 1 yellow onion, sliced
- ½ cup soy sauce
- ½ cup brown sugar
- 3 tbsp regular chili paste
- 2 tbsp sesame seeds
- 3 tsp black pepper
- Red pepper flakes to taste

Preparation
1. Take a zip-lock bag, add all the Ingredients. Shake well and refrigerate for 6-8 hours to marinate.
2. Take Ninja Foodi Grill, orchestrate it over your kitchen stage, and open the top.
3. Mastermind the barbecue mesh and close the top cover.
4. Click "GRILL" and choose the "MED" temperature setting. Modify the clock to 8 minutes and afterward press "START/STOP." Ninja Foodi will begin to warm up.
5. Ninja Foodi is preheated and prepared to cook when it begins to signal. After you hear a signal, open the top.
6. Fix finely sliced pork on the Grill Grate.
7. Cover and cook for 4 minutes. Then open the cover, switch the side of the pork.
8. Cover it and cook for another 4 minutes.

Serving Suggestion: Serve warm with chopped lettuce.

Variation Tip: for spiciness use Korean red chili paste.

Nutritional Information Per Serving:
Calories: 621| Fat: 31g|Carbohydrates: 29g|Fiber: 3g| Sodium: 1428mg| Protein: 53g

Grilled Steak Salad with Tomatoes & Eggplant

Prep time: 40 minutes
Cook time: 40 minutes
Servings: 4

Ingredients
- 1 tablespoon dried oregano
- 1pound flank steak, trimmed
- 1 small eggplant cut lengthwise into ½-inch-thick slices
- 4 tbsp extra-virgin olive oil, divided
- 1 tsp salt, divided
- ¾ tsp freshly ground pepper, divided
- 2 sweet Italian peppers, cut into 2-inch-wide strips
- 2 large tomatoes, cut into wedges
- 1 small red onion, thinly sliced
- 1 small clove garlic, minced
- 3 tbsp red-wine vinegar

Preparation
1.
2. Cook the oregano in a small skillet on medium heat and keep stirring until it is toasted, which will be about two minutes. Transfer it to a bowl.
3. Cut the steak in half, lengthwise; season it with half tsp each salt and pepper. Brush the peppers and eggplant with one tablespoon oil.
4. Insert Grill Grate in the unit and close the hood. Select the option GRILL, set the temperature to LOW, and set time to 30 minutes. Select the option START/STOP to begin preheating.
5. Grill the steak for 30 minutes, flipping halfway for even cooking.
6. Add the tomatoes, garlic, and onion to a bowl with the oregano. Drizzle them with vinegar and the remaining 3 tsp oil. Season them with the remaining half tsp salt and quarter tsp pepper; toss to combine. Chop the eggplant and peppers and cut the steak across the grain into thin slices; add to the bowl and toss to combine.

Serving Suggestion: Serve warm.

Variation Tip: add your favorite veggies for the salad.

Nutritional Information Per Serving:
Calories 177.6 | Carbohydrates 25.5g | Protein 5 g | Fat 8.9g | Sodium 286.5mg| Fiber 2.5g

Chili-Spiced Ribs

Prep time: 15 minutes.
Cook time: 63 minutes.
Serves: 6
Ingredients:
Glaze
- 1 cup of soy sauce
- 1 cup packed brown sugar
- ⅔ cup ketchup
- ⅓ cup lemon juice
- 1 ½ teaspoon fresh ginger root, minced
Ribs
- 6 lbs. pork baby back ribs
- 3 tablespoons packed brown sugar
- 2 tablespoons paprika
- 2 tablespoons chili powder
- 3 teaspoons ground cumin
- 2 teaspoons garlic powder
- 1 teaspoon salt
Preparation:
1. Take the first six ingredients in a suitable bowl and mix well.
2. Rub this mixture over the ribs, then covers them to refrigerate for 30 minutes of margination.
3. Preheat the Ninja Foodi Grill on the "Grill Mode" at MAX-temperature settings.
4. When the grill is preheated, open its hood and place the ribs in it.
5. Cover the grill's hood and grill for 30 minutes.
6. Flip the ribs after every 10 minutes for even cooking.
7. Meanwhile, prepare the sauce by cooking its ingredients for 8 minutes in a saucepan.
8. Pour this sauce over the grilled ribs in the Ninja Foodi grill.
9. Grill for another 5 minutes per side.
10. Serve.
Serving Suggestion: Serve the ribs with mashed potatoes.
Variation Tip: Use BBQ sauce for the change of taste.
Nutritional Information Per Serving:
Calories 305 | Fat 25g |Sodium 532mg | Carbs 2.3g | Fiber 0.4g | Sugar 2g | Protein 18.3g

Raspberry Pork Chops

Prep time: 15 minutes.
Cook time: 14 minutes.
Serves: 4
Ingredients:
- ½ cup seedless raspberry preserves
- 1 chipotle in adobo sauce, chopped
- ½ teaspoon salt
- 4 bone-in pork loin chops
Preparation:
1. Take a small pan and mix preserves with chipotle pepper sauce on medium heat.
2. Keep ¼ cup of this sauce aside and rub the remaining over the pork.
3. Sprinkle salt over the pork and mix well.
4. Preheat the Ninja Foodi Grill on the "Grill Mode" at MAX-temperature settings.
5. When the grill is preheated, open its hood and place the pork chops in it.
6. Cover the grill's hood and grill for 5-7 minutes per side.
7. Grill the remaining chops in the same method.
8. Serve with the reserved sauce.
9. Enjoy.
Serving Suggestion: Serve the pork chops with boiled rice or spaghetti.
Variation Tip: Use apple sauce or maple syrup for seasoning.
Nutritional Information Per Serving:
Calories 361 | Fat 16g |Sodium 515mg | Carbs 19.3g | Fiber 0.1g | Sugar 18.2g | Protein 33.3g

Beef with Pesto

Prep time: 15 minutes.
Cook time: 14 minutes.
Serves: 2
Ingredients:
- 2 cups penne pasta, uncooked
- 2 (6 oz.) beef tenderloin steaks
- ¼ teaspoon salt
- ¼ teaspoon black pepper
- 5 oz. fresh baby spinach, chopped
- 2 cups grape tomatoes, halved
- ⅓ cup pesto
- ¼ cup walnuts, chopped
- ¼ cup feta cheese, crumbled

Preparation:
1. At first, prepared the pasta as per the given instructions on the pack.
2. Drain and rinse, then keep this pasta aside.
3. Now season the tenderloin steaks with salt and black pepper.
4. Preheat the Ninja Foodi Grill on the "Grill Mode" at MAX-temperature settings.
5. When the grill is preheated, open its hood and place the steaks in it.
6. Cover the grill's hood and grill for 7 minutes.
7. Flip the steaks and continue grilling for another 7 minutes
8. Toss the pasta with spinach, tomatoes, walnuts, and pesto in a bowl.
9. Slice the grilled steak and top the salad with the steak.
10. Garnish with cheese.
11. Enjoy.

Serving Suggestion: Serve the beef with toasted bread slices.
Variation Tip: Add crumbled bacon to the mixture.
Nutritional Information Per Serving:
Calories 325 | Fat 16g |Sodium 431mg | Carbs 22g | Fiber 1.2g | Sugar 4g | Protein 23g

Sweet Chipotle Ribs

Prep time: 15 minutes.
Cook time: 2 hrs. 25 minutes.
Serves: 8
Ingredients:
- 6 lbs. baby back ribs
Sauce
- 3 cups ketchup
- 2 (11.2 oz.) beer bottles
- 2 cups barbecue sauce
- ⅔ cup honey
- 1 small onion, chopped
- ¼ cup Worcestershire sauce
- 2 tablespoons Dijon mustard
- 2 tablespoons chipotle in adobo sauce, chopped
- 4 teaspoons ground chipotle pepper
- 1 teaspoon salt
- 1 teaspoon garlic powder
- ½ teaspoon black pepper

Preparation:
1. First, wrap the ribs in a large foil and keep it aside.
2. Preheat the Ninja Foodi Grill on the "Bake Mode" at 350 degrees F.
3. When the grill is preheated, open its hood and place the chipotle ribs in it.
4. Cover the grill's hood and roast for 1 ½ hour.
5. Take the rest of the ingredients in a saucepan and cook for 45 minutes on a simmer.
6. Brush the grilled ribs with the prepared sauce generously.
7. Place the ribs back into the grill and continue grilling for 10 minutes per side.
8. Serve.

Serving Suggestion: Serve these ribs with rice, pasta, or spaghetti.
Variation Tip: Add maple syrup instead of honey.
Nutritional Information Per Serving:
Calories 425 | Fat 14g |Sodium 411mg | Carbs 44g | Fiber 0.3g | Sugar 1g | Protein 8.3g

Pork with Salsa

Prep time: 15 minutes.
Cook time: 12 minutes.
Serves: 4
Ingredients:
- ¼ cup lime juice
- 2 tablespoons olive oil
- 2 garlic cloves, minced
- 1 ½ teaspoon ground cumin
- 1 ½ teaspoons dried oregano
- ½ teaspoon black pepper
- 2 lbs. pork tenderloin, ¾ inch slices

Salsa
- 1 jalapeno pepper, seeded and chopped
- ⅓ cup red onion, chopped
- 2 tablespoons fresh mint, chopped
- 2 tablespoons lime juice
- 4 cups pears, peeled and chopped
- 1 tablespoon lime zest, grated
- 1 teaspoon sugar
- ½ teaspoon black pepper

Preparation:
1. Season the pork with lime juice, cumin, oregano, oil, garlic, and pepper in a suitable bowl.
2. Cover to refrigerate for overnight margination.
3. Preheat the Ninja Foodi Grill on the "Grill Mode" at MAX-temperature settings.
4. When the grill is preheated, open its hood and place the pork in it.
5. Cover the grill's hood and grill for 6 minutes.
6. Flip the pork and continue grilling for another 6 minutes until al dente.
7. Mix the pear salsa ingredients into a separate bowl.
8. Serve the sliced pork with pear salsa.

Serving Suggestion: Serve the pork with mashed potatoes.

Variation Tip: Dust the pork chops with flour before grilling for more texture.

Nutritional Information Per Serving:
Calories 91 | Fat 5g |Sodium 88mg | Carbs 3g | Fiber 0g | Sugar 0g | Protein 7g

Bratwurst Potatoes

Prep time: 15 minutes.
Cook time: 40 minutes.
Serves: 6
Ingredients:
- 3 lbs. bratwurst links, uncooked
- 3 lbs. small red potatoes, wedged
- 1-lb. baby carrots
- 1 large red onion, sliced and rings
- 2 jars (4-½ oz.) whole mushrooms, drained
- ¼ cup butter, cubed
- 1 pack onion soup mix
- 2 tablespoons soy sauce
- ½ teaspoon black pepper

Preparation:
1. Place 2 foil packets on the working surface.
2. Divide the potatoes, carrots, onion, brats, and mushrooms with the foil.
3. Top them with butter, soup mix, pepper, and soy sauce.
4. Seal the foil packets by pinching their ends together.
5. Preheat the Ninja Foodi Grill on the "Grill Mode" at MED-temperature settings.
6. When the grill is preheated, open its hood and place the foil packet in it.
7. Cover the grill's hood and grill for 10 minutes per side.
8. Cook the other half of the brat's mixture in a similar way.
9. Open the packets carefully and be careful of the steam.
10. Serve.

Serving Suggestion: Serve the bratwurst potatoes with boiled peas, carrots, and potatoes on the side.

Variation Tip: Add butter to the potatoes for more taste.

Nutritional Information Per Serving:
Calories 345 | Fat 36g |Sodium 272mg | Carbs 41g | Fiber 0.2g | Sugar 0.1g | Protein 22.5g

Steak Bread Salad

Prep time: 15 minutes.
Cook time: 18 minutes.
Serves: 2

Ingredients:
- 2 teaspoons chili powder
- 2 teaspoons brown sugar
- ½ teaspoon salt
- ½ teaspoon black pepper
- 1 beef top sirloin steak, sliced
- 2 cups bread, cubed
- 2 tablespoons olive oil
- 1 cup ranch salad dressing
- 2 tablespoons horseradish, grated
- 1 tablespoon prepared mustard
- 3 large tomatoes, diced
- 1 medium cucumber, chopped
- 1 small red onion, thinly sliced

Preparation:
1. First, mix the chili powder with salt, pepper, and brown sugar in a bowl
2. Sauté the bread cubes with oil in a skillet for 10 minutes until golden.
3. Take a small bowl and mix horseradish with mustard and salad dressing.
4. Preheat the Ninja Foodi Grill on the "Grill Mode" at MAX-temperature settings.
5. When the grill is preheated, open its hood and place the steak slices in it.
6. Cover the grill's hood and grill for 4 minutes per side.
7. Toss the sautéed bread cubes with the rest of the ingredients and dressing mix in a salad bowl.
8. Slice the grilled steak and serve on top of the salad.
9. Enjoy.

Serving Suggestion: Serve the steak bread salad with crispy bacon on top.
Variation Tip: Grill bread cubes in the Ninja Foodi grill for more texture.
Nutritional Information Per Serving:
Calories 380 | Fat 20g |Sodium 686mg | Carbs 33g | Fiber 1g | Sugar 1.2g | Protein 21g

Ham Pineapple Skewers

Prep time: 15 minutes.
Cook time: 10 minutes.
Serves: 4

Ingredients:
- 1 can (20 oz.) pineapple chunks
- ½ cup orange marmalade
- 1 tablespoon mustard
- ¼ teaspoon ground cloves
- 1 lb. ham, diced
- ½-lb. Swiss cheese, diced
- 1 medium green pepper, cubed

Preparation:
1. Take 2 tablespoons of pineapple from pineapples in a bowl.
2. Add mustard, marmalade, and cloves; mix well and keep it aside.
3. Thread the pineapple, green pepper, cheese, and ham over the skewers alternatively.
4. Preheat the Ninja Foodi Grill on the "Grill Mode" at MED-temperature settings.
5. When the grill is preheated, open its hood and place the skewers in it.
6. Cover the grill's hood and grill for 10 minutes.
7. Continue rotating the skewers every 2 minutes.
8. Pour the sauce on top and serve.
Serving Suggestion: Serve the skewers with cream cheese dip.
Variation Tip: Serve the pineapple skewers on top of the fruit salad.
Nutritional Information Per Serving:
Calories 276 | Fat 21g |Sodium 476mg | Carbs 12g | Fiber 3g | Sugar 4g | Protein 10g

Beef Chimichurri Skewers

Prep time: 15 minutes.
Cook time: 12 minutes.
Serves: 4
Ingredients:
- ⅓ cup fresh basil
- ⅓ cup fresh cilantro
- ⅓ cup fresh parsley
- 1 tablespoon red wine vinegar
- Juice of ½ lemon
- 1 Garlic clove, minced
- 1 shallot, minced
- ½ teaspoon crushed red pepper flakes
- ½ cup olive oil, divided
- Salt to taste
- Black pepper to taste
- 1 red onion, cubed
- 1 red pepper, cubed
- 1 orange pepper, cubed
- 1 yellow pepper, cubed
- 1 ½ lb. sirloin steak, fat trimmed and diced

Preparation:
1. First, take basil, parsley, vinegar, lemon juice, red pepper, shallots, garlic, and cilantro in a blender jug.
2. Blend well, then add ¼ cup olive oil, salt, and pepper and mix again.
3. Now thread the steak, peppers, and onion on the skewers.
4. Drizzle salt, black pepper, and remaining oil over the skewers.
5. Preheat the Ninja Foodi Grill on the "Grill Mode" at MEDIUM-temperature settings.
6. When the grill is preheated, open its hood and place the skewers in it.
7. Cover the grill's hood and grill for 5-6 minutes per side.
8. Grill the skewers in a batch until all are cooked.
9. Serve warm with green sauce.
Serving Suggestion: Serve the skewers with fresh green and mashed potatoes.
Variation Tip: Add a drizzle of herbs on top of the skewers.
Nutritional Information Per Serving:
Calories 301 | Fat 5g |Sodium 340mg | Carbs 24.7g | Fiber 1.2g | Sugar 1.3g | Protein 15.3g

Korean Beef Steak

Prep time: 15 minutes.
Cook time: 12 minutes.
Serves: 2
Ingredients:
- ½ cup 1 tablespoon soy sauce
- ¼ cup 2 tablespoon vegetable oil
- ½ cup rice wine vinegar
- 4 garlic cloves, minced
- 2 tablespoon ginger, minced
- 2 tablespoon honey
- 3 tablespoon sesame oil
- 3 tablespoon Sriracha
- 1 ½ lb. flank steak
- 1 teaspoon sugar
- 1 teaspoon crushed red pepper flakes
- 2 cucumbers, cut lengthwise, seeded, and sliced
- Salt to taste

Preparation:
1. Mix ½ cup soy sauce, half of the rice wine, honey, ginger, garlic, 2 tablespoon Sriracha sauce, 2 tablespoon sesame oil, and vegetable oil in a large bowl.
2. Pour half of this sauce over the steak and rub it well.
3. Cover the steak and marinate for 10 minutes.
4. For the salad, mix remaining rice wine vinegar, sesame oil, sugar, red pepper flakes, Sriracha sauce, soy sauce, and salt in a salad bowl.
5. Preheat the Ninja Foodi Grill on the "Grill Mode" at MEDIUM-temperature settings.
6. When the grill is preheated, open its hood and place the steak in it.
7. Cover the grill's hood and grill for 6 minutes per side.
8. Slice and serve with cucumber salad.
Serving Suggestion: Serve the flank steak with sautéed vegetables and toasted bread slices.
Variation Tip: Use maple syrup instead of honey for a unique sweet taste.
Nutritional Information Per Serving:
Calories 309 | Fat 25g |Sodium 463mg | Carbs 9.9g | Fiber 0.3g | Sugar 0.3g | Protein 18g

Lamb Skewers

Prep time: 15 minutes.
Cook time: 16 minutes.
Serves: 4

Ingredients:
- 1 (10 oz.) pack couscous
- 1 ½ cup yogurt
- 1 tablespoon 1 teaspoon cumin
- 2 garlic cloves, minced
- Juice of 2 lemons
- Salt to taste
- Black pepper to taste
- 1 ½ lb. leg of lamb, boneless, diced
- 2 tomatoes, seeded and diced
- ½ English cucumber, seeded and diced
- ½ small red onion, chopped
- ¼ cup fresh parsley, chopped
- ¼ cup fresh mint, chopped
- 3 tablespoon olive oil
- Lemon wedges, for serving

Preparation:
1. First, cook the couscous as per the given instructions on the package, then fluff with a fork.
2. Whisk yogurt with garlic, cumin, lemon juice, salt, and black pepper in a large bowl.
3. Add lamb and mix well to coat the meat.
4. Separately toss red onion with cucumber, tomatoes, parsley, mint, lemon juice, olive oil, salt, and couscous in a salad bowl.
5. Thread the seasoned lamb on 8 skewers and drizzle salt and black pepper over them.
6. Preheat the Ninja Foodi Grill on the "Grill Mode" at MEDIUM-temperature settings.
7. When the grill is preheated, open its hood and place the lamb skewers in it.
8. Cover the grill's hood and grill for 7-8 minutes per side.
9. Cook the remaining skewers in a similar way.
10. Serve warm with prepared couscous.

Serving Suggestion: Serve the lamb skewers with quinoa salad.

Variation Tip: Add barbecue sauce to the lamb cube skewers.

Nutritional Information Per Serving:
Calories 448 | Fat 23g | Sodium 350mg | Carbs 18g | Fiber 6.3g | Sugar 1g | Protein 40.3g

Fajita Skewers

Prep time: 15 minutes.
Cook time: 14 minutes.
Serves: 4

Ingredients:
- 1 lb. sirloin steak, cubed
- 1 bunch scallions, cut into large pieces
- 1 pack flour tortillas, torn
- 4 large bell peppers, cubed
- 8 skewers
- Olive oil for drizzling
- Salt to taste
- Black pepper to taste

Preparation:
1. Thread the steak, tortillas, peppers, and scallions on the skewers.
2. Drizzle salt, black pepper, and olive oil over the skewers.
3. Preheat the Ninja Foodi Grill on the "Grill Mode" at MEDIUM-temperature settings.
4. When the grill is preheated, open its hood and place the skewers in it.
5. Cover the grill's hood and grill for 14 minutes.
6. Continue rotating the skewers every 4 minutes.
7. Cook the skewers in batches until all are grilled.
8. Serve warm.

Serving Suggestion: Serve the fajita skewers with mashed potatoes.

Variation Tip: Add more veggies of your choice to the skewers.

Nutritional Information Per Serving:
Calories 537 | Fat 20g | Sodium 719mg | Carbs 25.1g | Fiber 0.9g | Sugar 1.4g | Protein 37.8g

Teriyaki Beef Kebabs

Prep time: 15 minutes.
Cook time: 16 minutes.
Serves: 4

Ingredients:
- 1 tbsp. olive oil
- 1 tbsp. grated ginger
- 1 tbsp. minced garlic
- 1 tsp. red pepper flakes
- ¾ cup teriyaki sauce
- ¾ cup pineapple juice
- 2 tbsp. soy sauce
- 1 tbsp. dark brown sugar
- 1 tsp. sesame oil
- 1 ½ lbs. beef sirloin tips, cubed
- ½ pineapple, peeled, cored, cubed
- 1 large sweet onion, cubed
- 2 red bell peppers, cubed

Preparation:
1. Sauté red pepper, garlic and ginger with oil in a saucepan for 1 minute.
2. Stir in brown sugar, soy sauce, ¼ cup pineapple juice and teriyaki sauce then cook for 5 minutes on a simmer.
3. Remove from the heat and allow the sauce to cool.
4. Mix half of this marinade with ½ pineapple juice in a bowl.
5. Pour this mixture into a ziplock and add beef cubes.
6. Seal the bag, shake well and refrigerate for 5 hours.
7. Thread the beef, bell peppers, onion and pineapple on the wooden skewers, alternately.
8. Place the cooking pot in the Ninja Foodi Grill then set a grill grate inside.
9. Select the "Grill" Mode, set the temperature to MED.
10. Press the START/STOP button to initiate preheating.
11. Once preheated, place the skewers in the Ninja Foodi Grill.
12. Cover the hood and allow the grill to cook for 10 minutes, flipping halfway through.
13. Serve warm.

Serving Suggestion: Serve the kebabs with a kale cucumber salad.

Variation Tip: Add crumbled bacon on top before serving.

Nutritional Information Per Serving:
Calories 325 | Fat 16g |Sodium 431mg | Carbs 12g | Fiber 1.2g | Sugar 4g | Protein 23g

Moink Balls

Prep time: 15 minutes.
Cook time: 10 minutes.
Serves: 4

Ingredients:
- 1 ½ lb. ground beef chuck
- ¾ cup fresh breadcrumbs
- 2 large eggs, beaten
- 2 tsp. minced garlic
- ½ lb. bacon, halved
- ¼ cup rub
- 1 cup of barbecue sauce

Preparation:
1. Mix beef with garlic, eggs and breadcrumbs in a bowl.
2. Make 1 inch round balls out of this mixture.
3. Stick a toothpick in each ball and coat each with the bbq rub.
4. Place the cooking pot in the Ninja Foodi Grill then set a grill grate inside.
5.
6. Select the "Grill" Mode, set the temperature to MED.
7. Press the START/STOP button to initiate preheating.
8. Once preheated, place the moink balls in the Ninja Foodi Grill.
9. Cover the hood and cook for 5 minutes per side.
10. Serve warm.

Serving Suggestion: Serve the moink balls with cream cheese dip.

Variation Tip: Serve the balls on top of a lettuce bed.

Nutritional Information Per Serving:
Calories 376 | Fat 21g |Sodium 476mg | Carbs 12g | Fiber 3g | Sugar 4g | Protein 20g

Grilled Beef Skewers

Prep time: 10 minutes.
Cook time: 10 minutes.
Serves: 4

Ingredients:
- 4 tbsp. minced fresh lemongrass
- 3 fresh bay leaves, chopped
- 2 tsp. fresh thyme leaves
- 1 tsp. lemon zest
- 1 tsp. lime zest
- 2 tsp. fresh peeled ginger, diced
- 8 medium garlic cloves, crushed
- 1 ½ tsp. turmeric powder
- 1 ½ tsp. fresh juice from 1 lemon
- 1 tsp. kosher salt
- 1 tbsp. sugar
- 1 tsp. cinnamon
- 1 lb. beef sirloin steak, sliced
- 2 tsp. Asian fish sauce
- 1 tbsp. vegetable oil

Preparation:
1. Grind ginger, garlic, lime zest, lemon zest, thyme bay leaves and lemon grass in a mortar with a pestle.
2. Stir in cinnamon, sugar, salt, lemon juice and turmeric to form a paste.
3. Add this paste, oil, fish sauce and beef to a mixing bowl.
4. Mix well, and thread the beef on the wooden skewers.
5. Place the cooking pot in the Ninja Foodi Grill then set a grill grate inside.
6. Select the "Grill" Mode, set the temperature to MED.
7. Press the START/STOP button to initiate preheating.
8. Once preheated, place the skewers in the Ninja Foodi Grill.
9. Cover the hood and allow the grill to cook for 10 minutes, flipping halfway through.
10. Serve warm.

Serving Suggestion: Serve the skewers with mashed cauliflower.
Variation Tip: Use BBQ sauce for the change of taste.
Nutritional Information Per Serving:
Calories 305 | Fat 25g |Sodium 532mg | Carbs 13g | Fiber 0.4g | Sugar 2g | Protein 28.3g

Pork Tenderloin with Peach-Mustard Sauce

Prep time: 11 minutes.
Cook time: 12 minutes.
Serves: 4

Ingredients:
Peach-Mustard Sauce:
- 2 large ripe peaches, peeled, diced
- ¼ cup ketchup
- 3 tbsp. Dijon mustard
- 1 tsp. light brown sugar
- ½ tsp. black pepper
- ½ tsp. kosher salt

Pork:
- 2 pork tenderloins
- 4 tsp. kosher salt
- 1 tsp. black pepper
- Vegetable oil, for grill
- ½ cup peach preserves

Preparation:
1. Blend peaches with ½ tsp. salt, black pepper, brown sugar, mustard and ketchup in a blender.
2. Rub the pork with black pepper and salt then leave for 1 hour.
3. Place the cooking pot in the Ninja Foodi Grill then set a grill grate inside.
4. Select the "Grill" Mode, set the temperature to MED.
5. Press the START/STOP button to initiate preheating.
6. Once preheated, place the pork in the Ninja Foodi Grill.
7. Cover the hood and grill for 6 minutes per side.
8. Slice the pork and serve with peach sauce.

Serving Suggestion: Serve the pork with a fresh spinach salad.
Variation Tip: Add a drizzle of cheese on top of the pork.
Nutritional Information Per Serving:
Calories 445 | Fat 7.9g |Sodium 581mg | Carbs 14g | Fiber 2.6g | Sugar 0.1g | Protein 42.5g

Grilled Pork Chops with Plums

Prep time: 15 minutes.
Cook time: 12 minutes.
Serves: 4

Ingredients:
- 4 tbsp. olive oil
- 1 tsp. honey
- 4 bone-in pork rib chops (1" thick), patted dry
- Kosher salt and ground pepper, to taste
- 4 ripe medium plums, halved
- 1 lemon, halved, seeds removed
- 8 oz. Halloumi cheese, sliced
- 2 tbsp. torn oregano leaves
- Aleppo-style pepper flakes, for serving

Preparation:
1. Season the pork chops with black peppers, salt, 2 tbsp. oil and honey.
2. Toss plums with lemon, halloumi, salt, black pepper and 2 tbsp. oil in a bowl.
3. Place the cooking pot in the Ninja Foodi Grill then set a grill grate inside.
4. Select the "Grill" Mode, set the temperature to MED.
5. Press the START/STOP button to initiate preheating.
6. Once preheated, place the pork in the Ninja Foodi Grill.
7. Cover the hood and allow the grill to cook for 8 minutes, flipping halfway through.
8. Grill the lemon, plums and halloumi for 2 minutes per side.

9. Slice the pork chops and serve with grilled halloumi, plums and lemon.
10. Garnish with oregano, and peppers.
11. Enjoy.

Serving Suggestion: Serve the pork chops with steaming rice.

Variation Tip: Add 1 tbsp. lemon juice to the seasoning.

Nutritional Information Per Serving:
Calories 361 | Fat 16g | Sodium 189mg | Carbs 13g | Fiber 0.3g | Sugar 18.2g | Protein 33.3g

Parmesan Pork Chops

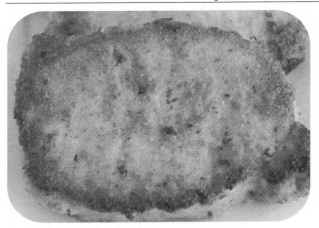

Prep time: 10 minutes
Cook time: 10 minutes
Serves: 2

Ingredients:
- 2 pork chops, boneless
- 3 tablespoons of Parmesan cheese, grated
- 1 tablespoon olive oil
- ⅓ cup almond flour
- 1 teaspoon Cajun seasoning
- 1 teaspoon dried mix herbs
- 1 teaspoon paprika
- Pepper
- Salt

Directions:
1. Place the cooking pot in the Ninja Foodi Grill Main Unit then place the Ninja Foodi Crisper Basket in the pot.
2. In a bowl, mix Parmesan cheese, paprika, mixed herbs, almond flour and Cajun seasoning.
3. Brush pork chops with oil and coat with cheese mixture.
4. Place coated pork chops into the Crisper Basket.
5. Press Air Crisp mode, set the temperature to 350°F, and set time to 10 minutes.
6. Cover with lid and press Start.

Serving Suggestion: Allow to cool completely then serve.

Variation Tip: You can also add Italian seasoning instead of dried herbs.

Nutritional Information per Serving:
Calories 319 | Fat 27g | Sodium 159mg | Carbs 0.6g | Fiber 0.4g | Sugar 0.1g | Protein 18.2g

Beer Bratwurst

Prep time: 15 minutes.
Cook time: 8 minutes.
Serves: 4

Ingredients:
- 2 lbs. boneless pork shoulder, cut into cubes
- ⅔ lb. boneless veal shoulder, cut into cubes
- ½ cup pale ale
- 1 tbsp. fine sea salt
- 1 tsp. sugar
- 1 tsp. caraway seeds
- ½ tsp. dry mustard powder
- 1 tsp. fresh thyme leaves
- ½ tsp. ground ginger
- ¼ tsp. freshly grated nutmeg
- Hog casings, rinsed

Preparation:
1. Mix nutmeg, ginger, thyme, mustard powder, caraway seeds, sugar and salt in a small bowl.
2. Grind the pork meat in a food processor then add semi frozen ale.
3. Stir in spice mixture, mix well and take 2 tbsp. of the beef mixture to make a sausage.
4. Make more sausages and keep them aside.
5. Place the cooking pot in the Ninja Foodi Grill then set a grill grate inside.
6.
7. Select the "Grill" Mode, set the temperature to MED.
8. Press the START/STOP button to initiate preheating.
9. Once preheated, place the pork in the Ninja Foodi Grill.
10. Cover the hood and allow the grill to cook for 8 minutes, flipping halfway through.
11. Serve warm.

Serving Suggestion: Serve the bratwurst with roasted veggies.
Variation Tip: Use toasted buns for serving.
Nutritional Information Per Serving:
Calories 384 | Fat 25g |Sodium 460mg | Carbs 16g | Fiber 0.4g | Sugar 2g | Protein 26g

Grilled Pork Chops with Pineapple Glaze

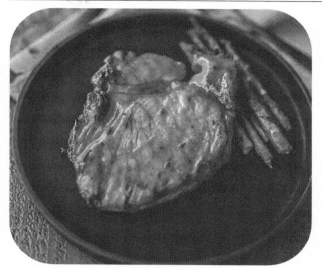

Prep time: 10 minutes.
Cook time: 14 minutes.
Serves: 4

Ingredients:
- ½ cup pineapple juice
- ¼ cup honey
- ¼ cup unseasoned rice vinegar
- 3 tbsp. Dijon mustard
- 1 tsp. crushed red pepper flakes
- ½ tsp. toasted sesame oil
- ½ tsp. ground turmeric
- 4 (1"-thick) bone-in pork chops
- Kosher salt, to taste

Preparation:
1. Mix pineapple juice, honey, rice vinegar, mustard, red pepper flakes, sesame oil and turmeric in a bowl.
2. Mix the pork chops with the marinade in a shallow tray, cover and refrigerate for 30 minutes.
3. Place the cooking pot in the Ninja Foodi Grill then set a grill grate inside.
4. Select the "Grill" Mode, set the temperature to MED.
5. Press the START/STOP button to initiate preheating.
6. Once preheated, place the pork in the Ninja Foodi Grill.
7.
8. Cover the hood and grill for 7 minutes per side.
9. Serve warm.

Serving Suggestion: Serve the pork chops with steamed rice.
Variation Tip: Add butter sauce on top of the pork.
Nutritional Information Per Serving:
Calories 419 | Fat 13g |Sodium 432mg | Carbs 19g | Fiber 3g | Sugar 1g | Protein 33g

Pork Cutlets with Cantaloupe Salad

Prep time: 15 minutes.
Cook time: 8 minutes.
Serves: 4

Ingredients:

- 4 (½ -inch–thick) pork cutlets
- Kosher salt, to taste
- 1 cup grated cantaloupe
- 4 tbsp. fresh lime juice
- 2 tbsp. olive oil
- 4 scallions, sliced
- 1 red chile, sliced
- ¼ cup cilantro, chopped
- 2 tbsp. fish sauce
- Crushed salted, roasted peanuts

Preparation:

1. Prick the pork with a fork and season with 2 tbsp. lime juice, and cantaloupe in a bowl.
2. Cover and refrigerate for 1 hour.
3. Place the cooking pot in the Ninja Foodi Grill then set a grill grate inside.
4. Select the "Grill" Mode, set the temperature to MED.
5. Press the START/STOP button to initiate preheating.
6. Once preheated, place the pork in the Ninja Foodi Grill.
7. Cover the hood and grill for 4 minutes per side.
8. Mix scallions and other ingredients in a bowl.
9. Serve the pork with the scallions mixture.

Serving Suggestion: Serve the pork with fresh herbs on top and a bowl of rice.

Variation Tip: You can serve the pork with cabbage slaw as well.

Nutritional Information Per Serving:
Calories 388 | Fat 8g |Sodium 611mg | Carbs 18g | Fiber 0g | Sugar 4g | Protein 13g

Curried Pork Skewers

Prep time: 10 minutes.
Cook time: 23 minutes.
Serves: 4

Ingredients:

- 1 (13 ½ -oz.) can unsweetened coconut milk
- 2 tbsp. fish sauce
- 2 tbsp. Thai thin soy sauce
- 1 tbsp. sugar
- 1 tsp. kosher salt
- ¾ tsp. white pepper
- ½ tsp. curry powder
- ½ tsp. ground turmeric
- ¾ cup sweetened condensed milk
- 1 (½ lb.) boneless pork shoulder, cut into 4x ½ " strips
- 4 oz. fatback, cut into ½ " pieces

Preparation:

1. Mix coconut milk, turmeric, curry powder, black pepper, salt, sugar, soy sauce and fish sauce in a pan.
2. Cook to a boil then reduce its heat and cook for 15 minutes on a simmer.
3. Allow this mixture to cool, then add black pepper, salt and pork.
4. Mix well, cover and refrigerate for 1 hour.
5. Place the cooking pot in the Ninja Foodi Grill then set a grill grate inside.
6. Select the "Grill" Mode, set the temperature to MED.
7. Press the START/STOP button to initiate preheating.
8. Once preheated, place the pork in the Ninja Foodi Grill.
9. Cover the hood and allow the grill to cook for 8 minutes, flipping halfway through.
10. Serve warm.

Serving Suggestion: Serve the skewers with roasted green beans and mashed cauliflower.

Variation Tip: Add chopped sautéed kale on top before serving.

Nutritional Information Per Serving:
Calories 429 | Fat 17g |Sodium 422mg | Carbs 15g | Fiber 0g | Sugar 1g | Protein 41g

Mojo-Marinated Pork Kebabs

Prep time: 15 minutes.
Cook time: 10 minutes.
Serves: 4

Ingredients:
Brined Pork:
- 2 quarts ice-cold water
- ⅓ cup kosher salt
- ¼ cup sugar
- 2 lbs. center-cut pork chops

Mojo Marinade
- 2 tbsp. garlic, minced
- ½ tsp. kosher salt
- ½ cup fresh sour orange juice
- ¼ cup olive oil
- ½ tsp. dried oregano
- ½ tsp. cumin
- Black pepper, to taste

Skewers:
- 2 whole mangos, peeled, cored, and cut into 1 ½ -inch squares

Preparation:
1. Mix salt, sugar and water in a large pan and soak the pork for 1 hour.
2. Mash garlic, with ½ tsp. salt, cumin, oregano, oil, and orange juice in a mortar.
3. Remove the pork from the brine and cut into cubes.
4. Mix the pork with the marinade in a bowl, cover and refrigerate for 1 hour.
5. Thread the pork and mango cubes on the wooden skewers.
6. Place the cooking pot in the Ninja Foodi Grill then set a grill grate inside.
7. Select the "Grill" Mode, set the temperature to MED.
8. Press the START/STOP button to initiate preheating.
9. Once preheated, place the pork in the Ninja Foodi Grill.
10. Cover the hood and allow the grill to cook for 10 minutes, flipping halfway through.
11. Serve warm.

Serving Suggestion: Serve the kebabs with cauliflower cheese casserole.
Variation Tip: Add cheese on top of the pork and then bake after grilling.

Nutritional Information Per Serving:
Calories 425 | Fat 15g |Sodium 345mg | Carbs 23g | Fiber 1.4g | Sugar 3g | Protein 33.3g

Grilled Pork Belly Kebabs

Prep time: 10 minutes.
Cook time: 10 minutes.
Serves: 4

Ingredients:
- 2 tbsp. gochujang
- 2 tbsp. honey
- 2 tsp. sake
- 2 tsp. soy sauce
- 1 tsp. vegetable oil
- 1 ¼ lb. boneless pork belly, cut into cubes
- 1 small zucchini, cut 1-inch-thick half-moons
- ½ pint cherry tomatoes
- 1 red bell pepper, seeded, and cut into 1-inch pieces

Preparation:
1. Mix oil, soy sauce, sake, honey and gochujang in a bowl and keep 2 tbsp. of this marinade aside.
2. Add pork to the bowl, mix well, cover and refrigerate for 1 hour.
3. Thread the pork, bell pepper, tomatoes and zucchini on the wooden skewers alternately.
4. Place the cooking pot in the Ninja Foodi Grill then set a grill grate inside.
5. Select the "Grill" Mode, set the temperature to MED.
6. Press the START/STOP button to initiate preheating.
7. Once preheated, place the pork in the Ninja Foodi Grill.
8. Cover the hood and allow the grill to cook for 10 minutes, flipping halfway through.
9. Pour the reserved marinade on top of the skewers and serve warm.

Serving Suggestion: Serve the kebabs with boiled cauliflower rice or grilled zucchini.
Variation Tip: Add crushed or sliced almonds to the serving.

Nutritional Information Per Serving:
Calories 361 | Fat 16g |Sodium 515mg | Carbs 13g | Fiber 0.1g | Sugar 18.2g | Protein 33.3g

Balinese Pork Satay

Prep time: 15 minutes.
Cook time: 15 minutes.
Serves: 4

Ingredients:
Spice Paste:
- 1 (1-inch) knob fresh turmeric, peeled
- 2 stalks lemongrass, sliced
- 8 garlic cloves, sliced
- 2 small shallots, sliced
- 3 wholes dried Pasilla chilli with seeds removed, chopped
- 2 tbsp. palm sugar
- 2 tsp. whole coriander seed
- 1 tbsp. whole white peppercorns
- Kosher salt, to taste
- 2 lbs. boneless pork shoulder, cut into cubes

Glaze
- 1 cup Kecap manis
- ¼ cup sugar
- One (2-inch) knob ginger, chopped
- 4 medium garlic cloves, chopped

Dipping Sauce
- 10 oz. roasted peanuts
- ¼ cup vegetable or canola oil
- 1 oz. tamarind pulp
- 1 tbsp. Kecap manis or fish sauce
- Water, as necessary
- Sugar, to taste

Preparation:
1. Blend all the spice paste ingredients in a mini-food processor.
2. Mix pork with the ¾ of the spice paste in a bowl.
3. Cover and refrigerate the pork for 45 minutes. Thread the pork on the wooden skewers.
4. Place the cooking pot in the Ninja Foodi Grill then set a grill grate inside.
5. Select the "Grill" Mode, set the temperature to MED.
6. Press the START/STOP button to initiate preheating.
7. Once preheated, place the pork in the Ninja Foodi Grill.
8. Cover the hood and allow the grill to cook for 10 minutes, flipping halfway through.
9. Meanwhile, mix the glaze ingredients and ⅓ spice paste in a saucepan and cook for 5 minutes

on a simmer. Pour this glaze over the skewers. Serve warm.

Serving Suggestion: Serve the pork with cauliflower rice.

Variation Tip: Add some BBQ sauce as well for seasoning.

Nutritional Information Per Serving:
Calories 425 | Fat 14g |Sodium 411mg | Carbs 24g | Fiber 0.3g | Sugar 1g | Protein 28.3g

Lamb Burger Patties

Prep time: 10 minutes
Cook time: 20 minutes
Serves: 4

Ingredients:
- 1 ½ pound ground lamb
- 1 tablespoon ginger garlic paste
- ¼ teaspoon paprika
- ½ teaspoon chili powder
- ¼ cup green onions, sliced
- Pepper
- Salt

Directions:
1. Place the cooking pot in the Ninja Foodi Grill Main Unit.
2. Add all ingredients into the bowl and mix until well combined.
3. Make patties from the meat mixture and place into the baking dish.
4. Press Bake mode, set the temperature to 375°F, and set time to 20 minutes. Press Start.
5. Once a unit is preheated then place the baking dish in the cooking pot.
6. Cover with lid and cook for 20 minutes.

Serving Suggestion: Allow to cool completely then serve.

Variation Tip: You can also add your choice of seasoning.

Nutritional Information per Serving:
Calories 320 | Fat 12.6g |Sodium 172mg | Carbs 0.7g | Fiber 0.3g | Sugar 0.2g | Protein 47.9g

Skirt Steak with Mojo Marinade

Prep time: 15 minutes.
Cook time: 10 minutes.
Serves: 4

Ingredients:
Steak:
- 2 lbs. skirt steak
- 2 tbsp. limes juice
- ¼ cup orange juice
- ⅔ cup olive oil
- 4 medium garlic cloves, minced
- 1 tsp. ground cumin
- Kosher salt and black pepper, to taste
- ¼ cup chopped cilantro leaves

Preparation:
1. Add skirt steak, ½ tsp. black pepper, 1 tsp. salt, cumin, garlic, ⅔ cup olive oil, orange and lime juice in a sealable bag.
2. Refrigerate the steak for 1 hour then remove it from the heat.
3. Cook the marinade in a saucepan and cook until reduced to half.
4. Place the cooking pot in the Ninja Foodi Grill then set a grill grate inside.
5. Select the "Grill" Mode, set the temperature to MAX.
6. Press the START/STOP button to initiate preheating.
7. Once preheated, place the steak in the Ninja Foodi Grill.
8. Cover the hood and cook for 10 minutes, flipping halfway through.
9. Slice and serve the chicken with the prepared sauce and cilantro on top.
10. Enjoy.

Serving Suggestion: Serve the beef with avocado guacamole and cauliflower rice.
Variation Tip: Add sweet paprika for a tangy taste.
Nutritional Information Per Serving:
Calories 440 | Fat 14g |Sodium 220mg | Carbs 12g | Fiber 0.2g | Sugar 1g | Protein 37g

Cumin Lamb Skewers

Prep time: 15 minutes.
Cook time: 10 minutes.
Serves: 4

Ingredients:
- 1 tbsp. red chili flakes
- 1 tbsp. whole cumin seed
- 2 tsp. whole fennel seed
- 1 tsp. kosher salt
- 2 tsp. granulated garlic
- 2 lbs. boneless lamb shoulder, cubed
- 1 tbsp. vegetable or canola oil
- 2 tsp. Shaoxing wine

Preparation:
1. Grind all the spices, garlic, and salt, in a mortar.
2. Mix the spice-mixture with wine, and oil in a large bowl.
3. Toss in the lamb cubes, mix well to coat and cover then refrigerate for 30 minutes.
4. Thread the lamb cubes on the wooden skewers.
5. Place the cooking pot in the Ninja Foodi Grill then set a grill grate inside.
6. Select the "Grill" Mode, set the temperature to MED.
7. Press the START/STOP button to initiate preheating.
8. Once preheated, place the skewers in the Ninja Foodi Grill.
9. Cover the hood and allow the grill to cook for 10 minutes, flipping halfway through.
10. Serve warm.

Serving Suggestion: Serve the skewers with grilled zucchini salad.
Variation Tip: Add crushed red pepper on top before serving.
Nutritional Information Per Serving:
Calories 380 | Fat 20g |Sodium 686mg | Carbs 13g | Fiber 1g | Sugar 1.2g | Protein 21g

Jalapeño Steak Sandwiches

Prep time: 15 minutes.
Cook time: 14 minutes.
Serves: 2

Ingredients:
Cotija Mayo
- ¼ cup mayonnaise
- ⅓ cup cotija cheese, grated
- 2 tbsp. sour cream
- 1 tbsp. lime juice
- 1 tsp. chili powder
- ½ tsp. cayenne pepper

Marinade
- ⅓ cup juice from about 4 limes
- 3 tbsp. olive oil
- 2 medium jalapeños, chopped
- 2 tsp. minced garlic
- 1 tbsp. dark brown sugar
- 1 tbsp. soy sauce
- 1 tbsp. apple cider vinegar
- 1 tsp. Kosher salt
- 1 tsp. black pepper
- 1 lb. hanger steak, butterflied
- 1 medium onion, cut into ½ -inch slices
- 1 handful fresh cilantro leaves
- 1 baguette, sliced
- Olive oil, for brushing

Preparation:
1. Mix all the cotija mayo ingredients in a bowl.
2. Add and whisk all the marinade ingredients in a blender until smooth.
3. Place the steak in a plastic bag and add the prepared marinade.
4. Seal the bag, and refrigerate for 1 hour.
5. Place the cooking pot in the Ninja Foodi Grill then set a grill grate inside.
6. Select the "Grill" Mode, set the temperature to MED.
7. Press the START/STOP button to initiate preheating.
8. Once preheated, place the steak in the Ninja Foodi Grill.
9. Cover the hood and cook for 5 minutes per side.
10. Slice the cooked steak against the grain.
11. Sauté onion with oil in a skillet for 5 minutes.
12. Slice the baguette and top half of the slices with steak, onion and cotija mojito.
13. Once preheated, place the remaining bread slices on top.
14. Grill the sandwiches for 2 minutes per side.
15. Serve.

Serving Suggestion: Serve the steak with cucumber salad.
Variation Tip: Add 1 tbsp. lime juice to the seasoning and marinate.
Nutritional Information Per Serving:
Calories 380 | Fat 8g |Sodium 339mg | Carbs 16g | Fiber 1g | Sugar 2g | Protein 21g

Colombian-Style Beef Tenderloin

Prep time: 15 minutes.
Cook time: 12 minutes.
Serves: 4

Ingredients:
- 1 ½ to 2 lbs. kosher salt
- 6 to 8 sprigs oregano, rosemary, or thyme
- 1 center-cut trimmed beef tenderloin (2 ½ lbs.)
- ¼ cup chimichurri sauce

Preparation:
1. Season the beef with herbs and salt.
2. Place the cooking pot in the Ninja Foodi Grill then set a grill grate inside.
3. Select the "Grill" Mode, set the temperature to MAX.
4. Press the START/STOP button to initiate preheating.
5. Once preheated, place the beef in the Ninja Foodi Grill.
6. Cover the hood and cook for 6 minutes per side.
7. Pour the chimichurri sauce over the beef and serve.

Serving Suggestion: Serve the steak with roasted veggies on the side.
Variation Tip: Add sweet paprika for a more spicy taste.
Nutritional Information Per Serving:
Calories 334 | Fat 16g |Sodium 462mg | Carbs 13g | Fiber 0.4g | Sugar 3g | Protein 35.3g

Steakhouse Kebabs

Prep time: 10 minutes.
Cook time: 10 minutes.
Serves: 4

Ingredients:
- ¼ cup olive oil
- ¼ cup Worcestershire sauce
- 3 tbsp. soy sauce
- 1 tbsp. lemon juice
- 1 tbsp. Dijon mustard
- 1 tbsp. minced garlic
- 2 tsp. dark brown sugar
- 2 tsp. black pepper
- 1 ½ lbs. beef sirloin tips, cubed
- 8 oz. cremini mushrooms, halved
- 1 large red onion, cubed

Preparation:
1. Mix black pepper, brown sugar, garlic, mustard, lemon juice, soy sauce, oil and Worcestershire sauce in a bowl.
2. Add this mixture to a ziplock bag and Once preheated, place the beef and mushrooms in the bag.
3. Seal the bag, shake well and refrigerate for 1 hour.
4. Thread mushrooms and beef on the skewer alternately.
5. Place the cooking pot in the Ninja Foodi Grill then set a grill grate inside.
6.
7. Select the "Grill" Mode, set the temperature to MED.
8. Press the START/STOP button to initiate preheating.
9. Once preheated, place the skewers in the Ninja Foodi Grill.
10. Cover the hood and allow the grill to cook for 10 minutes, flipping halfway through.
11. Serve warm.

Serving Suggestion: Serve the kebabs with mashed cauliflower.

Variation Tip: Dust the beef with almond flour before grilling for more texture.

Nutritional Information Per Serving:
Calories 391 | Fat 5g |Sodium 88mg | Carbs 3g | Fiber 0g | Sugar 0g | Protein 27g

Colombian-Style Beef Ribs Recipe

Prep time: 10 minutes.
Cook time: 45 minutes.
Serves: 6

Ingredients:
- 12 beef rib bones (two 6-bone racks)
- Kosher salt
- Black pepper, to taste

Preparation:
1. Rub the ribs with black pepper and salt.
2. Place the cooking pot in the Ninja Foodi Grill then set a grill grate inside.
3. Select the "Grill" Mode, set the temperature to MAX.
4. Press the START/STOP button to initiate preheating.
5. Place the ribs in the Ninja Foodi Grill.
6. Cover the hood and allow the grill to cook for 20 minutes.
7. Flip the beef ribs and grill again for 25 minutes.
8. Serve warm.

Serving Suggestion: Serve the beef ribs with roasted veggies and mashed cauliflower.

Variation Tip: Add dried herbs to the seasoning.

Nutritional Information Per Serving:
Calories 405 | Fat 20g |Sodium 941mg | Carbs 21g | Fiber 0.9g | Sugar 0.9g | Protein 45.2g

Beef Cheese Burgers

Prep time: 15 minutes.
Cook time: 20 minutes.
Serves: 4

Ingredients:
- ½ cup shredded cheddar cheese
- 6 tablespoons chili sauce, divided
- 1 tablespoon chili powder
- 1-lb. ground beef

To serve
- 4 hamburger buns, split
- Lettuce leaves, tomato slices, and mayonnaise,

Preparation:
1. First, take all the ingredients for patties in a bowl.
2. Thoroughly mix them together, then make 4 of the ½ inch patties out of it.
3. Preheat the Ninja Foodi Grill on the "Grill Mode" at MAX-temperature settings.
4. When the grill is preheated, open its hood and place the patties in it.
5. Cover the grill's hood and grill for 5 minutes per side.
6. Grill the remaining patties in a similar way.
7. Serve with buns, lettuce, tomato, and mayonnaise.

Serving Suggestion: Serve the beef cheeseburgers with mayo dip.
Variation Tip: Add butter to the patties before cooking.
Nutritional Information Per Serving:
Calories 405 | Fat 22.7g |Sodium 227mg | Carbs 26.1g | Fiber 1.4g | Sugar 0.9g | Protein 45.2g

Crusted Beef Burger

Prep time: 15 minutes.
Cook time: 20 minutes.
Serves: 4

Ingredients:
- ½ cup seasoned bread crumbs
- 1 large egg, beaten
- ½ teaspoon salt
- ½ teaspoon black pepper
- 1-lb. ground beef
- 1 tablespoon olive oil
- 4 sesame seed hamburger buns, split

Preparation:
1. Take all the ingredients for a burger in a suitable bowl except the oil and the buns.
2. Mix them thoroughly together and make 4 of the ½ inch patties.
3. Brush these patties with olive oil.
4. Preheat the Ninja Foodi Grill on the "Grill Mode" at LOW-temperature settings.
5. When the grill is preheated, open its hood and place the patties in it.
6. Cover the grill's hood and grill for 5 minutes per side.
7. Grill the remaining 2 patties in the same way.
8. Serve with buns.

Serving Suggestion: Serve the burgers with sautéed green beans and mashed potatoes.
Variation Tip: Insert a cheese cube to the center of each patty.
Nutritional Information Per Serving:
Calories 395 | Fat 9.5g |Sodium 655mg | Carbs 13.4g | Fiber 0.4g | Sugar 0.4g | Protein 28.3g

Delicious Beef Meatballs

Prep time: 10 minutes
Cook time: 10 minutes
Serves: 4

Ingredients:
- 1 egg, lightly beaten
- 1 pound ground beef
- 1 tablespoon garlic, minced
- ½ cup Cheddar cheese, shredded
- ¼ cup fresh parsley, chopped
- ¼ cup onion, chopped
- 2 tablespoons taco seasoning
- Pepper
- Salt

Directions:
1. Place the cooking pot in the Ninja Foodi Grill Main Unit then place the Ninja Foodi Crisper

Basket in the pot.
2. Add meat and remaining ingredients into the bowl and mix until well combined.
3. Make small balls from the meat mixture and place into the Crisper Basket.
4. Press Air Crisp mode, set the temperature to 400°F, and set time to 10 minutes.
5. Cover with lid and press Start.
Serving Suggestion: Serve warm.
Variation Tip: Add your choice of seasonings.
Nutritional Information per Serving:
Calories 291 | Fat 12.9g |Sodium 219mg | Carbs 1.9g | Fiber 0.3g | Sugar 0.5g | Protein 39.6g

Crispy Pork Chops

Prep time: 10 minutes
Cook time: 30 minutes
Serves: 3
Ingredients:
- 1 egg, lightly beaten
- 3 pork chops, boneless
- ½ cup crackers, crushed
- 4 tablespoons ofParmesan cheese, grated
- 2 tablespoons milk
- Pepper
- Salt

Directions:
1. Place the cooking pot in the Ninja Foodi Grill Main Unit.
2. In a small bowl, whisk egg with milk.
3. In a shallow dish, mix cheese, crackers, pepper and salt.
4. Dip pork chops in egg then coat with cheese mixture and place into the baking dish.
5. Press Bake mode, set the temperature to 350°F, and set time to 30 minutes. Press Start.
6. Once a unit is preheated then place the baking dish in the cooking pot.
7. Cover with lid and cook for 30 minutes. Turn pork chops halfway through.
Serving Suggestion: Garnish with fresh coriander and serve.
Variation Tip: None
Nutritional Information per Serving:
Calories 334 | Fat 24.2g |Sodium 219mg | Carbs 6.9g | Fiber 0.2g | Sugar 0.8g | Protein 20.9g

Flavorful Lamb Chops

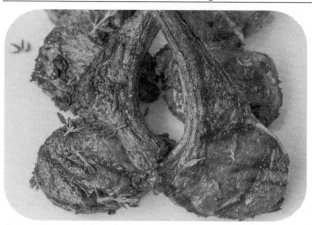

Prep time: 10 minutes
Cook time: 30 minutes
Serves: 4
Ingredients:
- 4 lamb chops
- 1 teaspoon ginger
- 1 teaspoon cinnamon
- 1 ½ teaspoon tarragon
- ¼ cup brown sugar
- 1 teaspoon garlic powder
- Pepper
- Salt

Directions:
1. Place the cooking pot in the Ninja Foodi Grill Main Unit.
2. Add lamb chops and remaining ingredients into the zip-lock bag. Seal bag and place in the refrigerator for overnight.
3. Place lamb chops into the baking dish.
4. Press Bake mode, set the temperature to 375°F, and set time to 30 minutes. Press Start.
5. Once a unit is preheated then place the baking dish in the cooking pot.
6. Cover with lid and cook for 30 minutes. Turn lamb chops after 20 minutes.
Serving Suggestion: Serve warm.
Variation Tip: Once cooked sprinkle with chopped parsley.
Nutritional Information per Serving:
Calories 649 | Fat 24g |Sodium 290mg | Carbs 10.3g | Fiber 0.5g | Sugar 9g | Protein 92.1g

Lemon Garlic Lamb Chops

Prep time: 10 minutes
Cook time: 10 minutes
Serves: 4

Ingredients:
- 1 ½ pound lamb chops
- 2 teaspoons oregano
- 1 lemon zest
- ¼ cup olive oil
- 4 garlic cloves, minced
- 1 lemon juice
- Pepper
- Salt

Directions:
1. Place the cooking pot in the Ninja Foodi Grill Main Unit then place the grill plate in the pot.
2. Add lamb chops and remaining ingredients into the zip-lock bag. Seal bag and place in the refrigerator for overnight.
3. Press Grill mode, set the temperature to HIGH, and set time to 10 minutes. Press Start.
4. Once a unit is preheated then place marinated lamb chops on the grill plate.
5. Cover with lid and cook for 10 minutes.

Serving Suggestion: Serve warm.
Variation Tip: Add chili powder for a spicy flavor.
Nutritional Information per Serving:
Calories 431 | Fat 25.2g |Sodium 169mg | Carbs 1.5g | Fiber 0.4g | Sugar 0.1g | Protein 48g

Honey Garlic Pork Chops

Prep time: 10 minutes

Cook time: 12 minutes
Serves: 4

Ingredients:
- 4 pork chops
- 2 tablespoons grainy mustard
- 2 tablespoons Dijon mustard
- ¼ cup honey
- 3 garlic cloves, chopped
- 1 tablespoon soy sauce
- 2 tablespoons vinegar
- Pepper
- Salt

Directions:
1. Place the cooking pot in the Ninja Foodi Grill Main Unit then place the grill plate in the pot.
2. Add pork chops and remaining ingredients into the zip-lock bag. Seal bag and place in the refrigerator for 30 minutes.
3. Press Grill mode, set the temperature to HIGH, and set time to 12 minutes. Press Start.
4. Once a unit is preheated then place pork chops on the grill plate.
5. Cover with lid and cook for 12 minutes. Turn pork chops halfway through.

Serving Suggestion: Serve warm.
Variation Tip: None
Nutritional Information per Serving:
Calories 338 | Fat 20.5g |Sodium 444mg | Carbs 19.5g | Fiber 0.4g | Sugar 17.6g | Protein 18.8g

Lemon Basil Pork Chops

Prep time: 10 minutes
Cook time: 12 minutes
Serves: 4

Ingredients:
- 4 pork chops
- 1 cup fresh basil
- 2 garlic cloves
- 2 tablespoons olive oil
- 2 tablespoons fresh lemon juice
- Pepper
- Salt

Directions:
1. Place the cooking pot in the Ninja Foodi Grill Main Unit then place the grill plate in the pot.
2. Add basil, lemon juice, oil, garlic, pepper and salt into the blender and blend until smooth.

3. Add pork chops and basil mixture into the zip-lock bag. Seal bag and place in the refrigerator for 30 minutes.

4. Press Grill mode, set the temperature to HIGH, and set time to 12 minutes. Press Start.

5. Once a unit is preheated then place marinated pork chops on the grill plate.

6. Cover with lid and cook for 12 minutes.

Serving Suggestion: Serve warm.

Variation Tip: You can also add your choice of seasoning.

Nutritional Information per Serving:
Calories 322 | Fat 27g |Sodium 97mg | Carbs 0.8g | Fiber 0.2g | Sugar 0.2g | Protein 18.3g

Flavorful Pork Chops

Prep time: 10 minutes
Cook time: 14 minutes
Serves: 4

Ingredients:
- 4 pork loin chops

For Rub:
- 1 teaspoon paprika
- 2 tablespoons brown sugar
- ½ teaspoonCayenne
- ½ teaspoon ground mustard
- Pepper
- Salt

Directions:
1. Place the cooking pot in the Ninja Foodi Grill Main Unit then place the grill plate in the pot.

2. In a small bowl, mix all rub ingredients and rub all over pork chops.

3. Press Grill mode, set the temperature to HIGH, and set time to 14 minutes. Press Start.

4. Once a unit is preheated then place pork chops on the grill plate.

5. Cover with lid and cook for 14 minutes.

6. Serve and enjoy.

Serving Suggestion: Garnish with parsley and serve.

Variation Tip: Add your choice of seasonings.

Nutritional Information per Serving:
Calories 277 | Fat 20.1g |Sodium 96mg | Carbs 5g | Fiber 0.3g | Sugar 4.5g | Protein 18.2g

Greek Lamb Meatballs

Prep time: 10 minutes
Cook time: 15 minutes
Serves: 4

Ingredients:
- 1 egg
- 1 pound ground lamb
- 1 teaspoon Italian seasoning
- ¼ teaspoon coriander
- ½ teaspoon ground cumin
- 2 teaspoons dried oregano
- 1 tablespoon mint, chopped
- ¼ cup parsley, chopped
- ½ cup breadcrumbs
- 2 ½ teaspoons garlic, minced
- ¼ cup onion, grated
- Pepper
- Salt

Directions:
1. Place the cooking pot in the Ninja Foodi Grill Main Unit.

2. Add all ingredients into the bowl and mix until well combined.

3. Make small balls from the meat mixture and place into the baking dish.

4. Press Bake mode, set the temperature to 400°F, and set time to 15 minutes. Press Start.

5. Once a unit is preheated then place the baking dish in the cooking pot.

6. Cover with lid and cook for 15 minutes.

Serving Suggestion: Garnish with chopped coriander and serve.

Variation Tip: Add ¼ teaspoon of crushed red pepper flakes.

Nutritional Information per Serving:
Calories 294 | Fat 10.7g |Sodium 243mg | Carbs 12.2g | Fiber 1.4g | Sugar 1.4g | Protein 35.5g

Garlic Rosemary Lamb Chops

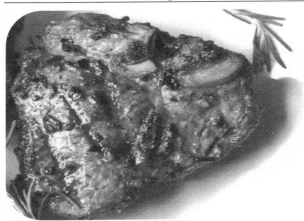

Prep time: 10 minutes
Cook time: 10 minutes
Serves: 6

Ingredients:
- 2 pounds of lamb chops
- 1 tablespoon rosemary, chopped
- ¼ cup olive oil
- 1 tablespoon garlic, minced
- 1 lemon zest
- Pepper
- Salt

Directions:
1. Place the cooking pot in the Ninja Foodi Grill Main Unit then place the grill plate in the pot.
2. Add lamb chops and remaining ingredients into the zip-lock bag. Seal bag and place in the refrigerator overnight.
3. Press Grill mode, set the temperature to HIGH, and set time to 10 minutes. Press Start.
4. Once a unit is preheated then place lamb chops on the grill plate.
5. Cover with lid and cook for 10 minutes.
Serving Suggestion: Serve warm.
Variation Tip: None
Nutritional Information per Serving:
Calories 357 | Fat 19.6g |Sodium 143mg | Carbs 0.8g | Fiber 0.3g | Sugar 0g | Protein 42.6g

Cheese Beef Meatballs

Prep time: 10 minutes
Cook time: 10 minutes
Serves: 4

Ingredients:
- 1 egg
- 1 pound ground beef
- ¼ cup onions, chopped
- ½ cup Cheddar cheese, shredded
- 2 tablespoons taco seasoning
- Pepper
- Salt

Directions:
1. Place the cooking pot in the Ninja Foodi Grill Main Unit then place the Ninja Foodi Crisper Basket in the pot.
2. Add all ingredients into the bowl and mix until well combined.
3. Make small balls from the meat mixture and place in the Ninja Foodi Crisper Basket.
4. Press Air Crisp mode, set the temperature to 400°F, and set time to 10 minutes.
5. Cover with lid and press Start.
Serving Suggestion: Garnish with parsley and serve.
Variation Tip: Add your choice of seasonings.
Nutritional Information per Serving:
Calories 286 | Fat 12.9g |Sodium 217mg | Carbs 1g | Fiber 0.2g | Sugar 0.5g | Protein 39.4g

Black Diamond-Style Steak

Prep time: 10 minutes.
Cook time: 10 minutes.
Serves: 6

Ingredients:
- ¼ cup 2 tbsp. Worcestershire sauce
- ¼ cup 2 tbsp. soy sauce
- 2 tbsp. balsamic vinegar
- ¼ tsp. garlic powder
- ¼ tsp. onion powder
- Black pepper, to taste
- 3 lbs. steak

Preparation:
1. Mix black pepper, onion powder, garlic powder, balsamic vinegar, soy sauce, and Worcestershire sauce in a ziplock bag.
2. Add steak to the bag, mix well and seal it to refrigerate for 1 hour.
3. Place the cooking pot in the Ninja Foodi Grill

then set a grill grate inside.

4. Select the "Grill" Mode, set the temperature to MAX.

5. Press the START/STOP button to initiate preheating.

6. Once preheated, place the steak in the Ninja Foodi Grill.

7. Cover the hood and cook for 10 minutes, flipping halfway through.

8. Serve warm.

Serving Suggestion: Serve the steaks with fresh cucumber salad.

Variation Tip: Coat the beef with pork rinds before cooking.

Nutritional Information Per Serving:
Calories 352 | Fat 2.4g |Sodium 216mg | Carbs 16g | Fiber 2.3g | Sugar 1.2g | Protein 27g

Grilled Stuffed Flank Steak

Prep time: 15 minutes.
Cook time: 10 minutes.
Serves: 2

Ingredients:
- ¼ cup vegetable oil
- 2 cups thinly sliced scallions
- 3 tbsp. minced fresh ginger
- 1 (2 ½ lbs.) whole flank steak
- Kosher salt and black pepper, to taste
- 1 cup teriyaki sauce

Preparation:
1. Sauté ginger and scallions with oil in a skillet for 30 seconds then allow them to cool.

2. Cut the steak in ½ inch thick slices and cut each slice into 2-3 smaller rectangles.

3. Season the steaks with black pepper and salt then top each piece with the scallion mixture.

4. Roll the steak pieces and secure them a toothpick.

5. Place the cooking pot in the Ninja Foodi Grill then set a grill grate inside.

6. Select the "Grill" Mode, set the temperature to HI.

7. Press the START/STOP button to initiate preheating.

8. Once preheated, place the steak in the Ninja Foodi Grill.

9. Cover the hood and grill for 10 minutes, flipping halfway through.

10. Serve warm.

Serving Suggestion: Serve the steaks with scallions on top.

Variation Tip: Add 1 tbsp. lime juice to the seasoning.

Nutritional Information Per Serving:
Calories 431 | Fat 20.1g |Sodium 364mg | Carbs 13g | Fiber 1g | Sugar 1.4g | Protein 25g

Grill Lamb Chops

Prep time: 10 minutes
Cook time: 10 minutes
Serves: 4

Ingredients:
- 2 pounds of lamb chops
- ¼ cup fresh lime juice
- ¼ cup olive oil
- ¼ teaspoon red pepper flakes, crushed
- 2 teaspoons garlic, minced
- 2 teaspoons dried oregano
- ½ teaspoon pepper
- 1 teaspoon salt

Directions:
1. Place the cooking pot in the Ninja Foodi Grill Main Unit then place the Ninja Foodi Crisper Basket in the pot.

2. Add lamb chops and remaining ingredients into the zip-lock bag. Seal bag and place in the refrigerator overnight.

3. Add marinated lamb chops in the Ninja Foodi Crisper Basket.

4. Press Air Crisp mode, set the temperature to 400°F, and set time to 10 minutes.

5. Cover with lid and press Start. Turn lamb chops halfway through.

Serving Suggestion: Serve warm.

Variation Tip: Add your choice of seasonings.

Nutritional Information per Serving:
Calories 535 | Fat 29.3g |Sodium 754mg | Carbs 1.1g | Fiber 0.4g | Sugar 0g | Protein 63.9g

Seekh Kebabs

Prep time: 15 minutes.
Cook time: 9 minutes.
Serves: 4

Ingredients:

Spice Blend:
- 2 tsp. whole black peppercorns
- 1 ½ tsp. whole coriander seeds
- 1 tsp. whole cumin seed
- 2 whole cloves
- 2 whole bay leaves
- 2 tsp. sweet paprika
- ½ tsp. cayenne pepper
- 3 tsp. kosher salt
- 1 tsp. amchur powder

Aromatics:
- 1 red onion, chopped
- 2 cups fresh cilantro leaves
- 4 medium garlic cloves, chopped
- 1 ½ tbsp. fresh ginger, chopped
- 4 green Thai bird chilies
- 1 ½ tsp. sugar
- 2 lbs. ground lamb

To Serve:
- Shredded cabbage
- Sliced cucumbers
- Tomatoes, sliced
- Lime wedges

Preparation:
1. Add peppercorns, coriander seeds, cumin seeds and cloves to a hot pan for 1 minute.
2. Grind the spices in a food processor then add bay leaves, sugar, chilies, ginger, garlic, cilantro, red onion, amchur, salt, cayenne and paprika.
3. Blend again and add ground lamb, onion, cilantro, garlic, ginger, bird chilies, and sugar.
4. Mix again and thread the beef mixture over the wooden skewers to make long kebabs.

5. Place the cooking pot in the Ninja Foodi Grill then set a grill grate inside.
6. Select the "Grill" Mode, set the temperature to MAX.
7. Press the START/STOP button to initiate preheating.
8. Once preheated, place the kebabs in the Ninja Foodi Grill.
9. Cover the hood and cook for 4 minutes per side.
10. Serve warm.

Serving Suggestion: Serve the steaks with toasted bread slices and cabbage slaw.
Variation Tip: Add canned adobo peppers to season the kebabs.
Nutritional Information Per Serving:
Calories 301 | Fat 16g |Sodium 412mg | Carbs 13g | Fiber 0.2g | Sugar 1g | Protein 28.2g

Juicy Pork Chops

Prep time: 10 minutes
Cook time: 10 minutes
Serves: 4

Ingredients:
- 4 pork chops, boneless
- 1 teaspoon Italian seasoning
- 1 teaspoon olive oil
- ¼ teaspoon garlic powder
- Pepper
- Salt

Directions:
1. Place the cooking pot in the Ninja Foodi Grill Main Unit then place the Ninja Foodi Crisper Basket in the pot.
2. In a small bowl, mix oil, Italian seasoning, garlic powder, pepper and salt.
3. Brush pork chops with oil mixture and place in theNinja Foodi Crisper Basket.
4. Press Air Crisp mode, set the temperature to 400°F, and set time to 10 minutes.
5. Cover with lid and press start.

Serving Suggestion: Garnish with chopped coriander and serve.
Variation Tip: None
Nutritional Information per Serving:
Calories 270 | Fat 21.4g |Sodium 95mg | Carbs 0.3g | Fiber 0g | Sugar 0.1g | Protein 18g

Ninja Foodi Asparagus Steak Tips

Prep time: 10 minutes
Cook time: 15 minutes
Serves: 4

Ingredients:

- 2 pounds steak cubes
- ¼ teaspoon cayenne pepper
- 1 teaspoon dried onion powder
- 2 pounds asparagus, tough ends trimmed
- 3 teaspoons olive oil
- 1 teaspoon dried garlic powder
- Salt and black pepper, to taste

Preparation:

1. Insert grill grate in the unit and close hood. Select GRILL, set temperature to MEDIUM, and set time to 15 minutes. Select START/STOP to begin preheating.
2. Meanwhile, in a Ziploc bag, add steak cubes, cayenne pepper, garlic powder, salt, black pepper, and onion powder. Shake vigorously.
3. In a mixing dish, combine asparagus, salt, and olive oil. Mix thoroughly. When the Ninja Foodi Grill shows "Add Food", place steak cubes in it and cook for 10 minutes.
4. After 10 minutes, add the seasoned asparagus and simmer for another 5 minutes.
5. Remove from the oven and serve immediately.

Serving Suggestions: You can serve with vinegar on the top.

Variation Tip: You can also add chili sauce for spicy taste.

Nutritional Information per Serving:
Calories: 404 |Fat: 17.3g|Sat Fat: 6g|Carbohydrates: 9.9g|Fiber: 4.9g|Sugar: 4.7g|Protein: 53.8g

Ninja Foodi Korean BBQ Beef

Prep time: 10 minutes
Cook time: 15 minutes
Serves: 4

Ingredients:

- 2 pounds steak
- ½ cup cornstarch
- 1 cup soy sauce
- 2 tablespoons barbeque sauce
- 2 teaspoons water
- 2 teaspoons ground ginger
- 1 cup brown sugar
- 4 tablespoons white wine vinegar
- 1 teaspoon sesame seeds
- 2 garlic cloves, crushed
- Salt and pepper, to taste

Preparation:

1. Whisk together the cornstarch and water until the sauce thickens. Remove the item and place it away.
2. In a skillet, combine all of the remaining ingredients, except the steak. Cook to perfection.
3. Insert grill grate in the unit and close hood. Select GRILL, set temperature to MEDIUM, and set time to 10 minutes. Select START/STOP to begin preheating.
4. Cover steak with cornstarch and place it in the Ninja Foodi Grill when it shows "Add Food".
5. Cook for 10 minutes at medium pressure and take out.
6. Top with barbeque sauce and serve.

Serving Suggestions: Top with fresh cilantro before serving.

Variation Tip: You can use chopped green bell pepper to enhance taste.

Nutritional Information per Serving:
Calories: 708 |Fat: 11.8g|Sat Fat: 4g|Carbohydrates: 59.3g|Fiber: 0.9g|Sugar: 38.4g|Protein: 86.3g

Ninja Foodi Herbed Pork Chops

Prep time: 10 minutes
Cook time: 12 minutes
Serves: 4

Ingredients:
- 2 pounds pork loin chops
- 2 tablespoons herb and garlic seasoning
- 2 teaspoons olive oil

Preparation:
1. Insert crisper basket in the unit. Select AIR CRISP, set temperature to 350°F, and set time to 12 minutes. Select START/STOP to begin preheating
2. In a mixing dish, combine the pork loin chops, olive oil, herb, and garlic seasoning. Mix thoroughly.
3. Place pork chops in Ninja Foodi Grill when it says "Add Food" and cook for 12 minutes.
4. Remove the dish from the unit and serve immediately.

Serving Suggestions: Serve with chopped cilantro on the top.
Variation Tip: Olive oil can be replaced with coconut oil.
Nutritional Information per Serving:
Calories: 751 |Fat: 58.7g|Sat Fat: 21.5g|Carbohydrates: 1g|Fiber: 0g|Sugar: 0g|Protein: 51g

Ninja Foodi Pork Ribs

Prep time: 5 minutes
Cook time: 20 minutes
Serves: 3

Ingredients:
- ½ tablespoon sweet paprika

- ¼ teaspoon mustard powder
- ½ teaspoon garlic powder
- ½ teaspoon onion powder
- 1 pound pork ribs
- ½ tablespoon dark brown sugar
- ½ teaspoon poultry seasoning
- Salt and black pepper, to taste

Preparation:
1. Insert grill grate in the unit and close hood. Select GRILL, set temperature to MEDIUM, and set time to 20 minutes. Select START/STOP to begin preheating.
2. In a large mixing bowl, add everything except the pork ribs. Mix thoroughly.
3. Set aside pork ribs that have been dipped in the mixture.
4. Place pork ribs in the Ninja Foodi Grill when it shows "Add Food" and cook for 20 minutes.
5. Turn halfway through and serve.
6. Finally, serve and enjoy!

Serving Suggestions: Serve with chopped cilantro on the top.
Variation Tip: Add in chopped red bell pepper to enhance taste.
Nutritional Information per Serving:
Calories: 427 |Fat: 27g|Sat Fat: 9.6g|Carbohydrates: 3.1g|Fiber: 0.6g|Sugar: 1.9g|Protein: 40.4g

Ninja Foodi Crispy Pork Belly

Prep time: 5 minutes
Cook time: 20 minutes
Serves: 2

Ingredients:
- 1 pound pork belly, cubed
- ¼ teaspoon fish sauce
- 2 tablespoons Sriracha sauce
- ¼ cup coconut aminos
- ¼ cup coconut vinegar
- Salt, to taste

Preparation:
1. Insert crisper basket in the unit. Select AIR CRISP, set temperature to 390°F, and set time to 20 minutes. Select START/STOP to begin preheating
2. In a Ziploc bag, combine all of the ingredients and leave aside for 2 hours.
3. Place pork belly cubes in the Ninja Foodi Grill

when it says "Add Food" and cook for 20 minutes, flipping halfway through.

4. Remove the dish from the oven and serve immediately.

Serving Suggestions: Serve with chopped bell peppers on the top.

Variation Tip: Fish sauce can be replaced with BBQ sauce.

Nutritional Information per Serving:
Calories: 1077 |Fat: 61.1g|Sat Fat: 26.2g|Carbohydrates: 6.2g|Fiber: 0g|Sugar: 0g|Protein: 104.7g

Ninja Foodi Beef Satay

Prep time: 10 minutes
Cook time: 15 minutes
Serves: 4

Ingredients:
- 4 tablespoons olive oil
- 2 tablespoons fish sauce
- 2 tablespoons sugar
- ½ cup peanuts, roasted and chopped
- 2 tablespoons garlic, minced
- 1 cup chopped cilantro
- 2 pounds beef steak, cubed
- 2 tablespoons minced ginger
- 2 teaspoons ground coriander
- 2 tablespoons soy sauce
- 2 teaspoons Sriracha sauce
- Salt, to taste

Preparation:
1. Insert grill grate in the unit and close hood. Select GRILL, set temperature to MEDIUM, and set time to 15 minutes. Select START/STOP to begin preheating.

2. In a mixing bowl, combine all of the ingredients except the beef steak and olive oil. Mix thoroughly.

1. Dip beefsteak in the mixture and place them in the "Crisper Basket" when the Ninja Foodi Grill shown "Add food."

3. Drizzle with olive oil and cook for 15 minutes on the grill.

4. Turn halfway through and serve.

5. Finally, serve and enjoy!

Serving Suggestions: Serve with rice.

Variation Tip: Add red chili powder to enhance taste.

Nutritional Information per Serving:

Calories: 691 |Fat: 37.3g|Sat Fat: 8.6g|Carbohydrates: 13.4g|Fiber: 2.2g|Sugar: 7.4g|Protein: 75.1g

Ninja Foodi Basil Pork Loin

Prep time: 5 minutes
Cook time: 20 minutes
Serves: 3

Ingredients:
- 3 teaspoons dried basil
- 1 pound pork loin
- ½ teaspoon garlic powder
- 1½ tablespoons sugar
- Salt, to taste

Preparation:
1. In a mixing dish, combine basil, sugar, garlic powder, and salt. Mix thoroughly.

2. Rub the pork loin with the mixture and put it aside.

3. Insert crisper basket in the unit. Select AIR CRISP, set temperature to 400°F, and set time to 20 minutes. Select START/STOP to begin preheating

4. When it appears "Add Food", place pork loin in it and cook for 20 minutes at 400 degrees F.

5. Flip halfway through and dish out.

6. Serve and enjoy!

Serving Suggestions: Serve with herbed butter on the top.

Variation Tip: Garlic powder can be omitted.

Nutritional Information per Serving:
Calories: 430 |Fat: 25.5g|Sat Fat: 5.7g|Carbohydrates: 10.2g|Fiber: 2.1g|Sugar: 3.6g|Protein: 38.8g

Ninja Foodi Bacon Wrapped Filet Mignon

Prep time: 10 minutes
Cook time: 15 minutes
Serves: 4

Ingredients:
- 4 bacon slices
- 2 teaspoons avocado oil
- 4 filet mignon
- Salt and black pepper, to taste

Preparation:
1. Season mignon fillets with salt, pepper, and avocado oil before wrapping them in bacon pieces.
2. Insert grill grate in the unit and close hood. Select "AIR CRISP", set temperature to 375 degrees F, and set time to 15 minutes. Select START/STOP to begin preheating.
3. When it shows "Add Food," add the fillets de mignon and cook for 15 minutes at 375°F.
4. Remove from the oven and serve immediately.

Serving Suggestions: Squeeze with lemon before serving.

Variation Tip: You can also add cayenne pepper to enhance taste.

Nutritional Information per Serving:
Calories: 258 |Fat: 13.8g|Sat Fat: 4.8g|Carbohydrates: 0.4g|Fiber: 0.1g|Sugar: 0g|Protein: 30.9g

Ninja Foodi Buttered Beef Steak

Prep time: 5 minutes
Cook time: 8 minutes
Serves: 2

Ingredients:

- 1 tablespoon melted butter
- 1 pound beef steak
- Salt and black pepper, to taste

Preparation:
1. Season the beef steak with salt, pepper, and butter that has been melted. Set aside.
2. Insert grill grate in the unit and close hood. Select GRILL, set temperature to HIGH, and set time to 8 minutes. Select START/STOP to begin preheating.
3. When "Add Food" appears, add the beefsteak and grill for around 8 minutes.
4. Remove halfway through and flip.
5. Finally, serve and enjoy!

Serving Suggestions: Top with chopped mint leaves serving.

Variation Tip: You can add more butter if you want.

Nutritional Information per Serving:
Calories: 472 |Fat: 19.9g|Sat Fat: 9g|Carbohydrates: 0g|Fiber: 0g|Sugar: 0g|Protein: 68.9g

Ninja Foodi Herbed Beef Steak

Prep time: 15 minutes
Cook time: 8 minutes
Serves: 8

Ingredients:
- 4 tablespoon melted butter
- 4 (¾ pounds) strip steaks
- 4 tablespoons herb and garlic seasoning
- Salt and black pepper, to taste

Preparation:
1. Season the beef steak with salt, pepper, and butter that has been melted. Set aside.
2. Insert grill grate in the unit and close hood. Select GRILL, set temperature to HIGH, and set time to 8 minutes. Select START/STOP to begin preheating.
3. When "Add Food" appears, add the beefsteak and simmer for around 8 minutes.
6. Remove halfway through and flip.
7. Finally, serve and enjoy!

Serving Suggestions: Top with yogurt before serving.

Variation Tip: You can add green chili sauce to enhance taste.

Nutritional Information per Serving:
Calories: 372 |Fat: 16.4g|Sat Fat: 7.7g|Carbohydrates: 1g|Fiber: 0g|Sugar: 0g|Protein: 51.7g

Ninja Foodi Herbed Lamb Chops

Prep time: 5 minutes
Cook time: 12 minutes
Serves: 2

Ingredients:
- 1 pound lamb chops
- 1 tablespoon herb and garlic seasoning
- 1 teaspoon olive oil
- 2 tablespoons herbed butter
- Salt and black pepper, to taste

Preparation:
1. Insert crisper basket in the unit. Select AIR CRISP, set temperature to 350°F, and set time to 12 minutes. Select START/STOP to begin preheating
2. In a mixing bowl, combine the lamb chops, herbed butter, olive oil, herb, and garlic seasoning. Mix thoroughly.
3. When the Ninja Foodi Grill shows "Add Food", place lamb chops in it and cook for 12 minutes.
4. Dish out and serve warm.

Serving Suggestions: Serve with chopped mint leaves on the top.
Variation Tip: You can add some herbs to enhance taste.
Nutritional Information per Serving:
Calories: 797 |Fat: 45g|Sat Fat: 17.3g|Carbohydrates: 4g|Fiber: 0g|Sugar: 1g|Protein: 86.7g

Ninja Foodi Lamb Leg Roast

Prep time: 5 minutes
Cook time: 1 hour 15 minutes
Serves: 2

Ingredients:

- 2 pounds lamb leg
- 2 tablespoons olive oil
- 1 tablespoon fresh rosemary
- ½ tablespoon black pepper
- 1½ tablespoons fresh thyme
- Salt, to taste

Preparation:
1. Preheat the Ninja Foodi Grill to 300 degrees F and press the "ROAST" button.
2. Fill it with the "Crisper Basket" and set the timer for 15 minutes.
3. To begin preheating, press START/STOP.
4. In a small bowl, combine rosemary, olive oil, black pepper, and thyme. Mix thoroughly.
5. Rub the thyme mixture all over the lamb leg and set it aside.
6. Cook for 75 minutes with the lamb leg in the "Crisper Basket."
7. Remove from the oven and cover with foil.
8. Finally, serve and enjoy!

Serving Suggestions: Serve with lime wedges on the top.
Variation Tip: Olive oil can be replaced with vegetable oil.
Nutritional Information per Serving:
Calories: 739 |Fat: 36.7g|Sat Fat: 10.1g|Carbohydrates: 6.9g|Fiber: 3.9g|Sugar: 0.1g|Protein: 93.1g

Ninja Foodi Herbed Lamb Leg

Prep time: 10 minutes
Cook time: 1 hour
Serves: 3

Ingredients:
- 2 pounds lamb leg
- 1 fresh thyme sprig
- 1 tablespoon olive oil
- 1 fresh rosemary sprig
- Salt and black pepper, to taste

Preparation:
1. In a mixing dish, combine the thyme, rosemary, salt, black pepper, and olive oil. Mix thoroughly.
2. Rub the thyme mixture all over the lamb leg and set it aside.
3. Insert crisper basket in the unit. Select AIR CRISP, set temperature to 300°F, and set time to 60 minutes. Select START/STOP to begin preheating.
4. When it shows "Add Food", place lamb leg in it and cook for 60 minutes at 300 degrees F.
5. Take out and serve hot.

Serving Suggestions: Serve with rice.
Variation Tip: Black pepper can be replaced with cayenne pepper.
Nutritional Information per Serving:
Calories: 587 |Fat: 24.9g|Sat Fat: 7.9g|Carbohydrates: 0.5g|Fiber: 0.3g|Sugar: 0g|Protein: 85.2g

Ninja Foodi Garlic Lamb Chops

Prep time: 10 minutes
Cook time: 15 minutes
Serves: 2
Ingredients:
- 2 garlic cloves
- ½ teaspoon olive oil
- ½ tablespoon lemon juice
- 4 lamb chops
- ½ tablespoon garlic powder
- Salt and black pepper, to taste

Preparation:
1. In a large mixing basin, combine all of the ingredients, stir well, and set away.
2. Insert crisper basket in the unit. Select AIR CRISP, set temperature to 400°F, and set time to 15 minutes. Select START/STOP to begin preheating.
3. Preheat the oven to 400 degrees Fahrenheit and set the timer for 15 minutes.
4. To begin preheating, press START/STOP.
5. When "Add Food" appears, add the lamb chops and cook for 15 minutes at 400 degrees F.
6. Turn halfway through and serve.
7. Finally, serve and enjoy!

Serving Suggestions: Serve with mint leaves on the top.
Variation Tip: You can add more garlic cloves for strong garlicy taste.
Nutritional Information per Serving:
Calories: 1079 |Fat: 59.2g|Sat Fat: 33.5g|Carbohydrates: 22.3g|Fiber: 3.1g|Sugar: 2.4g|Protein: 109.5g

Grilled Salmon with Mustard & Herbs

Prep time: 15 minutes
Cook time: 40 minutes
Servings: 4

Ingredients

- 2 lemons, thinly sliced,
- 20-30 sprigs mixed fresh herbs, plus 2 tbsp chopped, divided
- 1 tablespoon Dijon mustard
- 1 pound center-cut salmon, skinned
- 1 clove garlic
- ¼ tsp salt

Preparation

1. Preheat the grill for 8 minutes.

2. Lay the 2 9-inch pieces of heavy-duty foil on top of one another and place it on a baking sheet. Arrange the lemon slices in two layers in the center of the foil. Spread the herb sprigs on the lemons. With the chef's knife, mash the garlic with salt and form a paste. Transfer it to a small dish and then stir in mustard and the remaining two tsp of chopped herbs. Spread the mixture on double sides of the salmon. Place the salmon on top of the herb sprigs.

3. Slide off the foil and salmon from the baking sheet onto the grill Insert grill grate in the unit and close the hood. Select the option GRILL, set the temperature to MAX and time to 24 minutes. Select the option START/STOP to begin cooking.

4. Cook the fish for 20 minutes from each side. Work in batches.

Serving Suggestion: Divide the salmon into four portions and serve it with lemon wedges.

Variation Tip: use chopped dill for garnish.

Nutritional Information Per Serving:
Calories 197.3 | Carbohydrates 21.5g | Protein 2.5g | Fat 11.6g | Sodium 59.8mg| Fiber 1 g

Teriyaki-Marinated Salmon

Prep time: 5 minutes
Cook time: 8 minutes
Servings: 4

Ingredients

- 4 uncooked skinless salmon fillets (6 ounces each)
- 1 cup teriyaki marinade

Preparation

1. Put the fish fillets and teriyaki sauce in a big resalable plastic bag. Move the fillets around to coat everywhere with sauce. Refrigerate it for one to twelve hours as per your need.

2. Insert the grill grate in the unit and close the hood. Select the option GRILL, set the temperature to MAX, and set the time to 8 minutes. Press START/STOP to begin preheating.

3. When the unit signals that it has preheated, put fillets on the grill, gently press them to maximize the grill marks. Close the hood and cook it for 6 minutes. There isn't a need to flip the fish while cooking.

4. After 6 minutes, check the fillets if done; the internal temperature should come at least 140°F. If necessary, close the hood and continue to cook for 2 more minutes.

5. After cooking, serve the fillets immediately.

Serving Suggestion: Serve with lemon wedges.

Variation Tip: use chopped dill for garnish.

Nutritional Information per Serving:
Calories 190 | Carbohydrates 26g | Protein 4g | Fat 9g | Sodium 105mg| Fiber 3g

Grilled Fish Tacos

Prep time: 30 minutes
Cook time: 50minutes
Servings: 6

Ingredients

- 4 tsp chili powder
- 2 tbsp lime juice
- 2 tbsp extra-virgin olive oil
- 1 tsp ground cumin
- 1 tsp onion powder
- 1 tsp garlic powder
- 1 tsp salt
- ½ tsp freshly ground pepper
- 2 pounds mahi-mahi, ¾ inch thick, skinned and cut into 4 portions
- ¼ cup reduced-fat sour cream
- ¼ cup low-fat mayonnaise
- 2 tbsp chopped fresh cilantro
- 1 tsp lime zest
- Freshly ground pepper
- 3 cups finely shredded red or green cabbage
- 2 tbsp lime juice
- 1 tsp sugar
- ⅛ tsp salt
- 12 corn tortillas, warmed

Preparation

1. To prepare the fish: Combine lime juice, chili powder, oil, cumin, onion powder, salt and pepper, garlic powder in a bowl. Rub the adobo over all the fish. Let it stand 20 to 30 minutes for the fish to absorb the flavor.

2. To prepare the coleslaw: Add lime juice, sour cream, mayonnaise, cilantro, lime zest, salt and pepper, sugar, in a medium bowl; mix them until smooth and creamy. Add the cabbage and toss it to combine. Refrigerate until ready to use.

3. Preheat the grill for 8 minutes before use.

4. Insert Grill Grate in the unit and close the hood. Select the option GRILL, set the temperature to LOW, and set time to 15 minutes. Select the option START/STOP to begin cooking.

5. Transfer the fish to a plate and then separate it into large chunks.

Serving Suggestion: Serve the tacos by passing the fish, tortillas, coleslaw and taco garnishes separately.

Variation Tip: use chopped dill for garnish.

Nutritional Information per Serving:
Calories 215.3 | Carbohydrates 19.4g | Protein 3.7g | Fat 14.7g | Sodium 83.8mg| Fiber 1.1g

Paprika Grilled Shrimp

Prep time: 5-10 minutes
Cook time: 6 minutes
Servings: 4

Ingredients

- 1-pound jumbo shrimps, peeled and deveined
- 2 tbsp brown sugar
- 1 tablespoon paprika
- 1 tablespoon garlic powder
- 2 tbsp olive oil
- 1 tsp garlic salt
- ½ tsp black pepper

Preparation

1. Add listed Ingredients into a mixing bowl.
2. Mix them well.
3. Let it chill and marinate for 30-60 minutes.
4. Pre-heat Ninja Foodi by pressing the "GRILL" option and setting it to "MED.".
5. Set the timer to 6 minutes.
6. Let it pre-heat until you hear a beep.
7. Arrange prepared shrimps over the Grill Grate.
8. Lock lid and cook for 3 minutes.
9. Then flip and cook for 3 minutes more.
10. Serve and enjoy!

Serving Suggestion: Serve with dill garnishing or enjoy as it is.

Variation Tip: use hot chili powder for spicier.

Nutritional Information per Serving:
Calories: 370| Fat: 27 g| Carbohydrates: 23 g| Fiber: 8 g| Sodium: 182 mg| Protein: 6 g

Grilled Seafood Platter

Prep time: 30 minutes
Cook time: 10 minutes
Servings: 6

Ingredients

- 1 cup extra virgin olive oil
- 2 garlic cloves, finely chopped
- 2 tbsp chopped basil
- Zest and juice of 2 lemons
- 4 blue swimmer crabs, halved, claws cracked
- 4 lobster tails or small whole lobsters, halved, cleaned
- 24 scampi, peeled (tails intact), deveined
- 32 green prawns, peeled (tails intact), deveined
- 350g clams
- 12 scallops in the half shell
- 2 tbsp chopped flat-leaf parsley
- Avocado cream
- 2 ripe avocados, peeled, stoned, roughly chopped
- ½ cup thickened cream
- 1 garlic clove, chopped
- Juice of 1 lime

Seafood sauce

- 200ml whole-egg mayonnaise
- 1 small lime, zest grated, juiced
- 1 tbsp sweet chilli sauce
- 1 tbsp tomato sauce

Preparation

1. Combine the oil, garlic, basil, lemon juice and zest in a bowl, then season. Brush the marinade over the seafood.
2. Preheat the Ninja Foodi Grill for 5 minutes at the GRILL function at MEDIUM heat setting.
3. Heat a ninja grill over MEDIUM heat. Cook the crab and lobster for 2 minutes, then add the scampi and cook for a further 2 minutes. Add the prawns and clams, and cook for 3-4 minutes, then add the scallops. When the clams open and the prawns and scallops are opaque, transfer all seafood to a platter. Serve with parsley, avocado and seafood sauces.
4. **To make the avocado cream**: Pulse ingredients in a food processor until smooth. Season to taste with sea salt and freshly ground black pepper.

5. **To make the seafood sauce**: Whisk the ingredients together. Season with salt and pepper.

Serving Suggestion: Serve the platter with yummy sauce.

Variation Tip: use your favorite fish.

Nutritional Information Per Serving:
Calories 664 | Carbohydrates 11g | Protein 68g | Fat 38g | Sodium 1459mg| Fiber 0.6g

Easy BBQ Roast Shrimp

Prep time: 5-10 minutes
Cook time: 7 minutes
Servings: 2

Ingredients

- ½ pound shrimps, large
- 3 tbsp chipotle in adobo sauce, minced
- ½ orange, juiced
- ¼ cup BBQ sauce
- ¼ tsp salt

Preparation

1. Add listed Ingredients into a mixing bowl.
2. Mix them well.
3. Keep it aside.
4. Pre-heat Ninja Foodi Grill by pressing the "ROAST" option and setting it to "400 Degrees F.".
5. Set the timer to 7 minutes.
6. Let it pre-heat until you hear a beep.
7. Arrange shrimps over Grill Grate and lock lid.
8. Cook for 7 minutes.
9. Serve and enjoy!

Serving Suggestion: Serve with dill garnishing.

Variation Tip: use chopped dill for garnish.

Nutritional Information Per Serving:
Calories: 173|Fat: 2 g| Carbohydrates: 21 g| Fiber: 2 g| Sodium: 1143 mg| Protein: 17 g

Ginger Salmon with Cucumber Lime Sauce

Prep time: 30 minutes
Cook time: 10 minutes
Servings: 10

Ingredients
- 1 tablespoon grated lime zest
- 4 tsp sugar
- ½ tsp salt
- ¼ cup lime juice
- 2 tbsp olive oil
- 2 tbsp rice vinegar or white wine vinegar
- ½ tsp ground coriander
- ½ tsp freshly ground pepper
- 2 tsp minced fresh ginger root
- 2 garlic cloves, minced
- 2 medium cucumbers, peeled, seeded and chopped
- ⅓ cup chopped fresh cilantro
- 1 tablespoon finely chopped onion

Salmon
- 1 tablespoon olive oil
- ½ tsp salt
- ⅓ cup minced fresh ginger root
- 1 tablespoon lime juice
- ½ tsp freshly ground pepper
- 10 salmon fillets (6 ounces each)

Preparation
1. Place the first 13 Ingredients of the list in a blender. Cover and process until pureed.
2. In a bowl, combine ginger, oil, salt, lime juice, and pepper. Rub over flesh side of salmon fillets.
3. Preheat the grill for 5 minutes.
4. Lightly oil the grill. Place salmon on grill, skin side down. Grill while covered over MEDIUM heat 10-12 minutes or until fish just begins to flake easily with a fork.

Serving Suggestion: Serve with sauce.
Variation Tip: use chopped dill for garnish.

Nutritional Information per Serving:
Calories 248 | Carbohydrates 40.7g | Protein 2.5g | Fat 10.8g | Sodium 120.4mg| Fiber 0.7g

Grilled Shrimp Cocktail with Yellow Gazpacho Salsa

Prep time: 40 minutes
Cook time: 60 minutes
Servings: 4

Ingredients
- 4 medium yellow tomatoes, seeded and finely chopped
- 1 stalk celery, finely chopped
- ½ small red onion, finely chopped
- 1 yellow bell pepper, finely chopped
- 1 medium cucumber, peeled, seeded and finely chopped
- 1 tablespoon Worcestershire sauce
- ½ tsp freshly ground pepper
- 2 tbsp minced fresh chives
- 2 tbsp white-wine vinegar
- 2 tbsp lemon juice
- ¼ tsp salt
- Several dashes hot sauce, to taste
- 1pound raw shrimp, peeled and deveined
- 2 cloves garlic, minced
- 2 tsp minced fresh thyme

Preparation
1. Preheat the grill for 8 minutes.
2. Mix the tomatoes, cucumber, celery, bell pepper, onion, vinegar, lemon juice, chives, Worcestershire sauce, salt and pepper, and hot sauce in a big bowl. Cover it and chill for at least twenty minutes or for a single day.
3. Mix the shrimp, garlic, and thyme in a medium bowl; cover it and refrigerate for twenty minutes.
4. Insert grill grates in the unit and close the hood. Select the option GRILL, set the temperature to LOW, and set time to 4 minutes. Select the option START/STOP to begin cooking. Cook 2 minutes per side.

Serving Suggestion: Serve the shrimp with salsa in martini glasses.
Variation Tip: use chicken chips with same method.

Nutritional Information Per Serving:
Calories 251.8 | Carbohydrates 33.7g | Protein 2.6g | Fat 12.3g | Sodium 185.7mg| Fiber 0.6g

Shrimp with Tomatoes

Prep time: 15 minutes.
Cook time: 8 minutes.
Serves: 6

Ingredients:
- ⅔ cup fresh arugula
- ⅓ cup lemon juice
- 2 tablespoons olive oil
- 2 garlic cloves, minced
- ½ teaspoon grated lemon zest
- 1-lb. uncooked shrimp, peeled and deveined
- 2 green onions, sliced
- ¼ cup plain yogurt
- 2 teaspoons 2% milk
- 1 teaspoon cider vinegar
- 1 teaspoon Dijon mustard
- ½ teaspoon sugar
- ½ teaspoon salt, divided
- 12 cherry tomatoes
- ¼ teaspoon black pepper

Preparation:
1. Season the shrimp with lemon juice, lemon zest, oil, and garlic in a suitable bowl.
2. Let it for 10 minutes of margination.
3. Now arugula, yogurt, milk, green onion, sugar, vinegar, mustard, and ¼ teaspoon salt in a blender.
4. Thread the seasoned shrimp and tomatoes on the skewers alternately.
5. And season the skewers with salt and black pepper.
6. Preheat the Ninja Foodi Grill on the "Grill Mode" at MEDIUM-temperature settings.
7. When the grill is preheated, open its hood and place the skewers in it.
8. Cover the grill's hood and grill for 2 minutes per side.
9. Cook the shrimp in batches.
10. Serve with the prepared sauce.

Serving Suggestion: Serve the shrimp tomatoes meal on top of the rice risotto.
Variation Tip: Add paprika for more spice.
Nutritional Information Per Serving:
Calories 448 | Fat 13g |Sodium 353mg | Carbs 31g | Fiber 0.4g | Sugar 1g | Protein 29g

Pistachio Pesto Shrimp

Prep time: 15 minutes.
Cook time: 6 minutes.
Serves: 4

Ingredients:
- ¾ cup fresh arugula
- ½ cup parsley, minced
- ⅓ cup shelled pistachios
- 2 tablespoons lemon juice
- 1 garlic clove, peeled
- ¼ teaspoon lemon zest, grated
- ½ cup olive oil
- ¼ cup Parmesan cheese, shredded
- ¼ teaspoon salt
- 1/8 teaspoon black pepper
- 1- ½ lbs. jumbo shrimp, peeled and deveined

Preparation:
1. Start by adding the first 6 ingredients in a blender until smooth.
2. Add salt, pepper, Parmesan cheese, and mix well.
3. Toss in shrimp and mix well, then cover to refrigerate for 30 minutes.
4. Thread these shrimps on the skewers.
5. Preheat the Ninja Foodi Grill on the "Grill Mode" at LOW-temperature settings.
6. When the grill is preheated, open its hood and place the shrimp skewers in it.
7. Cover the grill's hood and grill for 6 minutes.
8. Continue rotating skewers after every 2 minutes.
9. Cook the skewers in batches.
10. Serve.

Serving Suggestion: Serve the pesto shrimp with fresh greens and chili sauce on the side.
Variation Tip: Roll the shrimp in breadcrumbs for a crispy touch.
Nutritional Information Per Serving:
Calories 457 | Fat 19g |Sodium 557mg | Carbs 19g | Fiber 1.8g | Sugar 1.2g | Protein 32.5g

Lemon-Garlic Salmon

Prep time: 15 minutes.
Cook time: 12 minutes.
Serves: 4

Ingredients:
- 2 garlic cloves, minced
- 2 teaspoons lemon zest, grated
- ½ teaspoon salt
- ½ teaspoon fresh rosemary, minced
- ½ teaspoon black pepper
- 4 (6 oz.) salmon fillets

Preparation:
1. Take the first five ingredients in a bowl and mix well.
2. Leave the mixture for 15 minutes, then rub the salmon with this mixture.
3. Preheat the Ninja Foodi Grill on the "Grill Mode" at MEDIUM-temperature settings.
4. When the grill is preheated, open its hood and place the salmon in it.
5. Cover the grill's hood and grill for 6 minutes per side.
6. Serve warm.

Serving Suggestion: Serve the lemon garlic salmon with butter sauce on top.
Variation Tip: Grill the veggies on the side to serve with the salmon.Nutritional Information Per Serving:
Calories 392 | Fat 16g |Sodium 466mg | Carbs 3.9g | Fiber 0.9g | Sugar 0.6g | Protein 48g

Shrimp Stuffed Sole

Prep time: 15 minutes.
Cook time: 14 minutes.
Serves: 4

Ingredients:
- ¼ cup soft bread crumbs
- ¼ cup butter, melted
- 2 tablespoons whipped cream cheese
- 2 teaspoons chives, minced
- 1 garlic clove, minced
- 1 teaspoon lemon zest, grated
- 1 can (6 oz.) crabmeat, drained
- 1 teaspoon parsley, minced
- 4 sole fillets (6 oz.), cut from a side and insides removed
- ½ cup shrimp, cooked, peeled, and chopped
- 1- ½ cups cherry tomatoes
- 2 tablespoons chicken broth
- 2 tablespoons lemon juice
- ½ teaspoon salt
- ½ teaspoon black pepper

Preparation:
1. Thoroughly mix crab with shrimp, cream cheese, chives, lemon zest, garlic, parsley, 2 tablespoon butter, and breadcrumbs in a small bowl.
2. Stuff ¼ of this filling into each fillet and secure the ends by inserting the toothpicks.
3. Mix tomatoes with salt, pepper, wine, and lemon juice in a separate bowl.
4. Place each stuffed fillet in a foil sheet and top with tomato mixture.
5. Cover and seal the fillets in the foil.
6. Preheat the Ninja Foodi Grill on the "Grill Mode" at MEDIUM-temperature settings.
7. When the grill is preheated, open its hood and place the foil packets in it.
8. Cover the grill's hood and grill for 7 minutes per side.
9. Cook the remaining fillets in a similar way.
10. Serve warm.

Serving Suggestion: Serve the shrimp stuffed with the sole with fried rice.
Variation Tip: Serve the sole fish with breadcrumbs and butter sauce on top.
Nutritional Information Per Serving:
Calories 321 | Fat 7.4g |Sodium 356mg | Carbs 9.3g | Fiber 2.4g | Sugar 5g | Protein 37.2g

Blackened Salmon

Prep time: 15 minutes.
Cook time: 20 minutes.
Serves: 2

Ingredients:
- 1 lb. salmon fillets
- 3 tablespoons melted butter
- 1 tablespoon lemon pepper
- 1 teaspoon seasoned salt
- 1½ tablespoon smoked paprika
- 1 teaspoon cayenne pepper
- ¾ teaspoon onion salt
- ½ teaspoon dry basil
- ½ teaspoon ground white pepper
- ½ teaspoon ground black pepper
- ¼ teaspoon dry oregano
- ¼ teaspoon ancho chili powder
- olive oil cooking spray
- fresh dill sprigs, to serve
- lemon wedges

Preparation:
1. Liberally season the salmon fillets with butter and other ingredients.
2. Preheat the Ninja Foodi Grill on the "Bake Mode" at 300 degrees F.
3. When the grill is preheated, open its hood and place the fish packets in it.
4. Cover the grill's hood and cook for 10 minutes per side.
5. Serve warm.

Serving Suggestion: Serve the blackened salmon with fresh greens.

Variation Tip: Drizzle lemon juice on top for a rich taste.

Nutritional Information Per Serving:
Calories 351 | Fat 4g |Sodium 236mg | Carbs 19.1g | Fiber 0.3g | Sugar 0.1g | Protein 36g

Grilled Ahi Tuna

Prep time: 10 minutes.
Cook time: 9 minutes.
Serves: 2

Ingredients:
- 1 cup labneh yogurt
- ⅓ cup chives, chopped
- 2 garlic cloves, minced
- 2 tsp. lemon zest
- 1 tbsp. fresh lemon juice
- 1 ½ tsp. kosher salt
- 3 tbsp. olive oil
- ¼ tsp. black pepper
- 2 (6-oz.) ahi tuna steaks, 1 ½ "-thick
- 10 oz. broccolini, stems trimmed
- ¼ tsp. crushed red pepper

Preparation:
1. Mix labneh, chives, garlic, lemon zest and juice, and ½ tsp. salt in a small bowl.
2. Season the turn steaks wit 1 tbsp. oil, ¼ tsp. black pepper, and ½ tsp. salt.
3. Place the cooking pot in the Ninja Foodi Grill then set a grill grate inside.
4. Select the "Grill" Mode, set the temperature to MED.
5. Press the START/STOP button to initiate preheating.
6. Once preheated, place the tuna fillets in the Ninja Foodi Grill.
7. Cover the hood and grill for 4 minutes, flipping halfway through.
8. Toss broccolini with red pepper, ½ tsp. salt and 2 tbsp. olive oil in a bowl.
9. Grill them for 5 minutes in the Ninja Smart grill.
10. Serve the turn steaks with labneh, and broccolini.

Serving Suggestion: Serve the tuna with butter sauce on top.

Variation Tip: Grill the veggies on the side to serve with the tuna.

Nutritional Information Per Serving:
Calories 392 | Fat 16g |Sodium 466mg | Carbs 19g | Fiber 0.9g | Sugar 0.6g | Protein 48g

Salmon Lime Burgers

Prep time: 15 minutes.
Cook time: 20 minutes.
Serves: 4

Ingredients:
- 1-lb. salmon fillets, cubed
- 2 tablespoons grated lime zest
- 1 tablespoon Dijon mustard
- 3 tablespoons shallot, chopped
- 2 tablespoons fresh cilantro, minced
- 1 tablespoon soy sauce
- 1 tablespoon honey
- 3 garlic cloves, minced
- ½ teaspoon salt
- ¼ teaspoon black pepper
- 4 hamburger buns, split

Preparation:
1. Thoroughly mix all the ingredients for burgers in a bowl except the buns.
2. Make four of the ½ patties out of this mixture.
3. Preheat the Ninja Foodi Grill on the "Grill Mode" at medium-temperature settings.
4. When the grill is preheated, open its hood and place the patties in it.
5. Cover the grill's hood and grill for 5 minutes per side.
6. Grill the remaining patties in a similar way.
7. Serve warm with buns.

Serving Suggestion: Serve the salmon lime burgers with vegetable rice.
Variation Tip: Add canned corn to the burgers.
Nutritional Information Per Serving:
Calories 258 | Fat 9g |Sodium 994mg | Carbs 1g | Fiber 0.4g | Sugar 3g | Protein 16g

Ginger Salmon

Prep time: 15 minutes.
Cook time: 12 minutes.
Serves: 10

Ingredients:
- 2 tablespoons rice vinegar
- 4 teaspoons sugar
- ½ teaspoon salt
- 1 tablespoon lime zest, grated
- ¼ cup lime juice
- 2 tablespoons olive oil
- ½ teaspoon ground coriander
- ½ teaspoon black pepper
- ⅓ cup fresh cilantro, chopped
- 1 tablespoon onion, chopped
- 2 teaspoons fresh ginger root, minced
- 2 garlic cloves, minced
- 2 medium cucumbers, peeled, seeded, and chopped

SALMON
- ⅓ cup minced fresh gingerroot
- 1 tablespoon lime juice
- 1 tablespoon olive oil
- ½ teaspoon salt
- ½ teaspoon freshly ground pepper
- 10 (6 oz.) salmon fillets

Preparation:
1. Start by blending the first 13 ingredients in a blender until smooth.
2. Season the salmon fillets with ginger, oil, salt, black pepper, lime juice.
3. Preheat the Ninja Foodi Grill on the "Grill Mode" at MEDIUM-temperature settings.
4. When the grill is preheated, open its hood and place the salmon in it.
5. Cover the grill's hood and grill for 6 minutes per side.
6. Cook the remaining fillets in a similar way.
7. Serve with the prepared sauce.

Serving Suggestion: Serve the ginger salmon with crispy onion rings on the side.
Variation Tip: Add honey for seasoning.
Nutritional Information Per Serving:
Calories 376 | Fat 17g |Sodium 1127mg | Carbs 24g | Fiber 1g | Sugar 3g | Protein 29g

Salmon Packets

Prep time: 15 minutes.
Cook time: 10 minutes.
Serves: 4

Ingredients:
- 4 (6 oz.) salmon steaks
- 1 teaspoon lemon-pepper seasoning

- 1 cup shredded carrots
- ½ cup julienned sweet yellow pepper
- ½ cup julienned green pepper
- 4 teaspoons lemon juice
- 1 teaspoon dried parsley flakes
- ½ teaspoon salt
- ¼ teaspoon black pepper

Preparation:

1. Season the salmon with lemon pepper, then place it on a 12-inch square foil sheet.
2. Top the salmon with the remaining ingredients, then seal the foil.
3. Preheat the Ninja Foodi Grill on the "Grill Mode" at MEDIUM-temperature settings.
4. When the grill is preheated, open its hood and place the fish packets in it.
5. Cover the grill's hood and grill for 5 minutes per side.
6. Cook the remaining fillets in a similar way.
7. Serve warm.

Serving Suggestion: Serve the salmon packets with lemon slices and fried rice.

Variation Tip: Use herbs to the seafood for a change of flavor.

Nutritional Information Per Serving:
Calories 378 | Fat 21g |Sodium 146mg | Carbs 7.1g | Fiber 0.1g | Sugar 0.4g | Protein 23g

Citrus-Soy Squid

Prep time: 15 minutes.

Cook time: 6 minutes.

Serves: 6

Ingredients:
- 1 cup mirin
- 1 cup soy sauce
- ⅓ cup yuzu juice
- 2 pounds squid tentacles, cut crosswise 1 inch thick

Preparation:

1. Toss squid with mirin, soy sauce, and water yuzu juice in a bowl.
2. Cover and marinate the squid for 4 hours in the refrigerator.
3. Preheat the Ninja Foodi Grill on the "Grill Mode" at LOW-temperature settings.
4. When the grill is preheated, open its hood and place the squids in it.

5. Cover the grill's hood and grill for 3 minutes per side.
6. Serve warm.

Serving Suggestion: Serve the grilled squid with mashed potatoes.

Variation Tip: Coat the squid with breadcrumbs.

Nutritional Information Per Serving:
Calories 378 | Fat 7g |Sodium 316mg | Carbs 16.2g | Fiber 0.3g | Sugar 0.3g | Protein 26g

Clams with Horseradish-Tabasco Sauce

Prep time: 15 minutes.

Cook time: 4 minutes.

Serves: 6

Ingredients:
- 4 tablespoons unsalted butter, softened
- 2 tablespoons drained horseradish
- 1 tablespoon Tabasco
- ¼ teaspoon lemon zest, grated
- 1 tablespoon fresh lemon juice
- ¼ teaspoon Spanish smoked paprika
- Salt, to taste
- 2 dozen littleneck clams, scrubbed
- Grilled slices of crusty white bread for serving

Preparation:

1. Blend butter with lemon zest, Tabasco, lemon juice, pimento de la Vera, salt, and horseradish in a small bowl.
2. Preheat the Ninja Foodi Grill on the "Grill Mode" at MEDIUM-temperature settings.
3. When the grill is preheated, open its hood and place the clams in it.
4. Cover the grill's hood and grill for 4 minutes.
5. Serve the clams with a horseradish mixture.

Serving Suggestion: Serve the clams with roasted broccoli florets.

Variation Tip: Drizzle lemon garlic butter on top before cooking.

Nutritional Information Per Serving:
Calories 415 | Fat 15g |Sodium 634mg | Carbs 14.3g | Fiber 1.4g | Sugar 1g | Protein 23.3g

Grill Cod

Prep time: 10 minutes
Cook time: 10 minutes
Serves: 4

Ingredients:
- 1 pound cod fillets, boneless & skinless
- 1 fresh lemon juice
- ¼ cup butter, melted
- ¼ teaspoon dried parsley
- Pepper
- Salt

Directions:
1. Place the cooking pot in the Ninja Foodi Grill Main Unit then place the grill plate in the pot.
2. In a small bowl, mix butter, lemon juice, parsley, pepper and salt.
3. Brush fish fillets with melted butter mixture.
4. Press Grill mode, set the temperature to HIGH, and set time to 10 minutes. Press Start.
5. Once a unit is preheated then place fish fillets on the grill plate.
6. Cover with lid and cook for 10 minutes. Turn fish fillets halfway through.

Serving Suggestion: Serve warm.
Variation Tip: None
Nutritional Information per Serving:
Calories 193 | Fat 12.5g |Sodium 191mg | Carbs 0g | Fiber 0g | Sugar 0g | Protein 20.4g

Honey Garlic Salmon

Prep time: 10 minutes
Cook time: 10 minutes
Serves: 2

Ingredients:
- 2 salmon fillets
- 2 tablespoon lemon juice
- 2 tablespoon honey
- 3 tablespoon brown mustard

- 1 tablespoon garlic, minced
- 1 Serrano pepper, diced
- ¼ cup olive oil
- ¼ teaspoon red pepper flakes, crushed

Directions:
1. Place the cooking pot in the Ninja Foodi Grill Main Unit then place the grill plate in the pot.
2. Add fish fillets and remaining ingredients into the zip-lock bag. Seal bag and place in the refrigerator for 30 minutes.
3. Press Grill mode, set the temperature to HIGH, and set time to 10 minutes. Press Start.
4. Once a unit is preheated then place marinated fish fillets on the grill plate.
5. Cover with lid and cook for 10 minutes. Turn fish fillets halfway through.

Serving Suggestion: Serve warm.
Variation Tip: Add one teaspoon dried oregano.
Nutritional Information per Serving:
Calories 529 | Fat 36.5g |Sodium 204mg | Carbs 21.3g | Fiber 0.7g | Sugar 17.8g | Protein 35.1g

Thai Fish Fillets

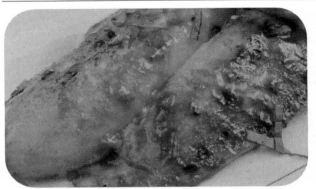

Prep time: 10 minutes
Cook time: 10 minutes
Serves: 4

Ingredients:
- 1 ½ poundTilapia fillets
- 2 teaspoons soy sauce
- 1 tablespoon fish sauce
- 1 tablespoon olive oil
- ¼ cup cilantro, chopped
- ½ teaspoon red pepper flakes
- 2 teaspoons garlic, minced
- 2 lime juice

Directions:
1. Place the cooking pot in the Ninja Foodi Grill Main Unit then place the grill plate in the pot.
2. Add fish fillets and remaining ingredients into the zip-lock bag. Seal bag and place in the refrigerator for 30 minutes.
3. Press Grill mode, set the temperature to HIGH, and set time to 10 minutes. Press Start.
4. Once a unit is preheated then place marinated fish fillets on the grill plate.
5. Cover with lid and cook for 10 minutes.

Serving Suggestion: Serve warm.
Variation Tip: None
Nutritional Information per Serving:
Calories 176 | Fat 5.1g |Sodium 558mg | Carbs 1g | Fiber 0.1g | Sugar 0.3g | Protein 32.2g

Baked Cajun Salmon

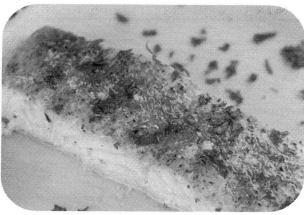

Prep time: 10 minutes
Cook time: 12 minutes
Serves: 4
Ingredients:
- 4 salmon fillets
- 4 tablespoons brown sugar
- 2 teaspoons Cajun seasoning
- Salt

Directions:
1. Place the cooking pot in the Ninja Foodi Grill Main Unit.
2. In a small bowl, mix brown sugar, Cajun seasoning and salt and rub over fish fillets.
3. Place fish fillets into the baking dish.
4. Press Bake mode, set the temperature to 400°F, and set time to 12 minutes. Press Start.
5. Once a unit is preheated then place the baking dish in the cooking pot.
6. Cover with lid and cook for 12 minutes.
Serving Suggestion: Serve warm.
Variation Tip: None
Nutritional Information per Serving:
Calories 270 | Fat 11g |Sodium 145mg | Carbs 8.8g | Fiber 0g | Sugar 8.7g | Protein 34.6g

Greek Salmon

Prep time: 10 minutes
Cook time: 20 minutes
Serves: 4
Ingredients:
- 4 salmon fillets
- 1 onion, chopped
- ½ cup Feta cheese, crumbled

- ½ cup basil pesto
- 2 cups cherry tomatoes, halved
- Pepper
- Salt

Directions:
1. Place the cooking pot in the Ninja Foodi Grill Main Unit.
2. Place fish fillets in a baking dish and top with tomatoes, onion, pesto, cheese, pepper and salt.
3. Press Bake mode, set the temperature to 350°F, and set time to 20 minutes. Press Start.
4. Once a unit is preheated then place the baking dish in the cooking pot.
5. Cover with lid and cook for 20 minutes.
Serving Suggestion: Serve warm.
Variation Tip: Add your choice of seasonings.
Nutritional Information per Serving:
Calories 313 | Fat 15.2g |Sodium 332mg | Carbs 6.9g | Fiber 1.7g | Sugar 4.3g | Protein 38.4g

Shrimp Casserole

Prep time: 10 minutes
Cook time: 8 minutes
Serves: 4
Ingredients:
- 1 pound shrimp, peeled and deveined
- 2 tablespoons white wine
- 1 tablespoon garlic, minced
- 2 tablespoons fresh parsley, chopped
- ½ cup breadcrumbs
- ¼ cup butter, melted
- Pepper
- Salt

Directions:
1. Place the cooking pot in the Ninja Foodi Grill Main Unit.
2. Add shrimp and remaining ingredients into the bowl and toss well.
3. Pour shrimp mixture into the baking dish.
4. Press Bake mode, set the temperature to 350°F, and set time to 8 minutes. Press Start.
5. Once a unit is preheated then place the baking dish in the cooking pot.
6. Cover with lid and cook for 8 minutes.
Serving Suggestion: Serve warm.
Variation Tip: Add your choice of seasonings.
Nutritional Information per Serving:
Calories 300 | Fat 14.2g |Sodium 498mg | Carbs 12.5g | Fiber 0.7g | Sugar 1g | Protein 28g

Garlic Rosemary Shrimp

Prep time: 10 minutes
Cook time: 10 minutes
Serves: 4
Ingredients:
- 1 pound shrimp, peeled and deveined
- 2 garlic cloves, minced
- 1 tablespoon olive oil
- ½ tablespoon fresh rosemary, chopped
- Pepper
- Salt

Directions:
1. Place the cooking pot in the Ninja Foodi Grill Main Unit.
2. Add shrimp and remaining ingredients into the bowl and toss well.
3. Transfer shrimp mixture into the baking dish.
4. Press Bake mode, set the temperature to 400°F, and set time to ten minutes. Press Start.
5. Once a unit is preheated then place the baking dish in the cooking pot.
6. Cover with lid and cook for ten minutes.
Serving Suggestion: Serve warm.
Variation Tip: Add ¼ teaspoon of crushed red pepper flakes.
Nutritional Information per Serving:
Calories 168 | Fat 5.5g |Sodium 316mg | Carbs 2.5g | Fiber 0.2g | Sugar 0g | Protein 26g

Shrimp and Vegetables

Prep time: 10 minutes
Cook time: 15 minutes
Serves: 4
Ingredients:
- 1 pound shrimp, peeled & deveined
- 1 tablespoon olive oil
- 1 bell pepper, sliced

- 1 zucchini, sliced
- ¼ cup Parmesan cheese, grated
- 1 tablespoon Italian seasoning
- 1 tablespoon garlic, minced
- Pepper
- Salt

Directions:
1. Place the cooking pot in the Ninja Foodi Grill Main Unit then place the Ninja Foodi Crisper Basket in the pot.
2. Add shrimp and remaining ingredients into the bowl and toss well.
3. Add shrimp and vegetable mixture into the Ninja Foodi Crisper Basket.
4. Press Air Crisp mode, set the temperature to 350°F, and set time to 15 minutes.
5. Cover with lid and press Start. Stir halfway through.
Serving Suggestion: Serve warm.
Variation Tip: Add your choice of seasonings.
Nutritional Information per Serving:
Calories 346 | Fat 15.6g |Sodium 923mg | Carbs 6.7g | Fiber 1g | Sugar 2.7g | Protein 38.9g

Dijon Fish Fillets

Prep time: 10 minutes
Cook time: 12 minutes
Serves: 4
Ingredients:
- 4 salmon fillets
- 2 tablespoons ground Dijon mustard
- 3 tablespoons maple syrup

Directions:
1. Place the cooking pot in the Ninja Foodi Grill Main Unit.
2. In a small bowl, mix mustard and maple syrup and brush over salmon fillets.
3. Place salmon fillets into the baking dish.
4. Press Bake mode, set the temperature to 390°F, and set time to 12 minutes. Press Start.
5. Once a unit is preheated then place the baking dish in the cooking pot.
6. Cover with lid and cook for 12 minutes.
Serving Suggestion: Serve warm.
Variation Tip: None
Nutritional Information per Serving:
Calories 282 | Fat 11g |Sodium 207mg | Carbs 10.1g | Fiber 0g | Sugar 8.9g | Protein 34.5g

Spicy Shrimp

Prep time: 10 minutes
Cook time: 6 minutes
Serves: 2

Ingredients:
- ½ pound shrimp, peeled and deveined
- ½ teaspoonCayenne
- 1 tablespoon olive oil
- ½ teaspoonOld bay seasoning
- ¼ teaspoonpaprika
- Pinch of salt

Directions:
1. Place the cooking pot in the Ninja Foodi Grill Main Unit then place the Ninja Foodi Crisper Basket in the pot.
2. Add shrimp and remaining ingredients into the bowl and toss well.
3. Add shrimp in the Ninja Foodi Crisper Basket.
4. Press Air Crisp mode, set the temperature to 390°F, and set time to 6 minutes.
5. Cover with lid and press Start.

Serving Suggestion: Serve warm.
Variation Tip: None
Nutritional Information per Serving:
Calories 197 | Fat 9g |Sodium 514mg | Carbs 2.1g | Fiber 0.2g | Sugar 0.1g | Protein 25.9g

Herb Salmon

Prep time: 10 minutes
Cook time: 15 minutes
Serves: 4

Ingredients:
- 1 pound salmon, cut into 4 pieces
- 1 tablespoon olive oil
- ¼ teaspoon dried basil
- ½ tablespoon dried rosemary
- Pepper
- Salt

Directions:
1. Place the cooking pot in the Ninja Foodi Grill Main Unit then place the Ninja Foodi Crisper Basket in the pot.
2. In a small bowl, mix olive oil, basil, chives and rosemary.
3. Brush salmon with oil mixture and place in the Ninja Foodi Crisper Basket.
4. Press Air Crisp mode, set the temperature to 400°F, and set time to 15 minutes.
5. Cover with lid and press Start.

Serving Suggestion: Serve warm.
Variation Tip: Add ¼ teaspoon of mix dried herbs.
Nutritional Information per Serving:
Calories 181 | Fat 10.6g |Sodium 89mg | Carbs 0.3g | Fiber 0.2g | Sugar 0g | Protein 22g

Grill Tuna Patties

Prep time: 10 minutes
Cook time: 12 minutes
Serves: 12

Ingredients:
- 2 eggs, lightly beaten
- 2 cans tuna, drained
- ¼ cup mayonnaise
- ½ cup breadcrumbs
- ½ onion, diced
- 2 tablespoons fresh lemon juice
- Pepper
- Salt

Directions:
1. Place the cooking pot in the Ninja Foodi Grill Main Unit then place the Ninja Foodi Crisper Basket in the pot.
2. Add all ingredients into the bowl and mix until well combined.
3. Make patties from the mixture and place into the Crisper Basket.
4. Press Air Crisp mode, set the temperature to 375°F, and set time to 12 minutes.
5. Cover with lid and press Start. Turn patties halfway through.

Serving Suggestion: Serve with dip.
Variation Tip: Add your choice of seasonings.
Nutritional Information per Serving:
Calories 105 | Fat 5g |Sodium 105mg | Carbs 5g | Fiber 0.3g | Sugar 0.9g | Protein 9.5g

Grilled Coconut and Pineapple Sweet Chili Shrimp

Prep time: 15 minutes.
Cook time: 6 minutes.
Serves: 4
Ingredients:
Sweet chili sauce:
- 3 tbsp. coconut cream
- 3 tbsp. pineapple sweet chili sauce
- 1 tsp. sriracha

Grilled shrimp
- 1 lb. shrimp, peeled and deveined
- 2 slices pineapple, cut into ½ inch pieces

Preparation:
1. Mix the chili sauce ingredients in a bowl.
2. Toss in shrimp and pineapple then mix well to coat.
3. Thread the shrimp and pineapple on the wooden skewers alternately.
4. Place the cooking pot in the Ninja Foodi Grill then set a grill grate inside.
5. Select the "Grill" Mode, set the temperature to MED.
6. Press the START/STOP button to initiate preheating.
7. Once preheated, place the skewers in the Ninja Foodi Grill.
8. Cover the hood and allow the grill to cook for 6 minutes, flipping halfway through.
9. Serve warm.
Serving Suggestion: Serve the shrimp with sautéed vegetables.

Variation Tip: Use some lemon juice as well for seasoning.
Nutritional Information Per Serving:
Calories 309 | Fat 25g |Sodium 463mg | Carbs 9.9g | Fiber 0.3g | Sugar 0.3g | Protein 18g

Grilled Calamari

Prep time: 15 minutes.
Cook time: 22 minutes.
Serves: 4
Ingredients:
- 1 garlic clove, chopped
- 2 ½ tbsp. olive oil
- 3 ¼ tsp. kosher salt
- 1 lb. (10 small) calamari
- 3 large red bell peppers, chopped
- 2 tsp. sherry vinegar
- 10 fresh mint leaves

Preparation:
1. Mix garlic with 1 ½ tbsp. oil, salt, and calamari in a bowl.
2. Cover and refrigerate them for 10 minutes.
3. Place the cooking pot in the Ninja Foodi Grill then set a grill grate inside.
4. Select the "Bake" Mode, set the temperature to 400 degrees F.
5. Set the cooking time to 20 minutes.
6. Press the START/STOP button to initiate preheating.
7. Once preheated, place the peppers in the Ninja Foodi Grill.
8. Cover the hood and allow the grill to cook then flip once cooked halfway through.
9. Cut the peppers in half, remove the seeds and cut into strips.
10. Mix these peppers with 1 tbsp. oil, ¼ tsp. salt, and vinegar in a bowl.
11. Grill the calamari in the Ninja Foodi Grill for 1 minute per side
12. Serve the calamari with peppers mixture and garnish with mint.
13. Enjoy.
Serving Suggestion: Serve the calamari on top of the cauliflower rice.
Variation Tip: Add paprika for more spice.
Nutritional Information Per Serving:
Calories 448 | Fat 13g |Sodium 353mg | Carbs 3g | Fiber 0.4g | Sugar 1g | Protein 29g

Tuna Burgers

Prep time: 10 minutes.
Cook time: 10 minutes.
Serves: 4

Ingredients:
- 1 ¼ lb. fresh tuna
- 2 scallions, chopped
- 12 pitted kalamata olives
- 1 tbsp. salted capers
- Salt, to taste
- Black pepper, to taste
- Olive oil, to taste
- ¼ cup mayonnaise
- 1 ½ tsp. anchovy paste
- 4 brioche buns
- Sliced tomatoes
- Arugula, to serve

Preparation:
1. Blend tuna with scallions, olives and oil in a food processor for 1 minute.
2. Make 4- 4 inch round patties out of this mixture.
3. Place the cooking pot in the Ninja Foodi Grill then set a grill grate inside.
4. Select the "Bake" Mode, set the temperature to 400 degrees F.
5. Press the START/STOP button to initiate preheating.
6. Once preheated, place the patties in the Ninja Foodi Grill.
7. Cover the hood and allow the grill to cook for 10 minutes, flipping halfway through.
8. Top the bottom half of the buns with mayo, anchovy paste, burgers, tomatoes, and rest of the ingredients.
9. Once preheated, place the other half of the buns on top.
10. Serve.
Serving Suggestion: Serve the burger with crispy onion rings on the side.
Variation Tip: Add roasted vegetables on the side.
Nutritional Information Per Serving:
Calories 376 | Fat 17g |Sodium 1127mg | Carbs 24g | Fiber 1g | Sugar 3g | Protein 29g

Grilled Scallops

Prep time: 15 minutes.
Cook time: 6 minutes.
Serves: 6

Ingredients:
- ⅓ cup mayonnaise
- 2 tsp. fresh lime juice
- Kosher salt, to taste
- 1 toasted nori sheet
- 1 tsp. ground coriander
- ½ tsp. ground ginger
- 2 tbsp. vegetable oil
- 12 large dry sea scallops
- ½ lime
- 3 scallions, sliced
- 1 tsp. Aleppo pepper flakes

Preparation:
1. Mix mayonnaise with 1 tbsp. water, 1 pinch of salt, and lime juice in a bowl.
2. Grind nori and mix half of it with ginger, coriander, and 2 tbsp. oil in a bowl
3. Stir in scallops, mix well to coat and thread them on the wooden skewers.
4. Place the cooking pot in the Ninja Foodi Grill then set a grill grate inside.
5. Select the "Grill" Mode, set the temperature to MED.
6. Press the START/STOP button to initiate preheating.
7. Once preheated, place the scallops in the Ninja Foodi Grill.
8. Cover the hood and allow the grill to cook for 6 minutes, flipping halfway through.
9. Spread lime mayo on a plate and top it with scallop skewers and garnish with nori, pepper, lime juice and scallions.
10. Serve warm.
Serving Suggestion: Serve the scallops with mayo dip.
Variation Tip: Add butter to the scallops before serving.
Nutritional Information Per Serving:
Calories 405 | Fat 22.7g |Sodium 227mg | Carbs 6.1g | Fiber 1.4g | Sugar 0.9g | Protein 45.2g

Grilled Shrimp Tostadas with Guacamole

Prep time: 10 minutes.
Cook time: 14 minutes.
Serves: 8

Ingredients:
- 8 (6") corn tortillas
- Cooking spray
- 3 ripe avocados, diced
- 1 small shallot, minced
- 7 tbsp. lime juice
- 3 tbsp. freshly chopped cilantro
- Kosher salt, to taste
- 2 tsp. cumin
- ½ tsp. cayenne
- ¼ cup olive oil
- 24 medium shrimp, peeled and deveined
- Black pepper, to taste
- ¼ cup red cabbage, shredded
- ¾ cup carrots, shredded
- Cilantro leaves, for serving
- Lime wedges, for serving

Preparation:
1. Place the cooking pot in the Ninja Foodi Grill then set a grill grate inside.
2. Select the "Grill" Mode, set the temperature to MED.
3. Press the START/STOP button to initiate preheating.
4. Use the arrow keys to set the cooking time to 4 minutes.
5. Once preheated, grill the tortillas in the Ninja Foodi Grill then transfer to a plate.
6. Mash avocados with salt, cilantro, 3 tbsp. lime juice, and shallot in a bowl.
7. Mix shrimp with oil, black pepper, salt, 2 tbsp. oil, 2 tbsp. lime juice, cayenne and cumin in a bowl.
8. Place the shrimp in the Ninja Foodi Grill.
9. Cover the Ninja Foodi Grill's hood, select the Bake Mode, set the temperature to 350 degrees F and cook for 3 minutes.
10. Flip the shrimp and cook again for 3

minutes.
11. Toss carrots and cabbage with 2 tbsp. lime juice, black pepper, salt and 2 tbsp. oil.
12. Divide the cabbage mixture, guacamole and shrimp in the tortillas.
13. Serve warm.
Serving Suggestion: Serve the tostada with yogurt dip.
Variation Tip: Add butter to the shrimp for a more rich taste.
Nutritional Information Per Serving:
Calories 345 | Fat 36g |Sodium 272mg | Carbs 21g | Fiber 0.2g | Sugar 0.1g | Protein 22.5g

Grilled Salmon Packets

Prep time: 5 minutes
Cook time: 15-20 minutes
Servings: 4

Ingredients
- 4 salmon steaks (6 ounces each)
- 1 tsp lemon-pepper seasoning
- 1 cup shredded carrots
- 1 tsp dried parsley flakes
- ½ cup julienned sweet yellow pepper
- ½ cup julienned green pepper
- 4 tsp lemon juice
- ½ tsp salt
- ¼ tsp pepper

Preparation
1. Preheat the grill for 5 minutes.
2. Sprinkle the salmon with a lemon-pepper. Place each of the salmon steaks on a double thickness of heavy-duty foil (about 12 in. square). Top with carrots and peppers. Sprinkle with remaining Ingredients.
3. Fold foil around fish and seal them tightly. Select GRILL mode, covered, grill over MEDIUM heat for 15-20 minutes or until fish flakes easily with a fork.
Serving Suggestion: Serve with dill garnishing or enjoy as it is.
Variation Tip: use chopped dill for garnish.
Nutritional Information Per Serving:
Calories 98 | Carbohydrates 7.1g | Protein 1.3g | Fat 6.5g | Sodium 154.6mg| Fiber 0g

Shrimp Boil

Prep time: 10 minutes.
Cook time: 6 minutes.
Serves: 6

Ingredients:
- 1 ½ lb. large shrimp, peeled and deveined
- 2 garlic cloves, minced
- 2 smoked andouille sausages, sliced
- 2 ears corn, cut into 4 pieces
- 1 lb. red bliss potatoes, chopped
- 2 tbsp. olive oil
- 3 tsp. Old Bay seasoning
- 1 lemon, sliced into thin wedges
- 4 tbsp. butter, melted
- Kosher salt, to taste
- Black pepper, to taste
- 2 tbsp. fresh parsley leaves, chopped

Preparation:
1. Boil potatoes with water and a pinch of salt in a saucepan and cook until soft.
2. Mix shrimp with 1 tbsp. parsley, 2 tsp. old bay, garlic, and oil in a bowl.
3. Toss potatoes with 1 tbsp. parsley, 1 tsp. old bay, melted and melted butter then mix well.
4. Thread the shrimp, potatoes, corn and sausage on the wooden skewers.
5. Set a grill grate in the Ninja Foodi Grill' cooking pot.
6. Select the "Grill" Mode, set the temperature to HI.
7. Press the START/STOP button to initiate preheating.
8. Once preheated, place the shrimp skewers in the Ninja Foodi Grill.
9. Cook for 6 minutes. Flip the skewers once cooked halfway through.
10. Serve warm.

Serving Suggestion: Serve the shrimp boil with fresh greens and chili sauce on the side.

Variation Tip: Add lemon juice and lemon zest on top before cooking.

Nutritional Information Per Serving:
Calories 457 | Fat 19g |Sodium 557mg | Carbs 29g | Fiber 1.8g | Sugar 1.2g | Protein 32.5g

Pineapple Shrimp Skewers

Prep time: 10 minutes.
Cook time: 6 minutes.
Serves: 6-8

Ingredients:
- 3 cups pineapple, cubed
- 1 lb. shrimp, peeled and deveined
- 3 tbsp. olive oil
- 3 tbsp. sweet chili sauce
- 2 garlic cloves, minced
- 2 tsp. freshly grated ginger
- 2 tsp. toasted sesame oil crushed red pepper flakes
- ½ tsp. crushed red pepper flakes
- Kosher salt
- Toasted sesame seeds, for garnish
- Thinly sliced green onions, for garnish
- Lime wedges, for serving

Preparation:
1. Toss shrimp with the ingredients in a bowl.
2. Thread the shrimp and pineapple on the skewers.
3. Place the cooking pot in the Ninja Foodi Grill then set a grill grate inside.
4. Select the "Grill" Mode, set the temperature to MED.
5. Press the START/STOP button to initiate preheating.
6. Once preheated, place the skewers in the Ninja Foodi Grill.
7. Cover the hood and allow the grill to cook for 6 minutes, flipping halfway through.
8. Serve warm.

Serving Suggestion: Serve the shrimp skewers with fried cauliflower rice.

Variation Tip: Add some butter sauce on top.

Nutritional Information Per Serving:
Calories 321 | Fat 7.4g |Sodium 356mg | Carbs 19g | Fiber 2.4g | Sugar 5g | Protein 37.2g

Grilled Oysters

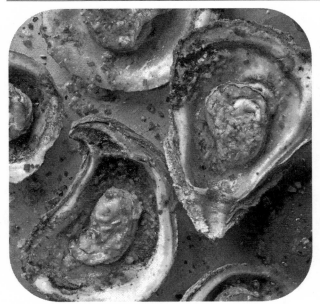

Prep time: 10 minutes.
Cook time: 7 minutes.
Serves: 4

Ingredients:
- 2 cups butter, softened
- ½ cup Parmesan cheese, grated
- ¼ cup parsley, chopped
- 2 garlic cloves, minced
- 1 tbsp. Worcestershire sauce
- 1 tsp. paprika
- ½ tsp. ground red pepper
- ½ tsp. hot sauce
- 2 dozen large fresh oysters on the half shell

Preparation:
1. Blend butter with parmesan cheese, parsley, garlic, paprika, red pepper, and hot sauce in a food processor.
2. Stuff the oysters with this mixture.
3. Place the cooking pot in the Ninja Foodi Grill then set a grill grate inside.
4. Select the "Grill" Mode, set the temperature to MED.
5. Use the arrow keys on the display to select the cooking time to 5 minutes.
6. Press the START/STOP button to initiate preheating.
7. Once preheated, place the oysters in the Ninja Foodi Grill.
8. Cover the hood and allow the grill to cook.
9. Serve warm.

Serving Suggestion: Serve the oysters with sautéed green beans and mashed cauliflower.

Variation Tip: Drizzle cheese on top before serving.

Nutritional Information Per Serving:
Calories 395 | Fat 9.5g |Sodium 655mg | Carbs 3.4g | Fiber 0.4g | Sugar 0.4g | Protein 28.3g

Grilled Salmon Soft Tacos

Prep time: 20 minutes
Cook time: 20 minutes
Servings: 4

Ingredients
- 2 tbsp extra-virgin olive oil
- 1 tablespoon ancho or New Mexico chile powder
- 4 4-ounce wild salmon fillets, about 1-inch thick, skin on
- 1 tablespoon fresh lime juice
- ¼ tsp kosher salt
- ⅛ tsp freshly ground pepper
- 8 6-inch corn or flour tortillas, warmed
- Cabbage Slaw
- Citrus Salsa
- Cilantro Crema

Preparation
1. Preheat the grill for eight minutes.
2. Combine chili powder, oil, lime juice, salt, and pepper in a bowl. Rub the spice mixture over salmon.
3. Cut each of the fillets lengthwise into two pieces and then remove the skin.
4. Insert grill grate in the unit and close the hood. Select the option START/STOP to begin cooking.
5. Cook fish for 10 minutes from each side. Serve.

Serving Suggestion: To serve, place two tortillas on each plate. Divide the fish, Citrus Salsa, Cabbage Slaw, and Cilantro Crema among the tortillas.

Variation Tip: use chopped dill for garnish.

Nutritional Information per Serving:
Calories 199.8 | Carbohydrates 25.6g | Protein 3.6g | Fat 2.2g | Sodium 147.6mg| Fiber 4.8g

Shrimp and Chorizo Grill

Prep time: 10 minutes.
Cook time: 46 minutes.
Serves: 4

Ingredients:

Cilantro-Sour Cream Sauce
- 1 ¼ cups sour cream
- 1 cup cilantro leaves with tender stems
- ¼ cup mayonnaise
- 1 small jalapeño, sliced
- 2 tbsp. fresh lime juice
- 1 ¼ tsp. kosher salt

Dressing
- 5 tbsp. olive oil
- ¼ cup fresh lime juice
- 1 garlic clove, grated
- 2 tbsp. cilantro, chopped
- 1 tsp. honey
- 1 tsp. kosher salt

Grilling and Assembly
- 1 ½ lb. jumbo or large shrimp, peeled, deveined
- ½ tsp. chili powder
- 1 ¼ tsp. kosher salt
- 1 head of green cabbage, cut into 4 wedges
- 6 links fresh chorizo sausage (1 ½ lb.)
- Canola oil (for grill)
- 2 bunches medium or large asparagus, tough ends trimmed
- Lime wedges (for serving)

Preparation:

1. Blend all the ingredients for sour cream sauce in a blender.
2. Mix lime juice and rest of the dressing ingredients in a bowl.
3. Season the shrimp with 1 tsp. salt, and chili powder in a bowl.
4. Place the cooking pot in the Ninja Foodi Grill then set a grill grate inside.
5.
6. Select the "Grill" Mode, set the temperature to MED.
7. Press the START/STOP button to initiate preheating.
8. Once preheated, place the shrimp in the Ninja Foodi Grill.
9. Cover the hood and allow the grill to cook for 20 minutes with flipping halfway through, then transfer to a plate.
10. Grill the sausages for 7 minutes per side and transfer to the plate.
11. Now grill the asparagus in the Ninja Foodi Smart Grill for 3 minutes per side then transfer them to plate.
12. Finally grill the shrimp for 3 minutes per side and add them to the veggies.
13. Garnish with the lime wedges.
14. Serve.

Serving Suggestion: Serve the grilled seafood with mashed cauliflower.

Variation Tip: Add more herbs of your choice to the shrimp.

Nutritional Information Per Serving:
Calories 337 | Fat 20g |Sodium 719mg | Carbs 11g | Fiber 0.9g | Sugar 1.4g | Protein 37.8g

Grilled Lemon-Garlic Salmon

Prep time: 10 minutes
Cook time: 15-20 minutes
Servings: 4

Ingredients
- 2 garlic cloves, minced
- ½ tsp minced fresh rosemary
- 2 tsp grated lemon zest
- ½ tsp salt
- ½ tsp pepper
- 4 salmon fillets (6 ounces each)

Preparation

1. Take a small bowl, mix the first five Ingredients, and rub over fillets. Let it stand for 15 minutes. Coat the grill with cooking oil.
2. Preheat the grill for 8 minutes before use. Place salmon on the grill with the skin side up. Grill while covered over MEDIUM heat or broil 4 in. From heat 4 minutes. Turn and grill 3 to 6 minutes longer or until fish just begins to flake easily with a fork.

Serving Suggestion: Serve with lemon wedges.

Variation Tip: use chopped dill for garnish.

Nutritional Information Per Serving:
Calories 280 | Carbohydrates 40g | Protein 4g | Fat 12g | Sodium 200mg| Fiber 1g

Scallops with Creamed Corn

Prep time: 10 minutes.
Cook time: 27 minutes.
Serves: 4

Ingredients:
- 3 dried Pasilla chiles, chopped
- 2 tbsp. dried thyme
- 1 tbsp. dried oregano
- 1 tbsp. ground coriander
- 1 tbsp. ground fennel
- 2 tsp. chipotle chile powder
- 2 tsp. black pepper
- 2 tsp. paprika
- 1 tsp. garlic powder
- 1 tsp. onion powder
- Zest of 1 lime
- 1 lb. large sea scallops
- 2 tbsp. olive oil
- 4 green garlic, sliced
- 1 medium shallot, chopped
- 1 garlic clove, sliced
- 4 ears of corn, husked, kernels grated
- 1 tbsp. unsalted butter
- Kosher salt, to taste
- Vegetable oil, for drizzling
- Lime wedges, for serving

Preparation:
1. Grind Pasilla chiles in a spice milk and mix them with onion power, garlic powder, paprika, black pepper, chile powder, fennel, coriander, oregano and thyme in a bowl.
2. Mix scallops with 2 tbsp. rub and lime zest in a bowl.
3. Sauté garlic, shallot and green garlic with oil in a saucepan for 8 minutes.
4. Stir in grated corn and cook for 5 minutes.
5. Add water and cook for 18 minutes until it is absorbed.
6. Stir in salt and butter for seasoning.
7. Thread the scallops on the skewers and season them with salt and oil.
8. Place the cooking pot in the Ninja Foodi Grill then set a grill grate inside.
9. Select the "Grill" Mode, set the temperature to LOW.
10. Press the START/STOP button to initiate preheating.
11. Cover the Ninja Foodi Grill's hood and cook for 3 minutes per side.
12. Serve the scallops on top of the creamed corn.

Serving Suggestion: Serve the scallops with fresh greens and mashed cauliflower.
Variation Tip: Add a drizzle of herbs on top.
Nutritional Information Per Serving:
Calories 301 | Fat 5g |Sodium 340mg | Carbs 27g | Fiber 1.2g | Sugar 1.3g | Protein 15.3g

Grilled Halibut

Prep time: 5 minutes
Cook time: 10 minutes
Servings: 4

Ingredients
For the halibut
- 4 (4-6-oz.) halibut steaks
- 2 tbsp. extra-virgin olive oil
- Kosher salt
- Freshly ground black pepper

For the mango salsa
- 1 mango, diced
- 1 red pepper, finely chopped
- ½ red onion, diced
- 1 jalapeno, minced
- 1 tbsp. freshly chopped cilantro
- Juice of 1 lime
- Kosher salt
- Freshly ground black pepper

Preparation
1. Select the GRILL function and adjust the temperature to HIGH heat, preheat the grill. Brush halibut with oil on both sides then season with salt and pepper.
2. Grill halibut until cooked through, about 5 minutes per side.
3. Make salsa: Mix together all ingredients in a medium bowl and season with salt and pepper. Serve salsa over halibut.

Serving Suggestion: Serve the fish with yummy mango salsa.
Variation Tip: Go for regular lime and tomato salsa for fun.
Nutritional Information Per Serving:
Calories 248 | Carbohydrates 40.7g | Protein 2.5g | Fat 10.8g | Sodium 120.4mg| Fiber 0.7g

Nigerian Skewers

Prep time: 10 minutes.
Cook time: 41 minutes.
Serves: 6

Ingredients:
Spice blend
- 3 tbsp. cayenne pepper
- 1 ½ tbsp. roasted peanuts
- 1 tbsp. paprika
- 1 tbsp. garlic powder
- 1 tbsp. onion powder
- ½ tbsp. ground ginger
- 2 tsp. kosher salt
- 2 Maggi bouillon cubes, crushed

Suya:
- 1 lb. jumbo shrimp, peeled and deveined
- 1 lb. Wagyu rib eye beef, thinly sliced
- 1 lb. boneless chicken thighs, cut into 2-inch pieces
- For the roasted tomato soubise:
- 2 medium vine-ripened tomatoes, stemmed
- 1 tbsp. olive oil
- Kosher salt, to taste
- 2 tbsp. canola oil
- 1 medium white onion, sliced
- 1 cup heavy cream

Preparation:
1. Blend cayenne pepper and other ingredients in a bowl.
2. Divide this marinade in three bowls and add chicken, beef and shrimp to the bowls.
3. Mix well to coat, cover and refrigerate them for 1 hour.
4. Toss tomatoes with salt and olive oil in a bowl.
5. Place the cooking pot in the Ninja Foodi Grill then set a grill grate inside.
6. Select the "Grill" Mode, set the temperature to MED.
7. Use the arrow keys to set the time to 14 minutes.
8. Press the START/STOP button to initiate preheating.
9. Once preheated, place the tomatoes in the Ninja Foodi Grill.
10. Cover the hood and allow the grill to cook then transfer to a plate.
11. Sauté onion with oil in a skillet for 6 minutes.
12. Stir in baked tomatoes and sauté for 10 minutes.
13. Add cream and blend this mixture with salt in a blender.
14. Thread the marinated chicken, beef and shrimp on the separated skewers.
15. Once preheated, place the skewers in the Ninja Foodi Grill.
16. Grill the beef skewers for 3 minutes per side, chicken for 4 minutes per side and shrimp 2 minutes per side.
17. Serve warm with the tomato soubise.

Serving Suggestion: Serve the skewers with kale cucumber salad.

Variation Tip: Add diced onion and bell peppers to the skewers as well.

Nutritional Information Per Serving:
Calories 248 | Fat 23g |Sodium 350mg | Carbs 18g | Fiber 6.3g | Sugar 1g | Protein 40.3g

Apricot-Chile Glazed Salmon

Prep time: 25 minutes
Cook time: 25 minutes
Servings: 4

Ingredients
- 2 tbsp red chili powder
- 3 tbsp apricot jam
- ½ tsp salt
- 1¼-1½ pounds center-cut wild salmon, skinned

Preparation
1. Preheat the grill for 8 minutes.
2. Combine the salt and chili powder in a bowl. Rub them onto both sides of salmon.
3. Place the jam in a saucepan; heat it over medium heat, keep stirring it until melted.
4. Insert grill grate in the unit and close the hood.
5. Select the option GRILL, set the temperature to MEDIUM, and set time to 10 minutes. Use a pastry brush, coat the top of the salmon with the jam. Close the grill; cook until the salmon easily flakes with a fork, 3 to 5 minutes more. To serve, cut into 4 portions.

Serving Suggestion: Serve with chilled drink.

Variation Tip: use any jam of your liking for glaze.

Nutritional Information Per Serving:
Calories 151 | Carbohydrates 19.46g | Protein 1.85g | Fat 7.54g | Sodium 95mg| Fiber 0.4g

Ninja Foodi Crispy Salmon

Prep time: 10 minutes
Cook time: 8 minutes
Serves: 4

Ingredients:
- 4 salmon fillets
- 8 teaspoons paprika
- 8 teaspoons avocado oil
- Salt and black pepper, to taste

Preparation:
1. Insert crisper basket in the unit. Select AIR CRISP, set temperature to 390°F, and set time to 8 minutes. Select START/STOP to begin preheating
2. Season salmon fillets with salt, pepper, paprika, and avocado oil, then place in Ninja Foodi Grill when "Add Food" appears.
3. Cook for 8 minutes, flipping halfway through.
4. Remove the dish from the oven and serve immediately.
Serving Suggestions: Serve with lemon wedges.
Variation Tip: You can also add parsley.
Nutritional Information per Serving:
Calories: 260 |Fat: 12.7g|Sat Fat: 1.9g|Carbohydrates: 2.9g|Fiber: 2g|Sugar: 0.5g|Protein: 35.3g

Grilled Shrimp with Miso Butter

Prep time: 15 minutes.
Cook time: 8 minutes.
Serves: 6
Ingredients:

- 1 stick unsalted butter, softened
- 2 tablespoons white miso
- ½ teaspoon lemon zest, grated
- 1 tablespoon lemon juice
- 1 tablespoon scallion, sliced
- 1-pound large shrimp, shelled and deveined
- 2 tablespoons canola oil
- 1 large garlic clove, minced
- 1 teaspoon Korean chile powder
- 1 teaspoon salt
- 1 ½ teaspoons mustard seeds, pickled

Preparation:
1. Blend butter with lemon juice, lemon zest, miso, 1 tablespoon scallion in a bowl.
2. Toss in shrimp, chile powder, salt, and garlic, then mix well.
3. Preheat the Ninja Foodi Grill on the "Grill Mode" at LOW-temperature settings.
4. When the grill is preheated, open its hood and place the shrimp in it.
5. Cover the grill's hood and grill for 4 minutes per side.
6. Serve warm.
Serving Suggestion: Serve the shrimp with potato salad.
Variation Tip: Add garlic salt to the sauce for more taste.
Nutritional Information Per Serving:
Calories 251 | Fat 17g |Sodium 723mg | Carbs 21g | Fiber 2.5g | Sugar 2g | Protein 7.3g

Ninja Foodi Spicy Salmon Fillets

Prep time: 5 minutes
Cook time: 8 minutes
Serves: 1
Ingredients:
- 1 salmon fillet
- 2 teaspoons paprika
- ½ teaspoon red chili powder
- ½ teaspoon onion powder
- ½ teaspoon garlic powder
- 2 teaspoons avocado oil
- 1 teaspoon dried parsley
- ½ teaspoon cayenne pepper
- Salt and black pepper, to taste

Preparation:
1. In a large mixing bowl, combine the salmon fillet, paprika, red chili powder, onion powder,

garlic powder, parsley, cayenne pepper, avocado oil, salt, and black pepper. Set aside after thoroughly mixing.

2. Insert crisper basket in the unit. Select AIR CRISP, set temperature to 390°F, and set time to 08 minutes. Select START/STOP to begin preheating.

3. When it shows "Add Food", place the salmon fillet in it and cook for 8 minutes, flipping halfway through.

4. Dish out and serve hot.

Serving Suggestions: Serve with melted butter.

Variation Tip: Lemon juice can also be added.

Nutritional Information per Serving:
Calories: 276 |Fat: 13.1g|Sat Fat: 2g|Carbohydrates: 6.2g|Fiber: 2.9g|Sugar: 1.4g|Protein: 36g

Ninja Foodi Broiled Tilapia

Prep time: 5 minutes
Cook time: 8 minutes
Serves: 4

Ingredients:
- 2 pounds tilapia fillets
- 2 teaspoons lemon pepper
- 4 teaspoons melted butter
- 2 teaspoons old bay seasoning
- Salt, to taste

Preparation:
1. In a mixing dish, combine the tilapia fillets, old bay seasoning, lemon pepper, melted butter, and salt. Mix thoroughly.

2. In the meantime, in a Ninja Foodi Grill, press the "ROAST" button and set the time to 8 minutes set temp 350°F.

3. To begin preheating, press START/STOP.

4. When "Add Food" appears, add the tilapia fillets and simmer for 8 minutes.

5. Remove the dish from the oven and serve immediately.

Serving Suggestions: Serve with lemon wedges.

Variation Tip: You can add lemon juice to enhance taste.

Nutritional Information per Serving:
Calories: 223 |Fat: 5.9g|Sat Fat:

3.3g|Carbohydrates: 0.7g|Fiber: 0.3g|Sugar: 0g|Protein: 42.3g

Ninja Foodi Southern Catfish

Prep time: 15 minutes
Cook time: 10 minutes
Serves: 8

Ingredients:
- 4 pounds catfish fillets
- 2 cups milk
- 1 cup cornmeal
- ½ cup all-purpose flour
- ½ teaspoon chili powder
- ½ teaspoon cayenne pepper
- 2 lemons, sliced
- 1 cup yellow mustard
- 4 tablespoons dried parsley
- ½ teaspoon onion powder
- ½ teaspoon garlic powder
- Salt and black pepper, to taste

Preparation:
1. Insert crisper basket in the unit. Select AIR CRISP, set temperature to 400°F, and set time to 10 minutes. Select START/STOP to begin preheating

2. In a separate bowl, combine the lemon juice, milk, and catfish. Refrigerate for about 15 minutes after thoroughly mixing.

3. In a large mixing bowl, whisk together cornmeal, parsley, all-purpose flour, salt, chili powder, onion powder, black pepper, garlic powder, and cayenne pepper. Mix thoroughly.

4. Coat the catfish fillets in the cornmeal mixture after rubbing them with mustard.

5. Place catfish fillets in the Ninja Foodi Grill when it says "Add Food" and cook for 10 minutes.

6. Turn halfway through and serve.

7. Finally, serve and enjoy!

Serving Suggestions: Serve with chopped mint leaves on the top.

Variation Tip: You can omit parsley.

Nutritional Information per Serving:
Calories: 448 |Fat: 20.5g|Sat Fat: 4.1g|Carbohydrates: 24.2g|Fiber: 2.9g|Sugar: 3.6g|Protein: 41g

Ninja Foodi Tuna Patties

Prep time: 10 minutes
Cook time: 10 minutes
Serves: 8
Ingredients:
- 3 tablespoons almond flour
- 3 tablespoons mayo
- 1 teaspoon onion powder
- 1½ pounds tuna
- 2 teaspoons garlic powder
- 2 teaspoons dried dill
- 1 lemon, squeezed
- Salt and black pepper, to taste

Preparation:
1. Insert grill grate in the unit and close hood. Select GRILL, set temperature to MEDIUM, and set time to 10 minutes. Select START/STOP to begin preheating.
2. In a separate bowl, combine the tuna, almond flour, mayonnaise, onion powder, garlic powder, dill, salt, black pepper, and lemon. Mix thoroughly.
3. Set aside tuna patties made from the ingredients.
4. Place the tuna patties in the Ninja Foodi Grill when it says "Add Food" and cook for 10 minutes, flipping halfway through.
5. Dish out, serve and have fun!

Serving Suggestions: Before serving, garnish with red chili flakes.
Variation Tip: You can add chopped mint leaves in the mixture.
Nutritional Information per Serving:
Calories: 623 |Fat: 28.3g|Sat Fat: 5.5g|Carbohydrates: 3.5g|Fiber: 0.6g|Sugar: 0.8g|Protein: 83.6g

Ninja Foodi Lime Chili Tilapia

Prep time: 10 minutes
Cook time: 10 minutes
Serves: 4
Ingredients:
- 2 cups bread crumbs
- 1 cup all-purpose flour
- 2 limes, squeezed
- 2 pounds tilapia fillets
- 2 tablespoons chili powder
- 4 eggs
- Salt and black pepper, to taste

Preparation:
1. Insert grill grate in the unit and close hood. Select GRILL, set temperature to MIDIUM, and set time to 10 minutes. Select START/STOP to begin preheating.
2. In a large mixing bowl, combine bread crumbs, salt, black pepper, and chili powder. Mix thoroughly.
3. Separate the eggs and flour into two bowls. Remove from the equation.
4. Coat the tilapia fillets in flour, then dip them in eggs, then bread crumbs.
5. Place the tilapia fillets in the Ninja Foodi Grill when it shows "Add Food" and cook for 10 minutes.
6. Serve with lime juice drizzled on top.
7. Finally, serve and enjoy!

Serving Suggestions: Serve with lemon slices.
Variation Tip: Black pepper can be replaced with cayenne pepper.
Nutritional Information per Serving:
Calories: 599 |Fat: 10.3g|Sat Fat: 3.1g|Carbohydrates: 68.7g|Fiber: 5.5g|Sugar: 4.6g|Protein: 58.9g

Ninja Foodi Breaded Shrimp

Prep time: 5 minutes
Cook time: 16 minutes
Serves: 2
Ingredients:
- 1 egg
- ¼ cup bread crumbs
- ½ teaspoon garlic powder
- ½ pound shrimp, peeled and deveined
- ½ teaspoon ginger
- ¼ cup diced onion
- Salt and black pepper, to taste

Preparation:
1. Insert crisper basket in the unit. Select AIR CRISP, set temperature to 350°F, and set time to 16 minutes. Select START/STOP to begin

preheating.

2. In a large mixing bowl, add bread crumbs, onions, garlic powder, ginger, salt, and pepper. Mix thoroughly.

3. In a separate bowl, whisk the egg and set it away.

4. Dip the shrimp in the egg mixture, then in the bread crumb mixture. Remove from the equation.

5. Place the shrimps in the Ninja Foodi Grill when it shows "Add Food" and cook for around 16 minutes.

6. Remove the dish from the oven and serve immediately.

Serving Suggestions: Top with chopped mint leaves before serving.

Variation Tip: You can also use onion powder to enhance taste.

Nutritional Information per Serving:
Calories: 229 |Fat: 4.9g|Sat Fat: 1.4g|Carbohydrates: 13.8g|Fiber: 1.1g|Sugar: 1.8g|Protein: 30.7g

Ninja Foodi Seasoned Catfish

Prep time: 5 minutes
Cook time: 12 minutes
Serves: 2

Ingredients:
- 2 tablespoons Louisiana fish seasoning
- 2 catfish fillets
- ½ tablespoon parsley
- ½ tablespoon olive oil

Preparation:
1. Insert grill grate in the unit and close hood. Select GRILL, set temperature to MEDIUM, and set time to 12 minutes. Select START/STOP to begin preheating.

2. In the meantime, combine catfish fillets, Louisiana fish seasoning, parsley, and olive oil in a mixing bowl. Remove from the equation.

3. Place the fillets in the Ninja Foodi Grill when it says "Add Food" and cook for 12 minutes.

4. Remove the dish from the oven and serve

immediately.

Serving Suggestions: Serve with butter topping.

Variation Tip: You can use oregano to enhance taste.

Nutritional Information per Serving:
Calories: 266 |Fat: 15.7g|Sat Fat: 2.7g|Carbohydrates: 5.1g|Fiber: 0g|Sugar: 0g|Protein: 24.9g

Ninja Foodi Teriyaki Salmon

Prep time: 5 minutes
Cook time: 8 minutes
Serves: 2

Ingredients:
- ½ cup teriyaki marinade
- 2 skinless salmon fillets

Preparation:
1. In a mixing bowl, combine the teriyaki marinade and the salmon fillets. Refrigerate for 3 hours after thoroughly mixing.

2. Insert grill grate in the unit and close hood. Select GRILL, set temperature to MEDIUM, and set time to 8 minutes. Select START/STOP to begin preheating.

3. Place the salmon fillets in the pan when it says "Add Food" and cook for 8 minutes.

4. Remove the dish from the oven and serve immediately.

Serving Suggestions: Serve with tomato sauce.

Variation Tip: You can also use sesame seeds to enhance taste.

Nutritional Information per Serving:
Calories: 280 |Fat: 12g|Sat Fat: 2.5g|Carbohydrates: 16g|Fiber: 0g|Sugar: 12g|Protein: 22g

Ninja Foodi Cajun Salmon

Prep time: 10 minutes
Cook time: 8 minutes
Serves: 4

Ingredients:
- 4 tablespoons Cajun seasoning
- 4 salmon steaks

Preparation:
1. Set aside for about 10 minutes after seasoning salmon steaks with Cajun seasoning.
2. Insert crisper basket in the unit. Select AIR CRISP, set temperature to 390°F, and set time to 8 minutes. Select START/STOP to begin preheating.
3. When "Add Food" appears, add the salmon steaks and cook for 8 minutes at 390 degrees F.
4. Turn halfway through.
5. Finally, serve and enjoy!

Serving Suggestions: Serve with coleslaw.
Variation Tip: You can add some sesame seeds to enhance taste.
Nutritional Information per Serving:
Calories: 235 |Fat: 11g|Sat Fat: 1.6g|Carbohydrates: 0g|Fiber: 0g|Sugar: 0g|Protein: 34.7g

Ninja Foodi Simple Cod Fillets

Prep time: 10 minutes
Cook time: 12 minutes
Serves: 4

Ingredients:
- 4 cod fillets
- Salt and black pepper, to taste

Preparation:
1. Sprinkle salt and pepper over the cod fillets. Set aside.
2. Insert grill grate in the unit and close hood. Select GRILL, set temperature to MEDIUM, and set time to 12 minutes. Select START/STOP to begin heating.
3. When "Add Food" appears, add the salmon fillets and simmer for around 12 minutes.
4. Remove from the oven and serve immediately.
5. Serving Suggestions: You can add melted butter on the top.
Variation Tip: You can also use cayenne pepper to enhance taste.
Nutritional Information per Serving:
Calories: 90 |Fat: 1g|Sat Fat: 0g|Carbohydrates: 0g|Fiber: 0g|Sugar: 0g|Protein: 20g

Ninja Foodi Buttered Scallops

Prep time: 10 minutes
Cook time: 4 minutes
Serves: 4

Ingredients:
- 1½ pounds sea scallops
- 1 tablespoon fresh thyme, minced
- 2 tablespoons melted butter
- Salt and black pepper, to taste

Preparation:
1. In a large mixing bowl, combine the scallops, thyme, butter, salt, and pepper. Mix thoroughly.
2. Insert crisper basket in the unit. Select AIR CRISP, set temperature to 390°F, and set time to 4 minutes. Select START/STOP to begin preheating.
3. When "Add Food" appears, add the sea scallops and cook for 4 minutes at 390°F.
4. Remove the dish from the oven and serve immediately.
Serving Suggestions: Serve with chopped parsley on the top.
Variation Tip: You can also add lemon juice to enhance taste.
Nutritional Information per Serving:
Calories: 602 |Fat: 10.6g|Sat Fat: 4.2g|Carbohydrates: 15.2g|Fiber: 0.3g|Sugar: 0g|Protein: 104.8g

Garlic Flavored Artichoke Meal

Honey Carrot Dish

Prep time: 10 minutes
Cook time: 10 minutes
Servings: 4

Ingredients
- 2 large artichokes, trimmed and halved
- 3 garlic cloves, chopped
- ½ a lemon, juiced
- ½ cup canola oil
- Salt and pepper to taste

Preparation
1. Select GRILL mode and set your Ninja Foodi Grill to "MAX."
2. Set the timer to 10 minutes.
3. Let it pre-heat until you hear a beep.
4. Add lemon juice, oil, garlic into a medium-sized bowl.
5. Season with salt and pepper.
6. Brush artichoke halves with lemon garlic mix.
7. Once ready, transfer artichokes to Grill.
8. Press them down to maximize grill mark.
9. Grill for 8-10 minutes; make sure to blister on all sides.

Serving Suggestion: Serve with dill garnishing or enjoy as it is.

Variation Tip: use chopped dill for garnish.

Nutritional Information per Serving:
Calories: 285| Fat: 28 g| Fat: 8 g
Carbohydrates: 10 g| Fiber: 3 g| Sodium: 137 mg| Protein: 3 g

Prep time: 15 minutes
Cook time: 10 minutes
Servings: 4

Ingredients
- 6 carrots, cut lengthwise
- 1 tablespoon rosemary, chopped
- 1 tablespoon honey
- 2 tbsp butter, melted
- 1 tablespoon parsley, chopped
- 1 tsp salt

Preparation
1. Take your Ninja Foodi Grill, open the lid.
2. Arrange grill grate and close top.
3. Pre-heat Ninja Foodi by pressing the "GRILL" option and setting it to "MAX.".
4. Then set the timer for 10 minutes.
5. Allow it pre-heat until it sounds a beep.
6. Arrange carrots over the grill grate.
7. Take the remaining Ingredients and spread them.
8. Drizzle honey, lock lid and cook for 5 minutes.
9. Then flip sausages and cook for 5 minutes more.
10. Once done, serve and enjoy!

Serving Suggestion: Serve with dill garnishing or enjoy as it is.

Variation Tip: use chopped dill for garnish.

Nutritional Information per Serving:
Calories: 80|, Fat: 4 g| Carbohydrates: 10 g| Fiber: 3 g| Sodium: 186 mg| Protein: 0.5 g

Grilled Veggies with Vinaigrette

Prep time: 15 minutes.
Cook time: 26 minutes.
Serves: 4
Ingredients:
Vinaigrette
- ¼ cup red wine vinegar
- 1 tablespoon Dijon mustard
- 1 tablespoon honey
- ½ teaspoon salt
- ⅛ teaspoon black pepper
- ¼ cup canola oil
- ¼ cup olive oil

Vegetables
- 2 large sweet onions, diced
- 2 medium zucchinis, diced
- 2 yellow summer squash, diced
- 2 red peppers, seeded and cut in half
- 1 bunch green onions, trimmed
- Cooking spray

Preparation:
1. Start by whisking the first 5 ingredients in a small bowl.
2. Gradually add oil while mixing the vinaigrette thoroughly.
3. Preheat the Ninja Foodi Grill on the "Grill Mode" at MEDIUM-temperature settings.
4. When the grill is preheated, open its hood and place the onion quarters in it.
5. Cover the grill's hood and grill for 5 minutes per side.
6. Grill squash, peppers, and zucchini for 7 minutes per side in the same grill.
7. Finally, grill the green onions for 1 minute per side.
8. Dice the grilled veggies and mix with vinaigrette.
9. Serve.
Serving Suggestion: Serve the vegetables with boiled rice or pasta.

Variation Tip: Top the veggies with feta cheese before serving.
Nutritional Information Per Serving:
Calories 341 | Fat 24g |Sodium 547mg | Carbs 36.4g | Fiber 1.2g | Sugar 1g | Protein 10.3g

Grilled Potato Rounds

Prep time: 15 minutes.
Cook time: 14 minutes.
Serves: 4
Ingredients:
- 4 large potatoes, baked and cooled
- ¼ cup butter, melted
- ¼ teaspoon salt
- ¼ teaspoon black pepper
- 1 cup sour cream
- 1- ½ cups cheddar cheese, shredded
- 8 bacon strips, cooked and crumbled
- 3 tablespoons chives, minced

Preparation:
1. First, cut the potatoes into 1-inch thick rounds.
2. Rub them with butter, salt, and black pepper.
3. Preheat the Ninja Foodi Grill on the "Grill Mode" at LOW-temperature settings.
4. When the grill is preheated, open its hood and place the potato slices in it.
5. Cover the grill's hood and grill for 7 minutes per side.
6. Serve warm with bacon, chives, cheese, and sour cream on top.
7. Enjoy.
Serving Suggestion: Serve the potatoes with tomato sauce.
Variation Tip: Add green beans around the potatoes before serving.
Nutritional Information Per Serving:
Calories 318 | Fat 15.7g |Sodium 124mg | Carbs 27g | Fiber 0.1g | Sugar 0.3g | Protein 4.9g

Zucchini Rolls with Goat Cheese

Prep time: 15 minutes.
Cook time: 12 minutes.
Serves: 4

Ingredients:
- 1 small bunch fresh chives
- 4 medium zucchinis, cut into ¼" slices
- 3 tbsp. olive oil
- Kosher salt, to taste
- Black pepper, to taste
- 4 oz. fresh goat cheese
- 1 small fresh mint leaves, chopped
- 2 tbsp. balsamic vinegar
- 1 handful baby arugula
- 2 Fresno peppers, cut into 1/8" matchsticks

Preparation:
1. Blanch chives in a saucepan filled with water for 30 seconds then drain.
2. Brush the zucchini slices with black pepper, salt and oil.
3. Place the cooking pot in the Ninja Foodi Grill then set a grill grate inside.
4. Select the "Grill" Mode, set the temperature to MED.
5. Use the arrow keys to set the cooking time to 6 minutes.
6. Press the START/STOP button to initiate preheating.
7. Once preheated, place the zucchini in the Ninja Foodi Grill.
8. Cover the hood and allow the grill to cook.
9. Flip the zucchini once cooked halfway through.
10. Divide the goat cheese mint, balsamic vinegar, arugula and pepper on top of the grilled zucchini.
11. Roll the zucchini slices and seal with a toothpick.
12. Serve.

Serving Suggestion: Serve the zucchini rolls with roasted mushrooms.
Variation Tip: Add lemon zest and lemon juice on top for a fresh taste.
Nutritional Information Per Serving:
Calories 224 | Fat 5g |Sodium 432mg | Carbs 3.1g | Fiber 0.3g | Sugar 1g | Protein 5.7g

Sweet Grilled Pickles

Prep time: 15 minutes.
Cook time: 10 minutes.
Serves: 4

Ingredients:
Brine:
- 1 ¼ cup distilled white vinegar
- 1 ¼ cup water
- 1 cup sugar
- 2 tbsp. Kosher salt
- 2 tsp. crushed red pepper

Pickles
- 5 large cucumbers, cut into 4 to 5-inch spears
- 1 white onion, sliced
- 6 sprigs dill
- 3 tsp. minced garlic
- 3 sanitized canning jars with lids

Preparation:
1. Place the cooking pot in the Ninja Foodi Grill then set a grill grate inside.
2. Select the "Grill" Mode, set the temperature to MED.
3. Use the arrow keys to set the cooking time to 6 minutes.
4. Press the START/STOP button to initiate preheating.
5. Once preheated, place the cucumber in the Ninja Foodi Grill.
6. Cover the hood and allow the grill to cook.
7. Flip the cucumber once cooked halfway through.
8. Mix the brine ingredients in a saucepan and divide into 2 canning jars.
9. Add 1 tsp. garlic and 2 dill sprigs to each jar.
10. Repeat the same steps with the onion.
11. Add cucumbers to one jar and onions to the other.
12. Close the lids and refrigerate them overnight.
13. Serve.

Serving Suggestion: Serve the grilled pickles with zucchini noodles.
Variation Tip: Add green beans to the pickles before serving.
Nutritional Information Per Serving:
Calories 318 | Fat 15.7g |Sodium 124mg | Carbs 27g | Fiber 0.1g | Sugar 0.3g | Protein 4.9g

Grilled Cauliflower with Miso Mayo

Prep time: 15 minutes.
Cook time: 14 minutes.
Serves: 6

Ingredients:
- 1 head of cauliflower, cut into florets
- ½ teaspoons kosher salt
- 4 tablespoons unsalted butter
- ¼ cup hot sauce
- 1 tablespoon ketchup
- 1 tablespoon soy sauce
- ½ cup mayonnaise
- 2 tablespoons white miso
- 1 tablespoon fresh lemon juice
- ½ teaspoons black pepper
- 2 scallions, sliced

Preparation:
1. Mix salt, butter, hot sauce, ketchup, soy sauce, miso, mayonnaise, lemon juice, and black pepper in a bowl.
2. Season the cauliflower florets with the marinade and mix well.
3. Preheat the Ninja Foodi Grill on the "Grill Mode" at MEDIUM-temperature settings.
4. When the grill is preheated, open its hood and place the cauliflower in it.
5. Cover the grill's hood and grill for 6 to 7 minutes per side.
6. Serve warm.

Serving Suggestion: Serve the cauliflower steaks with tomato sauce or guacamole.

Variation Tip: Add cheese on top of the grilled cauliflower.

Nutritional Information Per Serving:
Calories 391 | Fat 2.2g |Sodium 276mg | Carbs 27.7g | Fiber 0.9g | Sugar 1.4g | Protein 8.8g

Grilled Greens and Cheese on Toast

Prep time: 15 minutes.
Cook time: 36 minutes.
Serves: 4

Ingredients:
- 2 tablespoons olive oil
- 1 bunch, kale, stems removed
- ½ teaspoons kosher salt
- ½ teaspoons black pepper
- 6 oz. cherry tomatoes
- ½ lb. Halloumi cheese, sliced
- 1 lemon, halved crosswise
- 4 thick slices of country-style bread
- 1 large garlic clove, peeled, halved

Preparation:
1. Toss kale with olive oil, salt, black pepper, tomatoes, lemon juice, and garlic.
2. Preheat the Ninja Foodi Grill on the "Grill Mode" at LOW-temperature settings.
3. When the grill is preheated, open its hood and place the tomatoes in it.
4. Cover the grill's hood and grill for 5 minutes per side.
5. Grill the kale leaves for 2-3 minutes per side.
6. Transfer the veggies to a bowl.
7. Grill the bread slices for 4-5 minutes per side.
8. Grill the cheese slices for 3-5 minutes per side.
9. Divide the veggies and cheese on top of the bread slices.
10. Serve warm.

Serving Suggestion: Serve the bread slices with roasted mushrooms.

Variation Tip: Add lemon zest and lemon juice on top for better taste.

Nutritional Information Per Serving:
Calories 324 | Fat 5g |Sodium 432mg | Carbs 13.1g | Fiber 0.3g | Sugar 1g | Protein 5.7g

Mushroom Tomato Roast

Prep time: 10 minutes
Cook time: 15 minutes
Servings: 4

Ingredients

- 2 cups cherry tomatoes
- 2 cups cremini button mushrooms
- ¼ cup of vinegar or ¼ cup of red wine
- 2 garlic cloves, finely chopped
- ½ cup extra-virgin olive oil
- 3 tbsp chopped thyme
- Pinch of crushed red pepper flakes
- 1 tsp kosher salt
- ½ tsp black pepper
- 6 scallions, cut crosswise into 2-inch pieces

Preparation

1. Take a zip-lock bag; add black pepper, salt, red pepper flakes, thyme, vinegar, oil, and garlic. Add mushrooms, tomatoes, and scallions.
2. Shake well and refrigerate for 30-40 minutes to marinate.
3. Take Ninja Foodi Grill, orchestrate it over your kitchen stage, and open the top.
4. Press "ROAST" and alter the temperature to 400°F. Modify the clock to 12 minutes and afterward press "START/STOP." Ninja Foodi will begin preheating.
5. Ninja Foodi is preheated and prepared to cook when it begins to blare. After you hear a blare, open the top.
6. Arrange the mushroom mixture directly inside the pot.
7. Close the top lid and allow it to cook until the timer reads zero.
8. Arrange the mushroom mixture directly inside the Cooking Pot.

Serving Suggestion: Serve warm with chilled wine.

Variation Tip: use chopped dill for garnish.

Nutritional Information per Serving:

Calories: 253| Fat: 24g| Carbohydrates: 7g| Fiber: 2g| Sodium: 546mg| Protein: 1g

Tomato Salsa

Prep time: 5-10 minutes
Cook time: 10 minutes
Servings: 4

Ingredients

- 1 red onion, peeled, cut in quarters
- 1 jalapeño pepper, cut in half, seeds removed
- 5 Roma tomatoes, cut in half lengthwise
- 1 tablespoon kosher salt
- 2 tsp ground black pepper
- 2 tbsp canola oil
- 1 bunch cilantro, stems trimmed
- Juice and zest of 3 limes
- 3 cloves garlic, peeled
- 2 tbsp ground cumin

Preparation

1. In a blending bowl, join the onion, tomatoes, jalapeño pepper, salt, dark pepper, and canola oil.
2. Take Ninja Foodi Grill, mastermind it over your kitchen stage, and open the top. Mastermind the barbecue mesh and close the top cover.
3. Press "GRILL" and select the "MAX" flame broil work. Change the clock to 10 minutes and afterward press "START/STOP." Ninja Foodi will begin preheating.
4. Ninja Foodi is preheated and prepared to cook when it begins to blare. After you hear a signal, open the top cover.
5. Arrange the vegetables over the Grill Grate.
6. Close the top lid and cook for 5 minutes. Now open the top lid, flip the vegetables.
7. Close the top lid and cook for 5 more minutes.
8. Blend the mixture in a blender and serve as needed.

Serving Suggestion: Serve with dill garnishing or enjoy as it is.

Variation Tip: use chopped dill for garnish.

Nutritional Information per Serving:

Calories: 169| Fat: 9g|Carbohydrates: 12g| Fiber: 3g| Sodium: 321mg| Protein: 2.5g

Cheddar Cauliflower Meal

Prep time: 5-10 minutes
Cook time: 15 minutes
Servings: 2

Ingredients

- ½ tsp garlic powder
- ½ tsp paprika
- Ocean salt and ground dark pepper to taste
- 1 head cauliflower, stemmed and leaves removed
- 1 cup Cheddar cheese, shredded
- Ranch dressing, for garnish
- ¼ cup canola oil or vegetable oil
- 2 tbsp chopped chives
- 4 slices bacon, cooked and crumbled

Preparation

1. Cut the cauliflower into 2-inch pieces.
2. In a blending bowl, include the oil, garlic powder, and paprika. Season with salt and ground dark pepper; join well. Coat the florets with the blend.
3. Take Ninja Foodi Grill, mastermind it over your kitchen stage, and open the top cover.
4. Mastermind the flame broil mesh and close the top cover.
5. Press "GRILL" and select the "MAX" heat. Change the clock to 15 minutes and afterward press "START/STOP." Ninja Foodi will begin preheating.
6. Ninja Foodi is preheated and prepared to cook when it begins to signal. After you hear a blare, open the top.
7. Organize the pieces over the Grill Grate.
8. Close the top lid and cook for 10 minutes. Now open the top lid, flip the pieces and top with the cheese.
9. Close the top lid and cook for 5 more minutes.

Serving Suggestion: Serve warm with the chives and ranch dressing on top.

Variation Tip: use chili flakes for spice.

Nutritional Information per Serving:
Calories: 534| Fat: 34g |Carbohydrates: 14.5g| Fiber: 4g| Sodium: 1359mg| Protein: 31g

Cool Rosemary Potatoes

Prep time: 10 minutes
Cook time: 20 minutes
Servings: 4

Ingredients

- 2pounds baby red potatoes, quartered
- ½ tsp parsley, dried
- ¼ tsp celery powder
- 2 tbsp extra virgin olive oil
- ¼ cup onion flakes, dried
- ½ tsp garlic powder
- ½ tsp onion powder
- ½ tsp salt
- ¼ tsp freshly ground black pepper

Preparation

1. Add all listed Ingredients into a large bowl.
2. Toss well and coat them well.
3. Pre-heat your Ninja Foodi by pressing the "AIR CRISP" option and setting it to 390 Degrees F.
4. Set the timer to 20 minutes.
5. Allow it to pre-heat until it beeps.
6. Once preheated, add potatoes to the cooking basket.
7. Close the lid and cook for 10 minutes.
8. Shake the basket and cook for 10 minutes more.
9. Check the crispness if it is done or not.
10. Cook for 5 minutes more if needed.
11. Serve and enjoy!

Serving Suggestion: Serve with chilled beer.

Variation Tip: use shredded cheese for extra flavor.

Nutritional Information per Serving:
Calories: 232| Fat: 7 g| Carbohydrates: 39 g| Fiber: 6 g| Sodium: 249 mg| Protein: 4 g

Delicious Broccoli and Arugula

Prep time: 10 minutes
Cook time: 12 minutes
Servings: 4

Ingredients

- Pepper as needed
- ½ tsp salt
- Red pepper flakes
- 2 tbsp extra virgin olive oil
- 1 tablespoon canola oil
- ½ red onion, sliced
- 1 garlic clove, minced
- 1 tsp Dijon mustard
- 1 tsp honey
- 1 tablespoon lemon juice
- 2 tbsp parmesan cheese, grated
- 4 cups arugula, torn
- 2 heads broccoli, trimmed

Preparation

1. Pre-heat your Ninja Foodi Grill on GRILL mode at MAX heat and set the timer to 12 minutes.
2. Take a large-sized bowl and add broccoli, sliced onion, and canola oil, toss the mixture well until coated.
3. Once you hear the beep, it is pre-heated.
4. Arrange your vegetables over the grill grate; let them grill for 8-12 minutes.
5. Take a medium-sized bowl and whisk in lemon juice, olive oil, mustard, honey, garlic, red pepper flakes, pepper, and salt.
6. Once done, add the prepared veggies and arugula in a bowl.
7. Drizzle the prepared vinaigrette on top, sprinkle a bit of parmesan.
8. Stir and mix.
9. Enjoy!

Serving Suggestion: Serve warm with favorite drink.

Variation Tip: use cheese for taste.

Nutritional Information per Serving:

Calories: 168| Fat: 12 g| Carbohydrates: 13 g|
Fiber: 1 g| Sodium: 392 mg| Protein: 6 g

Mustard Green Veggie Meal

Prep time: 10 minutes
Cook time: 30-40 minutes
Servings: 4

Ingredients

Vinaigrette

- 2 tbsp Dijon mustard
- 1 tsp salt
- ¼ tsp black pepper
- ½ cup avocado oil
- ½ olive oil
- ½ cup red wine vinegar
- 2 tbsp honey

Veggies

- 4 sweet onions, quartered
- 4 yellow squash, cut in half
- 4 red peppers, seeded and halved
- 4 zucchinis, halved
- 2 bunches green onions, trimmed

Preparation

1. Take a small bowl and whisk mustard, pepper, honey, vinegar, and salt.
2. Add oil to make a smooth mixture.
3. Mastermind the flame broil mesh and close the top cover.
4. Pre-heat Ninja Foodi by pressing the "GRILL" option and setting it to "MEDIUM".
5. Let it pre-heat until you hear a beep.
6. Arrange the onion quarters over the grill grate, lock lid and cook for 5 minutes.
7. Flip the peppers and cook for 5 minutes more.
8. Grill the other vegetables in the same manner with 7 minutes each side for zucchini, pepper, and squash and 1 minute for onion.
9. Prepare the vinaigrette by mixing all the Ingredients under vinaigrette in a bowl.

Serving Suggestion: Serve the grilled veggies with vinaigrette on top.

Variation Tip: use your favorite veggies for fun.

Nutritional Information per Serving:

Calories: 326| Fat: 4.5 g| Carbohydrates: 35 g|
Fiber: 4 g| Sodium: 543 mg| Protein: 8 g

Vegetable Orzo Salad

Prep time: 15 minutes.
Cook time: 14 minutes.
Serves: 4

Ingredients:

- 1- ¼ cups orzo, uncooked
- ½-lb. fresh asparagus, trimmed
- 1 zucchini, sliced
- 1 sweet yellow, halved
- 1 portobello mushroom, stem removed
- ½ red onion, halved

Salad

- ½ teaspoon salt
- 1 cup grape tomatoes, halved
- 1 tablespoon minced fresh parsley
- 1 tablespoon minced fresh basil
- ¼ teaspoon black pepper
- 1 cup (4 oz.) feta cheese, crumbled

Dressing

- 4 garlic cloves, minced
- ⅓ cup olive oil
- ¼ cup balsamic vinegar
- 3 tablespoons lemon juice
- 1 teaspoon lemon-pepper seasoning

Preparation:

1. Cook the orzo as per the given instructions on the package, then drain.
2. Toss all the salad and dressing ingredients in a bowl until well coated.
3. Preheat the Ninja Foodi Grill on the "Grill Mode" at MEDIUM-temperature settings.
4. Place the mushrooms, pepper, and onion in the Ninja Foodi grill.
5. Cover the grill's hood and grill for 5 minutes per side.
6. Now grill zucchini and asparagus for 2 minutes per side.
7. Dice the grilled veggies and add them to the salad bowl.
8. Mix well, then stir in orzo.
9. Give it a toss, then serve.

Serving Suggestion: Serve the orzo salad with guacamole on top.

Variation Tip: Add olives or sliced mushrooms to the salad.

Nutritional Information Per Serving:
Calories 246 | Fat 15g |Sodium 220mg | Carbs 40.3g | Fiber 2.4g | Sugar 1.2g | Protein 12.4g

Buttery Spinach Meal

Prep time: 10 minutes
Cook time: 15 minutes
Servings: 4

Ingredients

- ⅔ cup olives, halved and pitted
- 1 and ½ cups feta cheese, grated
- 4 tbsp butter
- 2pounds spinach, chopped and boiled
- Pepper and salt to taste
- 4 tsp lemon zest, grated

Preparation

1. Take a mixing bowl and add spinach, butter, salt, pepper and mix well.
2. Pre-heat Ninja Foodi by pressing the "AIR CRISP" option and setting it to "340 Degrees F" and timer to 15 minutes.
3. Let it pre-heat until you hear a beep.
4. Arrange a reversible trivet in the Grill Pan, arrange spinach mixture in a basket and place basket in the trivet.
5. Let them cook until the timer runs out.
6. Serve and enjoy!

Serving Suggestion: Serve with your favorite dipping.

Variation Tip: use chopped cilantro for garnish.

Nutritional Information per Serving:
Calories: 250|Fat: 18 g| Carbohydrates: 8 g| Fiber: 3 g| Sodium: 309 mg| Protein: 10 g

Southwestern Potato Salad

Prep time: 15 minutes.
Cook time: 24 minutes.
Serves: 6

Ingredients:
- 1- ½ lbs. large red potatoes quartered lengthwise
- 3 tablespoons olive oil
- 2 poblano peppers
- 2 medium ears sweet corn, husks removed
- ½ cup buttermilk
- ½ cup sour cream
- 1 tablespoon lime juice
- 1 jalapeno pepper, seeded and minced
- 1 tablespoon minced fresh cilantro
- 1-½ teaspoons garlic salt
- 1 teaspoon ground cumin
- ¼ teaspoon cayenne pepper

Preparation:
1. Add water and potatoes to a large saucepan and cook for 5 minutes on a boil.
2. Drain and rub the potatoes with oil.
3. Preheat the Ninja Foodi Grill on the "Grill Mode" at MEDIUM-temperature settings.
4. When the grill is preheated, open its hood and place the corn ears in it.
5. Cover the grill's hood and grill for 5 minutes per side.
6. Now grill potatoes and corn for 7 minutes per side.
7. Peel the pepper and chop them.
8. Cut corn and potatoes as well and mix well peppers in a bowl.
9. Whisk the rest of the ingredients in a separate bowl, then add to the potatoes.
10. Mix well and serve.

Serving Suggestion: Serve the potato salad with pita bread.

Variation Tip: Add boiled chickpeas to the salad

Nutritional Information Per Serving:
Calories 338 | Fat 24g |Sodium 620mg | Carbs 58.3g | Fiber 2.4g | Sugar 1.2g | Protein 5.4g

Apple Salad

Prep time: 15 minutes.
Cook time: 10 minutes.
Serves: 4

Ingredients:
- 6 tablespoons olive oil
- ¼ cup cilantro, minced
- ¼ cup vinegar
- 2 tablespoons honey
- 1 garlic clove, minced
- ¼ cup orange juice
- ½ teaspoon salt
- ½ teaspoon Sriracha chili sauce
- 2 large apples, wedged
- 1 pack (5 oz.) salad greens
- 1 cup walnut halves, toasted
- ½ cup crumbled blue cheese

Preparation:
1. Whisk the first 8 ingredients in a bowl and add ¼ cup of this dressing to the apples.
2. Toss well and let them sit for 10 minutes.
3. Preheat the Ninja Foodi Grill on the "Grill Mode" at LOW-temperature settings.
4. When the grill is preheated, open its hood and place the apples in it.
5. Cover the grill's hood and grill for 5 minutes per side.
6. Toss the rest of the salad ingredients together in a salad bowl.
7. Add grilled apples and serve.

Serving Suggestion: Serve the apple salad with lemon wedges.

Variation Tip: Add breadcrumbs to the salad for a crispy texture.

Nutritional Information Per Serving:
Calories 93 | Fat 3g |Sodium 510mg | Carbs 12g | Fiber 3g | Sugar 4g | Protein 4g

Cajun Green Beans

Prep time: 15 minutes.
Cook time: 11 minutes.
Serves: 4

Ingredients:
- 1-lb. fresh green beans, trimmed
- ½ teaspoon Cajun seasoning
- 1 tablespoon butter

Preparation:
1. Add green beans to an 18-inch square sheet.
2. Drizzle Cajun seasoning and butter on top.
3. Cover and seal the foil over the green beans.
4. Preheat the Ninja Foodi Grill on the "Bake Mode" at 350 degrees F.
5. When the grill is preheated, open its hood and place the green beans in it.
6. Cover the grill's hood and cook on the "Bake Mode" for 11 minutes.
7. Serve warm

Serving Suggestion: Serve the green beans with crispy nachos and mashed potatoes.
Variation Tip: Add crispy dried onion for better taste.
Nutritional Information Per Serving:
Calories 304 | Fat 31g |Sodium 834mg | Carbs 21.4g | Fiber 0.2g | Sugar 0.3g | Protein 4.6g

Potatoes in a Foil

Prep time: 15 minutes.
Cook time: 25 minutes.
Serves: 4

Ingredients:
- 2 ½ lbs. potatoes, peeled and diced
- 1 medium onion, chopped
- 5 bacon strips, cooked and crumbled
- ¼ cup butter, melted
- ½ teaspoon salt
- ¼ teaspoon black pepper
- 6 slices American cheese
- Sour cream, to serve

Preparation:
1. Toss potatoes with salt, pepper, butter, bacon, and onion.
2. Add this mixture to a suitably sized foil sheet and wrap it well to seal.
3. Preheat the Ninja Foodi Grill on the "Bake Mode" at 350 degrees F.
4. When the grill is preheated, open its hood and place the potato pockets in it.
5. Cover the grill's hood and cook on the "Bake Mode" for 15-25 minutes.
6. Drizzle cheese over hot potatoes.
7. Serve warm.

Serving Suggestion: Serve the potatoes with butter sauce and bacon on top.
Variation Tip: Add boiled green beans to the potatoes before serving.
Nutritional Information Per Serving:
Calories 378 | Fat 3.8g |Sodium 620mg | Carbs 13.3g | Fiber 2.4g | Sugar 1.2g | Protein 5.4g

Jalapeño Poppers with Smoked Gouda

Prep time: 15 minutes.
Cook time: 10 minutes.
Serves: 6

Ingredients:
- 12 large jalapeño chiles
- 4 ounces cream cheese
- 1 cup smoked Gouda, shredded
- Salt, to taste
- Chopped fresh cilantro for serving

Preparation:
1. Cut the jalapenos chiles in half and remove the seeds.

2. Mix cream cheese, gouda, and salt in a bowl.

3. Stuff this cheese mixture in the chilies.

4. Preheat the Ninja Foodi Grill on the "Grill Mode" at MEDIUM-temperature settings.

5. When the grill is preheated, open its hood and place the chiles in it.

6. Cover the grill's hood and grill for 5 minutes.

7. Garnish with cilantro and serve warm.

Serving Suggestion: Serve the peppers with crispy bacon.

Variation Tip: Add shredded chicken to the filling.

Nutritional Information Per Serving:
Calories 136 | Fat 10g |Sodium 249mg | Carbs 8g | Fiber 2g | Sugar 3g | Protein 4g

Grilled Watermelon, Feta, and Tomato Salad

Prep time: 15 minutes.

Cook time: 10 minutes.

Serves: 8

Ingredients:
- 1 tablespoon olive oil
- 1 (4-pounds) watermelon, cut into slices
- 1 teaspoon salt
- 4 heirloom tomatoes, sliced
- ½ teaspoon black pepper
- 6 ounces feta, sliced

Preparation:
1. Season the tomatoes and watermelon with olive oil, salt, and black pepper.

2. Preheat the Ninja Foodi Grill on the "Grill Mode" at MEDIUM-temperature settings.

3. When the grill is preheated, open its hood and place the watermelon slices in it.

4. Cover the grill's hood and grill for 2 minutes per side.

5. Transfer the watermelons to a plate and grill the tomatoes for 3 minutes per side.

6. Transfer the tomatoes to the watermelon plate.

7. Add feta cheese on top.

8. Serve.

Serving Suggestion: Serve the salad with fresh herbs on top.

Variation Tip: Add canned corn to the salad.

Nutritional Information Per Serving:
Calories 351 | Fat 19g |Sodium 412mg | Carbs 43g | Fiber 0.3g | Sugar 1g | Protein 23g

Balsamic Vegetables

Prep time: 10 minutes

Cook time: 30 minutes

Serves: 3

Ingredients:
- 1 cup sweet potato, cut into chunks
- 1 cup broccoli, cut into chunks
- 1 cup beet, cut into chunks
- 1 tablespoonBalsamic vinegar
- 1 cup mushrooms, sliced
- 1 tablespoon olive oil
- 1 tablespoon honey
- Pepper
- Salt

Directions:
1. Place the cooking pot in the Ninja Foodi Grill Main Unit.

2. In a bowl, toss vegetables with oil, pepper and salt.

3. Transfer vegetables into the baking dish.

4. Press Bake mode, set the temperature to 390°F, and set time to 25 minutes. Press Start.

5. Once a unit is preheated then place the baking dish in the cooking pot.

6. Cover with lid and cook for 25 minutes.

7. Once veggies are baked then mix honey and vinegar and drizzle over vegetables and bake for five minutes more.

Serving Suggestion: Allow to cool completely then serve.

Variation Tip: Add your choice of seasonings.

Nutritional Information per Serving:
Calories 163 | Fat 5.1g |Sodium 130mg | Carbs 28.1g | Fiber 4.4g | Sugar 15.5g | Protein 3.9g

Parmesan Zucchini and Squash

Prep time: 10 minutes
Cook time: 30 minutes
Serves: 6

Ingredients:

- 2 medium zucchinis, sliced
- 2 yellow squash, sliced
- ¾ cup Parmesan cheese, shredded
- 3 tomatoes, sliced
- 1 tablespoon olive oil
- Pepper
- Salt

Directions:

1. Place the cooking pot in the Ninja Foodi Grill Main Unit.
2. Arrange sliced tomatoes, squash and zucchinis alternately in the baking dish.
3. Sprinkle cheese on top of vegetables and drizzle with oil. Season with pepper and salt.
4. Press Bake mode, set the temperature to 350°F, and set time to 30 minutes. Press Start.
5. Once a unit is preheated then place the baking dish in the cooking pot.
6. Cover with lid and cook for 30 minutes.

Serving Suggestion: Allow to cool completely then serve.

Variation Tip: Add your choice of seasonings.

Nutritional Information per Serving:
Calories 97 | Fat 6g |Sodium 263mg | Carbs 5g | Fiber 1.5g | Sugar 2.8g | Protein 6.4g

Rosemary Potatoes

Prep time: 10 minutes

Cook time: 15 minutes
Serves: 4

Ingredients:

- 4 cups of baby potatoes, cut into four pieces each
- 2 teaspoons dried rosemary, minced
- 1 tablespoon garlic, minced
- 3 tablespoons olive oil
- ¼ cup fresh parsley, chopped
- 1 tablespoon fresh lemon juice
- Pepper
- Salt

Directions:

1. Place the cooking pot in the Ninja Foodi Grill Main Unit then place the Ninja Foodi Crisper Basket in the pot.
2. In a bowl, toss potatoes with garlic, rosemary, oil, pepper and salt.
3. Add potatoes in the Ninja Foodi Crisper Basket.
4. Press Air Crisp mode, set the temperature to 400°F, and set time to 15 minutes.
5. Cover with lid and press Start.
6. Transfer potatoes to a large bowl and toss with parsley and lemon juice.

Serving Suggestion: Allow to cool completely then serve.

Variation Tip: You can use vegetable oil instead of olive oil.

Nutritional Information per Serving:
Calories 201 | Fat 10.8g |Sodium 51mg | Carbs 25g | Fiber 4.1g | Sugar 1.9g | Protein 2.8g

Baked Mushrooms

Prep time: 10 minutes
Cook time: 15 minutes
Serves: 4

Ingredients:

- 1 ½ pound mushrooms, sliced
- ¼ cup Parmesan cheese, grated
- ¼ cup fresh lemon juice
- 3 tablespoons olive oil
- 1 ½ teaspoon dried thyme
- 1 tablespoon garlic, minced
- 1 lemon zest
- Pepper
- Salt

Directions:
1. Place the cooking pot in the Ninja Foodi Grill Main Unit.
2. Add mushrooms and remaining ingredients into the bowl and toss well.
3. Transfer mushroom mixture into the baking dish.
4. Press Bake mode, set the temperature to 375°F, and set time to 15 minutes. Press Start.
5. Once a unit is preheated then place the baking dish in the cooking pot.
6. Cover with lid and cook for 15 minutes.

Serving Suggestion: Allow to cool completely then serve.

Variation Tip: Add your choice of seasonings.

Nutritional Information per Serving:
Calories 284 | Fat 20.2g |Sodium 652mg | Carbs 6.9g | Fiber 2g | Sugar 3.3g | Protein 17.6g

Baked Parmesan Zucchini

Prep time: 10 minutes
Cook time: 5 minutes
Serves: 4

Ingredients:
- 2 zucchini, cut into ½-inch slices
- 2 tablespoon olive oil
- ⅓ cup Parmesan cheese, grated
- ¼ cup breadcrumbs
- 1 teaspoon Italian seasoning
- Pepper
- Salt

Directions:
1. Place the cooking pot in the Ninja Foodi Grill Main Unit.
2. In a bowl, toss zucchini with remaining ingredients until well coated.
3. Add zucchini slices into the baking dish.
4. Press Bake mode, set the temperature to 400°F, and set time to 5 minutes. Press Start.
5. Once a unit is preheated then place the baking dish in the cooking pot.
6. Cover with lid and cook for 5 minutes.

Serving Suggestion: Allow to cool completely then serve.

Variation Tip: Add ¼ teaspoon of crushed red pepper flakes.

Nutritional Information per Serving:
Calories 156 | Fat 10.9g |Sodium 298mg | Carbs

8.3g | Fiber 1.4g | Sugar 2.2g | Protein 6.1g

Baked Zucchini andEggplant

Prep time: 10 minutes
Cook time: 35 minutes
Serves: 6

Ingredients:
- 3 medium zucchini, sliced
- 1 medium eggplant, sliced
- 1 tablespoon olive oil
- 1 tablespoon garlic, minced
- 1 cup cherry tomatoes, halved
- 3 ounces ofParmesan cheese, grated
- 4 tablespoons parsley, chopped
- 4 tablespoons basil, chopped
- Pepper
- Salt

Directions:
1. Place the cooking pot in the Ninja Foodi Grill Main Unit.
2. In a bowl, mix cherry tomatoes, eggplant, zucchini, oil, garlic, cheese, basil, pepper and salt.
3. Pour veggie mixture into the baking dish.
4. Press Bake mode, set the temperature to 350°F, and set time to 35 minutes. Press Start.
5. Once a unit is preheated then place the baking dish in the cooking pot.
6. Cover with lid and cook for 35 minutes.

Serving Suggestion: Garnish with parsley and serve.

Variation Tip: You can use vegetable oil instead of olive oil.

Nutritional Information per Serving:
Calories 109 | Fat 5.8g |Sodium 173mg | Carbs 10.1g | Fiber 4.3g | Sugar 4.8g | Protein 7g

Cheesy Cauliflower Casserole

Prep time: 10 minutes
Cook time: 15 minutes
Serves: 6
Ingredients:
- 1 cauliflower head, cut into florets &boil
- 2 ounces of cream cheese
- 1 cup heavy cream
- 2 cups Cheddar cheese, shredded
- 2 teaspoon Dijon mustard
- 1 teaspoon garlic powder
- Pepper
- Salt

Directions:
1. Place the cooking pot in the Ninja Foodi Grill Main Unit.
2. Add all ingredients into the bowl and mix until well combined.
3. Pour cauliflower mixture into the baking dish.
4. Press Bake mode, set the temperature to 375°F, and set time to 15 minutes. Press Start.
5. Once a unit is preheated then place the baking dish in the cooking pot.
6. Cover with lid and cook for 15 minutes.
Serving Suggestion: Serve warm and enjoy.
Variation Tip: None
Nutritional Information per Serving:
Calories 268 | Fat 23.3g |Sodium 329mg | Carbs 4.1g | Fiber 1.2g | Sugar 1.4g | Protein 11.5g

Baked Apple and Sweet Potatoes

Prep time: 5 minutes
Cook time: 30 minutes
Serves: 2
Ingredients:
- 2 sweet potatoes, diced
- 2 apples, diced
- 1 tablespoon olive oil
- 2 tablespoons honey

Directions:
1. Place the cooking pot in the Ninja Foodi Grill Main Unit.
2. In a bowl, add sweet potatoes, oil and apples and toss well.
3. Pour sweet potato and apple mixture into the baking dish.
4. Press Bake mode, set the temperature to 400°F, and set time to 30 minutes. Press Start.
5. Once a unit is preheated then place the baking dish in the cooking pot.
6. Cover with lid and cook for 30 minutes.
Serving Suggestion: Drizzle with honey and serve.
Variation Tip: Add ¼ teaspoon of ground cinnamon.
Nutritional Information per Serving:
Calories 240 | Fat 7.4g |Sodium 3mg | Carbs 48.1g | Fiber 5.4g | Sugar 40.5g | Protein 0.7g

Crispy Cauliflower Florets

Prep time: 10 minutes
Cook time: 10 minutes
Serves: 4
Ingredients:
- 1 small cauliflower head, cut into florets
- 2 tablespoons olive oil
- 1 tablespoon curry powder
- Pepper
- Salt

Directions:
1. Place the cooking pot in the Ninja Foodi Grill Main Unit then place the Ninja Foodi Crisper Basket in the pot.
2. In a bowl, toss cauliflower florets with oil, curry powder, pepper and salt.
3. Add cauliflower florets in the Ninja Foodi Crisper Basket.
4. Press Air Crisp mode, set the temperature to 350°F, and set time to 10 minutes.
5. Cover with lid and press Start.
Serving Suggestion: Allow to cool completely then serve.
Variation Tip: Add paprika for more spiciness.
Nutritional Information per Serving:
Calories 82 | Fat 7.3g |Sodium 59mg | Carbs 4.5g | Fiber 2.2g | Sugar 1.6g | Protein 1.5g

Charred Asparagus Tacos

Prep time: 15 minutes.
Cook time: 22 minutes.
Serves: 24
Ingredients:
- 2 ancho chilies, stemmed and seeded
- 2 tbsp. vegetable oil
- 1 small onion, sliced
- 2 garlic cloves, grated on
- 2 tsp. dried oregano
- 1 tbsp. cider vinegar
- 1 chipotle chili
- 1 tbsp. sauce from chipotles
- ⅔ cup sour cream or Mexican crema
- 2 tsp. fresh juice from 2 limes
- Kosher salt and black pepper, to taste
- 2 ½ lbs. asparagus, cut into 1-inch segments
- 24 corn tortillas warmed
- Pickled red onion, to serve
- Queso fresco or queso cotija, to serve
- Fresh cilantro leaves, to serve
- Lime wedges, to serve

Preparation:
1. Sauté ancho chilies in a saucepan for 3 minutes then soak in water for 3 minutes then drain and reserve the liquid.
2. Sauté onion with 1 tbsp. oil in a skillet for 8 minutes.
3. Stir in oregano and garlic then sauté for 30 seconds.
4. Add chili liquid, chili sauce, chipotle chile and vinegar, mix well then blend with lime juice, sour cream and soaked chilies in a blender.
5. Stir in black pepper and salt for seasoning.
6. Toss asparagus with oil, black pepper and salt in a bowl.
7. Place the cooking pot in the Ninja Foodi Grill.
8. Select the Bake Mode and set the temperature to 350 degrees F.
9. Use the Arrow keys to set the time to 10 minutes.
10. Press the START/STOP button to initiate preheating.
11. Once preheated, place the asparagus in the Ninja Foodi Grill.
12. Cover the hood and allow the grill to cook.

13. Divide the prepared sauce in the tortillas and add asparagus on top.
14. Garnish with lime wedges, cilantro, cheese and onions
15. Serve warm.
Serving Suggestion: Serve the tacos with lemon wedges.
Variation Tip: Add roasted broccoli on the side.
Nutritional Information Per Serving:
Calories 93 | Fat 3g |Sodium 510mg | Carbs 22g | Fiber 3g | Sugar 4g | Protein 4g

Eggplant Caprese

Prep time: 15 minutes.
Cook time: 10 minutes.
Serves: 2
Ingredients:
- 1 large eggplant, cut into ¼ -inch slices
- 1 ball fresh mozzarella, cut into ¼ -inch slices
- 2 large tomatoes, cut into ¼ -inch slices
- ¼ cup of basil chiffonade
- 1 tbsp. Kosher salt
- Olive oil, as required
- Balsamic vinegar, as required
- Black pepper, to taste

Preparation:
1. Keep eggplant slices in a colander and sprinkle salt on top then leave for leave for 30 minutes.
2. Place the cooking pot in the Ninja Foodi Grill.
3. Select the Bake Mode and set the temperature to 350 degrees F.
4. Use the Arrow keys to set the time to 10 minutes.
5. Press the Start/Stop button to initiate preheating.
6. Once preheated, place the eggplants in the Ninja Foodi Grill.
7. Cover the hood and allow the grill to cook.
8. Place one tomato slice and cheese slice on top of the eggplant slices.
9. Garnish with- basil and serve.
Serving Suggestion: Serve the eggplants with fresh herbs on top.
Variation Tip: Add a drizzle of red pepper flakes and parmesan on top.
Nutritional Information Per Serving:
Calories 351 | Fat 19g |Sodium 412mg | Carbs 13g | Fiber 0.3g | Sugar 1g | Protein 3g

Grilled Smashed Potatoes

Prep time: 15 minutes.
Cook time: 10 minutes.
Serves: 8
Ingredients:
- 16 small potatoes, skinned
- 2 tbsp. olive oil
- 2 tbsp. fresh rosemary leaves, chopped
- Kosher salt, to taste
- Black pepper, to taste

Preparation:
1. Add potatoes, water and a pinch of salt to a saucepan, cook on a simmer for 20 minutes then drain.
2. Lightly smash the potatoes with your palm without breaking them.
3. Brush them with black pepper, salt and oil.
4. Place the cooking pot in the Ninja Foodi Grill then set a grill grate inside.
5. Select the "Grill" Mode, set the temperature to MED.
6. Use the arrow keys to set the cooking time to 10 minutes.
7. Press the START/STOP button to initiate preheating.
8. Once preheated, place the potatoes in the Ninja Foodi Grill.
9. Cover the hood and allow the grill to cook.
10. Flip the potatoes once cooked halfway through.
11. Serve warm.

Serving Suggestion: Serve the potatoes with a drizzle of parmesan on top.
Variation Tip: Add shredded chicken to the potatoes.
Nutritional Information Per Serving:
Calories 136 | Fat 20g | Sodium 249mg | Carbs 44g | Fiber 2g | Sugar 3g | Protein 4g

Zucchini with Parmesan

Prep time: 15 minutes.
Cook time: 12 minutes.
Serves: 4
Ingredients:
- 4 medium zucchinis, split in half
- ¼ cup olive oil
- 1 tbsp. kosher salt
- 1 tbsp. black pepper
- 1 cup grated Parmesan cheese
- ½ cup garlic chili oil

Preparation:
1. Season the zucchini with black pepper, salt and oil.
2. Place the cooking pot in the Ninja Foodi Grill then set a grill grate inside.
3. Plug the thermometer into the appliance.
4. Place the cooking pot in the Ninja Foodi Grill then set a grill grate inside.
5. Select the "Grill" Mode, set the temperature to MED.
6. Use the arrow keys to set the cooking time to 10 minutes.
7. Press the START/STOP button to initiate preheating.
8. Once preheated, place the zucchini in the Ninja Foodi Grill.
9. Cover the hood and allow the grill to cook.
10. Flip the zucchini and add cheese on top and cover again then cook for 5 minutes.
11. Garnish with garlic chili oil.
12. Serve warm.

Serving Suggestion: Serve the zucchini with coconut shreds on top.
Variation Tip: Add a drizzle of sesame seeds and oil.
Nutritional Information Per Serving:
Calories 361 | Fat 20g | Sodium 218mg | Carbs 16g | Fiber 10g | Sugar 30g | Protein 14g

Grilled Brussels Sprouts with Bacon

Prep time: 10 minutes.
Cook time: 30 minutes.
Serves: 4

Ingredients:
- ⅓ lb. thick cut bacon, diced
- 1 ½ lbs. Brussels sprouts
- 2 medium shallots, sliced
- Kosher salt, to taste
- Black pepper, to taste

Preparation:
1. Add 1 pinch salt and water to a pan and cook brussels sprouts for 5 minutes then drain.
2. Sauté bacon in a skillet for 5-10 minutes until crispy then transfer to a plate.
3. Add shallots to the bacon grease and sauté until brown then transfer to the bacon.
4. Toss brussels sprouts with bacon fat, black pepper and salt in a bowl.
5. Place the cooking pot in the Ninja Foodi Grill then set a grill grate inside.
6. Select the "Grill" Mode, set the temperature to MED.
7. Use the arrow keys to set the cooking time to 10 minutes.
8. Press the START/STOP button to initiate preheating.
9. Once preheated, place the brussel sprouts in the Ninja Foodi Grill.
10. Cover the hood and allow the grill to cook.
11. Flip the sprouts once cooked halfway through.
12. Add the baked Brussel sprouts to the bacon and toss well
13. Serve.

Serving Suggestion: Serve the Brussels sprouts with boiled cauliflower rice.

Variation Tip: Top the Brussel sprouts with feta cheese before serving.

Nutritional Information Per Serving:
Calories 341 | Fat 24g |Sodium 547mg | Carbs 14g | Fiber 1.2g | Sugar 1g | Protein 10.3g

Cheddar Bacon Corn

Prep time: 15 minutes.
Cook time: 12 minutes.
Serves: 10

Ingredients:
- ½ cup butter, softened
- 1 packet ranch seasoning
- Black pepper, to taste
- 10 corn cobs
- 2 cups Cheddar, shredded
- 6 slices cooked bacon, crumbled
- Freshly chives, chopped
- Ranch, for drizzling

Preparation:
1. Mix butter with all the ingredients except the corn and cheese.
2. Place the cooking pot in the Ninja Foodi Grill.
3. Select the Bake Mode and set the temperature to 350 degrees F.
4. Use the Arrow keys to set the time to 10 minutes.
5. Press the Start/Stop button to initiate preheating.
6. Once preheated, place the corn in the Ninja Foodi Grill.
7. Cover the hood and allow the grill to cook.
8. Drizzle cheese on top and bake for 2 minutes.
9. Serve warm.

Serving Suggestion: Serve the corn with crispy bread.

Variation Tip: Add mozzarella cheese on top of the grilled corn.

Nutritional Information Per Serving:
Calories 391 | Fat 2.2g |Sodium 276mg | Carbs 27g | Fiber 0.9g | Sugar 1.4g | Protein 8.8g

Air Grilled Brussels

Prep time: 5-10 minutes
Cook time: 12 minutes
Servings: 4

Ingredients

- 6 slices bacon, chopped
- 1 pound Brussel sprouts, halved
- 2 tbsp olive oil, extra virgin
- 1 tsp salt
- ½ tsp black pepper, ground

Preparation

1. Add Brussels, olive oil, salt, pepper, and bacon into a mixing bowl.
2. Pre-heat Ninja Foodi Grill by pressing the "AIR CRISP" option and setting it to "390 degrees F.".
3. Set the timer to 12 minutes.
4. Allow it to pre-heat until it beeps.
5. Arrange Brussels over basket and lock lid.
6. Cook for 6 minutes.
7. Shake it and cook for 6 minutes more.
8. Serve and enjoy!

Serving Suggestion: Serve with chilled drink.
Variation Tip: use chopped dill for garnish.
Nutritional Information per Serving:
Calories: 279| Fat: 18 g| Carbohydrates: 12 g| Fiber: 4 g| Sodium: 874 mg| Protein: 1 g

Italian Squash Meal

Prep time: 5-10 minutes

Cook time: 16 minutes
Servings: 4

Ingredients

- 1 medium butternut squash, peeled, seeded and cut into ½ inch slices
- 1 and ½ tsp oregano, dried
- 1 tsp dried thyme
- 1 tablespoon olive oil
- ½ tsp salt
- ¼ tsp black pepper

Preparation

1. Add slices alongside other Ingredients into a mixing bowl.
2. Mix them well.
3. Pre-heat your Ninja Foodi by pressing the "GRILL" option and setting it to "MEDIUM.".
4. Set the timer to 16 minutes.
5. Allow it to pre-heat until it beep.
6. Arrange squash slices over the grill grate.
7. Cook for 8 minutes.
8. Flip and cook for 8 minutes more.
9. Serve and enjoy!

Serving Suggestion: Serve warm and enjoy.
Variation Tip: use chopped dill for garnish.
Nutritional Information per Serving:
Calories: 238| Fat: 12 g| Carbohydrates: 36 g| Fiber: 3 g| Sodium: 128 mg| Protein: 15 g

Honey Dressed Asparagus

Prep time: 5-10 minutes
Cook time: 15 minutes
Servings: 4

Ingredients

- 2pounds asparagus, trimmed
- 4 tbsp tarragon, minced
- ¼ cup honey
- 2 tbsp olive oil
- 1 tsp salt
- ½ tsp pepper

Preparation

1. Add asparagus, oil, salt, honey, pepper, tarragon into your bowl, Toss them well.
2. Pre-heat your Ninja Foodi by pressing the "GRILL" option and setting it to "MEDIUM".
3. Set the timer to 8 minutes.
4. Allow it pre-heat until it makes a beep sound.
5. Arrange asparagus over grill grate and lock lid.
6. Cook for 4 minutes.
7. Then flip asparagus and cook for 4 minutes more.
8. Serve and enjoy!

Serving Suggestion: Serve warm and enjoy.
Variation Tip: use chili flakes for extra spice.
Nutritional Information per Serving:
Calories: 240| Fat: 15 g| Carbohydrates: 31 g| Fiber: 1 g| Sodium: 103 mg| Protein: 7 g

Hearty Spinach Olive

Prep time: 5-10 minutes
Cook time: 15 minutes
Servings: 3
Ingredients
- 2 pounds spinach, chopped and boiled
- 1 and ½ cups feta cheese, grated
- 4 tbsp butter
- ⅔ cup olives, halved and pitted
- 4 tsp lemon zest, grated
- Pepper and salt to taste

Preparation
1. Add spinach, butter, salt, pepper into a mixing bowl, Mix them well.
2. Pre-heat your Ninja Foodi by pressing the "AIR CRISP" option and setting it to 340 Degrees F.
3. Set the timer to 15 minutes.
4. Allow it to pre-heat until it beeps.
5. Arrange a reversible trivet in the Grill Pan.
6. Arrange spinach mixture in a basket and place basket in the trivet.
7. Let them crisp for 15 minutes.
8. Serve and enjoy!

Serving Suggestion: Serve with chilled drink.

Variation Tip: add honey for extra fun.
Nutritional Information per Serving:
Calories: 250| Fat: 18 g| Carbohydrates: 8 g| Fiber: 4 g| Sodium: 339 mg| Protein: 10 g

Chinese Eggplant

Prep time: 10 minutes.
Cook time: 20 minutes.
Serves: 6
Ingredients:
- 3 tbsp. sugar
- 3 tbsp. sake
- 2 tbsp. mirin
- 1 tbsp. rice vinegar
- ⅓ cup Shiro miso
- 1 tbsp. fresh ginger, grated
- ¼ cup vegetable oil
- 1 tsp. dark sesame oil
- 6 Chinese eggplants, halved lengthwise
- Toasted sesame seeds for garnish

Preparation:
1. Toss eggplants with rest of the ingredients in a bowl.
2. Place the cooking pot in the Ninja Foodi Grill.
3. Select the Bake Mode and set the temperature to 350 degrees F.
4. Use the Arrow keys to set the time to 20 minutes.
5. Press the Start/Stop button to initiate preheating.
6. Once preheated, place the eggplants in the Ninja Foodi Grill.
7. Cover the hood and allow the grill to cook.
8. Serve warm with the rest of the marinade on top.

Serving Suggestion: Serve the eggplants with butter sauce and bacon on top.
Variation Tip: Add boiled green beans before serving.
Nutritional Information Per Serving:
Calories 378 | Fat 3.8g |Sodium 620mg | Carbs 33g | Fiber 2.4g | Sugar 1.2g | Protein 5.4g

Veggie Kabobs

Prep time: 10 minutes.
Cook time: 12 minutes.
Serves: 4

Ingredients:
- 2 medium zucchinis, cut into 1" thick half-moons
- 1 (10-oz.) package baby bella mushrooms, cleaned and halved
- 1 medium red onion, cut into wedges
- 2 small lemons, cut into eighths
- 3 tbsp. olive oil
- 1 garlic clove, grated
- 1 tsp. thyme, chopped
- Pinch of crushed red pepper flakes
- Kosher salt, to taste
- Black pepper, to taste

Preparation:
1. Toss all the veggies with other ingredients in a bowl.
2. Place the cooking pot in the Ninja Foodi Grill.
3. Select the Bake Mode and set the temperature to 350 degrees F.
4. Use the Arrow keys to set the time to 6 minutes.
5. Press the Start/Stop button to initiate preheating.
6. Once preheated, place the skewers in the Ninja Foodi Grill.
7. Cover the hood and allow the grill to cook.
8. Flip the skewers and cook again for 6 minutes.
9. Serve warm.

Serving Suggestion: Serve the kabobs with mashed cauliflower.

Variation Tip: Add crispy fried onions on top for a crunchier taste.

Nutritional Information Per Serving:
Calories 304 | Fat 31g |Sodium 834mg | Carbs 14g | Fiber 0.2g | Sugar 0.3g | Protein 4.6g

Ninja Foodi Stuffed Tomatoes

Prep time: 20 minutes
Cook time: 15 minutes
Serves: 4

Ingredients:
- 4 tomatoes
- 1 cup shredded cheddar cheese
- 1 teaspoon dried thyme
- 1 cup chopped broccoli
- 2 tablespoons unsalted butter, melted

Preparation:
1. Scoop out the pulp from the top of the tomato.
2. In a mixing dish, combine broccoli and cheese. Mix thoroughly.
3. Toss the broccoli mixture with the tomatoes and set them aside.
4. Meanwhile, in a Ninja Foodi Grill, arrange the "Crisper Basket" and press the "AIR CRISP" button. Preheat the oven to 355 degrees Fahrenheit and set the timer for 15 minutes.
5. To begin preheating, press START/STOP.
6. When the Ninja Foodi Grill showed "Add Food," put the tomatoes in the "Crisper Basket."
7. Drizzle with butter and bake at 355°F for 15 minutes.
8. Remove from the oven and sprinkle with dried thyme.
9. Finally, serve and enjoy!

Serving Suggestions: Top with chopped cilantro before serving.

Variation Tip: Mozzarella cheese can also be used.

Nutritional Information per Serving:
Calories: 195 |Fat: 15.5g|Sat Fat: 9.7g|Carbohydrates: 6.8g|Fiber: 2.2g|Sugar: 3.8g|Protein: 8.8g

Ninja Foodi Potato Gratin

Prep time: 20 minutes
Cook time: 20 minutes
Serves: 8

Ingredients:
- 4 potatoes, thinly sliced
- 4 eggs
- 1 cup grated cheddar cheese
- ¾ cup cream
- 2 tablespoons plain flour

Preparation:
1. Insert crisper basket in the unit. Select AIR CRISP, set temperature to 355°F, and set time to 10 minutes. Select START/STOP to begin preheating
2. Cook for 10 minutes with potato slices in the "Crisper Basket."
3. In a separate dish, whisk together the eggs, flour, and cream. Make sure everything is well combined.
4. Remove the potato slices from the oven and arrange them in 8 ramekins.
5. Pour the egg mixture over the ramekins and arrange them in the "Crisper Basket."
6. Cook for 10 minutes at 390 degrees F using the "AIR CRISP" option.
7. Remove from the oven and serve immediately.

Serving Suggestions: Top with chili flakes before serving.

Variation Tip: Replace cheddar cheese with mozzarella cheese.

Nutritional Information per Serving:
Calories: 183 |Fat: 8.3g|Sat Fat: 4.5g|Carbohydrates: 19.3g|Fiber: 2.6g|Sugar: 1.9g|Protein: 8.5g

Ninja Foodi Glazed Vegetables

Prep time: 20 minutes
Cook time: 25 minutes
Serves: 8

Ingredients:
- ½ cup cherry tomatoes, sliced
- 4 green bell peppers, seeded and chopped
- 4 tablespoons honey
- 2 teaspoons dried herbs
- 4 large zucchinis, chopped
- 1½ cups olive oil, divided
- 2 teaspoons Dijon mustard
- 2 teaspoons garlic paste
- Salt, to taste

Preparation:
1. Place the veggies in a baking dish lined with parchment paper and drizzle with half of the olive oil.
2. Insert crisper basket in the   unit. Select AIR CRISP, set temperature to 350°F, and set time to 20 minutes. Select START/STOP to begin preheating
3. lace the baking dish in a "Crisper Basket" when it says "Add Food."
4. In a mixing bowl, combine the remaining oil, mustard, honey, garlic, herbs, salt, and pepper. Mix thoroughly.
5. Pour the honey mixture over the vegetables and cook at 395°F for 5 minutes.
6. Remove from the oven and serve immediately.

Serving Suggestions: Serve with black cumin seeds on the top.

Variation Tip: Honey can be replaced with maple syrup.

Nutritional Information per Serving:
Calories: 1296 |Fat: 139.1g|Sat Fat: 19.9g|Carbohydrates: 19.4g|Fiber: 2.9g|Sugar: 14.7g|Protein: 2.8g

Ninja Foodi Tofu with Orange Sauce

Prep time: 20 minutes
Cook time: 20 minutes
Serves: 8

Ingredients:

- 2 pounds extra-firm tofu, pressed and cubed
- 2 tablespoons tamari
- ¾ cup fresh orange juice
- 2 teaspoons orange zest, grated
- 2 teaspoons fresh ginger, minced
- ½ teaspoon red pepper flakes
- 4 tablespoons cornstarch
- 1 cup water
- 2 tablespoons honey
- 2 teaspoons garlic, minced

Preparation:

1. In a mixing basin, combine two tablespoons of corn-starch, tofu, and tamari. Set aside for 15 minutes after thoroughly mixing.
2. Insert crisper basket in the unit. Select AIR CRISP, set temperature to 390°F, and set time to 10 minutes. Select START/STOP to begin preheating.
3. When it shows "Add Food," put the tofu mixture in the "Crisper Basket" and cook for 10 minutes. Remove the item and place it away.
4. In a separate pan, combine the water, orange juice, honey, orange zest, garlic, ginger, remaining corn-starch, and red pepper flakes. Cook for 10 minutes. Continue to stir constantly.
5. Toss the tofu mixture with the sauce and serve.

Serving Suggestions: Serve with sesame seeds on the top.

Variation Tip: You can omit red pepper flakes.

Nutritional Information per Serving:
Calories: 151 |Fat: 6.7g|Sat Fat: 0.6g|Carbohydrates: 13.7g|Fiber: 0.7g|Sugar: 7g|Protein: 12g

Ninja Foodi Crispy Chicken with Potatoes

Prep time: 10 minutes
Cook time: 15 minutes
Serves: 8

Ingredients:

- 2 teaspoons olive oil
- 1½ cups shredded cheddar cheese
- ½ teaspoon paprika
- 2 pounds potatoes, drained and sliced
- 2 pounds chicken breasts, cubed
- 8 bacon slices, cooked and cut into strips
- Salt and black pepper, to taste

Preparation:

1. In a large mixing bowl, combine the chicken, olive oil, salt, and pepper, as well as the potato slices. Toss well to coat.
2. In the meantime, in a Ninja Foodi Grill, press the "ROAST" button and set the time to 20 minutes and 350°F
3. To begin preheating, press START/STOP.
4. Place the potato mixture on top of the bacon and cheese when it says "Add Food."
5. Turn halfway through and serve.
6. Sprinkle with paprika before serving.

Serving Suggestions: Top with chopped mint leaves before serving.

Variation Tip: You can also mozzarella cheese to enhance taste.

Nutritional Information per Serving:
Calories: 720 |Fat: 43.4g|Sat Fat: 21.5g|Carbohydrates: 19.2g|Fiber: 2.8g|Sugar: 1.7g|Protein: 61.1g

Ninja Foodi Cheesy Spinach

Prep time: 20 minutes
Cook time: 15 minutes
Serves: 8

Ingredients:
- 2 pounds fresh spinach, chopped
- 2 teaspoons fresh lemon zest, grated
- 2 cups feta cheese, crumbled
- ½ cup melted butter
- Salt and black pepper, to taste

Preparation:
1. In a large mixing bowl, combine the butter, spinach, salt, and pepper. Mix thoroughly.
2. Insert crisper basket in the unit. Select AIR CRISP, set temperature to 340°F, and set time to 15 minutes. Select START/STOP to begin preheating.
3. Place the spinach combination in the "Crisper Basket" and cook for 15 minutes when the Ninja Foodi Grill is shown "Add Food."
4. Transfer the mixture to a mixing bowl and add the cheese and lemon zest.
5. Finally, serve and enjoy!

Serving Suggestions: Top with chopped mint leaves before serving.
Variation Tip: Replace feta cheese with mozzarella cheese.
Nutritional Information per Serving:
Calories: 227 |Fat: 19.9g|Sat Fat: 13g|Carbohydrates: 5.8g|Fiber: 2.5g|Sugar: 2.1g|Protein: 8.7g

Ninja Foodi Spicy Cauliflower

Prep time: 5 minutes
Cook time: 20 minutes
Serves: 2

Ingredients:
- ¼ cup sliced onion
- 2½ garlic cloves, thinly sliced
- ½ tablespoon sriracha sauce
- ¼ teaspoon coconut sugar
- ½ cauliflower head, cut into florets
- ½ tablespoon rice vinegar
- ¾ tablespoon tamari

Preparation:
1. Insert grill grate in the unit and close hood. Select GRILL, set temperature to MEDIUM, and set time to 20 minutes. Select START/STOP to begin preheating.
2. When it shows "Add Food", place the cauliflowers and cook for 10 minutes.
3. Cook for 5 minutes after adding the onion and garlic slices.
4. In a large mixing bowl, combine the soy sauce, sugar, rice vinegar, salt, pepper, and sriracha sauce. Mix thoroughly.
5. Cook for 5 minutes after pouring this mixture over the cauliflowers.
6. Remove from the unit and serve

Serving Suggestions: Top with chopped scallion before serving.
Variation Tip: You can also add red chili flakes to enhance taste.
Nutritional Information per Serving:
Calories: 64 |Fat: 0.2g|Sat Fat: 0g|Carbohydrates: 12.8g|Fiber: 2.4g|Sugar: 2.5g|Protein: 3.3g

Ninja Foodi Seasoned Asparagus

Prep time: 5 minutes
Cook time: 5 minutes
Serves: 4

Ingredients:
- ¼ teaspoon cayenne pepper
- 1 teaspoon dried onion powder

- 2 pounds asparagus
- 1 teaspoon olive oil
- 1 teaspoon dried garlic powder
- Salt and black pepper, to taste

Preparation:

1. Insert grill grate in the unit and close hood. Select GRILL, set temperature to MAX, and set time to 05 minutes. Select START/STOP to begin preheating.

2. In a large mixing bowl, combine the asparagus, cayenne pepper, onion powder, olive oil, garlic powder, salt, and pepper. Mix thoroughly.

3. Toss in the asparagus and simmer for about 5 minutes.

4. Remove the dish from the oven and serve immediately.

Serving Suggestions: Serve with lemon wedges.

Variation Tip: Cayenne pepper can be omitted.

Nutritional Information per Serving:
Calories: 60 |Fat: 1.5g|Sat Fat: 0.3g|Carbohydrates: 9.9g|Fiber: 4.9g|Sugar: 4.7g|Protein: 5.2g

Ninja Foodi Broccoli Chicken

Prep time: 10 minutes
Cook time: 20 minutes
Serves: 8

Ingredients:

- 2 tablespoons olive oil
- 1 pound broccoli, cut into bite-sized pieces
- 4 teaspoons hot sauce
- 1 onion, sliced
- 2 tablespoons fresh minced ginger
- 4 teaspoons rice vinegar
- 2 pounds boneless chicken breast, chopped
- 2 tablespoons low-sodium soy sauce
- 1 teaspoon garlic powder
- 2 teaspoons sesame seed oil
- Salt and black pepper, to taste

Preparation:

1. Insert grill grate in the unit and close hood. Select GRILL, set temperature to MEDIUM, and set time to 20 minutes. Select START/STOP to begin preheating.

2. In a large mixing bowl, combine the chicken,

broccoli, and onion. Mix thoroughly.

3. Toss in the remaining ingredients and toss well to coat.

4. Place the broccoli combination on the Ninja Foodi Grill when it shows "Add Food" and cook for 20 minutes.

5. Remove the dish from the oven and serve immediately

Serving Suggestions: Squeeze lemon juice on the top before serving.

Variation Tip: Soy sauce can be omitted.

Nutritional Information per Serving:
Calories: 289 |Fat: 13.3g|Sat Fat: 3g|Carbohydrates: 6.6g|Fiber: 2g|Sugar: 2g|Protein: 35g

Ninja Foodi Mushroom Steak

Prep time: 10 minutes
Cook time: 10 minutes
Serves: 8

Ingredients:

- 2 pounds beef sirloin steak, cubed
- 2 cups sliced mushrooms
- 2 teaspoons parsley flakes
- 2 teaspoons chili flakes, crushed
- ½ cup Worcestershire sauce
- 2 tablespoons olive oil
- 2 teaspoons paprika

Preparation:

1. In a large mixing bowl, combine the steak, olive oil, paprika, mushrooms, chili flakes, and Worcestershire sauce. Toss to evenly coat.

2. Wrap in foil and place in the refrigerator for 3 hours.

3. Insert crisper basket in the unit. Select AIR CRISP, set temperature to 400°F, and set time to 10 minutes. Select START/STOP to begin preheating

4. When it shows "Add Food", place the mixture and cook for 10 minutes.

5. Dish out and serve hot.

Serving Suggestions: Serve with chopped mint leaves on the top.

Variation Tip: Canola oil can also be used.

Nutritional Information per Serving:
Calories: 261 |Fat: 10.7g|Sat Fat: 3.2g|Carbohydrates: 3.9g|Fiber: 0.4g|Sugar: 3.4g|Protein: 35.1g

Delicious Grilled Honey Fruit Salad

Prep time: 5-10 minutes
Cook time: 5 minutes
Servings: 4

Ingredients

- 1 tablespoon lime juice, freshly squeezed
- 6 tbsp honey, divided
- 2 peaches, pitted and sliced
- 1 can (9 ounces) pineapple chunks, drained and juiced reserved
- ½ pound strawberries washed, hulled, and halved

Preparation

1. Take a shallow mixing bowl, then add respectively soy sauce, balsamic vinegar, oil, maple syrup and whisk well.
2. Then add broccoli and keep it aside.
3. Press the "GRILL" of the Ninja Foodi Grill and set it to "MAX" mode with 10 minutes timer.
4. Keep it in the preheating process.
5. When you hear a beat, add broccoli over the grill grate.
6. After then lock the lid and cook until the timer shows 0.
7. Lastly, garnish the food with pepper flakes and sesame seeds.
8. Enjoy!

Serving Suggestion: Serve topped with sesame seeds and pepper flakes.
Variation Tip: use chopped dill for garnish.
Nutritional Information per Serving:
Calories: 141| Fat: 7 g| Carbohydrate: 14 g|
Fiber: 4 g| Sodium: 853 mg| Protein: 4 g

Broccoli Maple Grill

Prep time: 5-10 minutes
Cook time: 10 minutes
Servings: 4

Ingredients

- 2 tsp maple syrup
- 4 tablespoons balsamic vinegar
- 2 tablespoon canola oil
- 4 tbsp soy sauce
- 2 heads broccoli, cut into floret
- Pepper flakes and sesame seeds for garnish

Preparation

1. Take a shallow mixing bowl, then add respectively soy sauce, balsamic vinegar, oil, maple syrup and whisk well.
2. Then add broccoli and keep it aside.
3. Press the "GRILL" of the Ninja Foodi Grill and set it to "MAX" mode with 10 minutes timer.
4. Keep it in the preheating process.
5. When you hear a beat, add broccoli over the grill grate.
6. After then lock the lid and cook until the timer shows 0.
7. Lastly, garnish the food with pepper flakes and sesame seeds.

Serving Suggestion: Serve topped with sesame seeds and chili flakes.
Variation Tip: use chopped dill for garnish.
Nutritional Information per Serving:
Calories: 141| Fat: 7 g| Carbohydrate: 14 g|
Fiber: 4 g| Sodium: 853 mg| Protein: 4 g

Grilled Potato Wedges

Prep time: 10 minutes.
Cook time: 20 minutes.
Serves: 6
Ingredients:
- 6 russet potatoes medium-sized, cut into wedges
- ½ cup cooking oil
- 2 tbsp. paprika
- ¼ cup salt
- 1 tbsp. black pepper
- ⅔ cup potato flakes

Preparation:
1. Toss potato wedges with black pepper and other ingredients in a bowl.
2. Place the cooking pot in the Ninja Foodi Grill then set a grill grate inside.
3. Select the "Grill" Mode, set the temperature to MED.
4. Use the arrow keys to set the cooking time to 10 minutes.
5. Press the START/STOP button to initiate preheating.
6. Once preheated, place the mushrooms in the Ninja Foodi Grill.
7. Cover the hood and allow the grill to cook.
8. Serve warm.
Serving Suggestion: Serve the potatoes with ketchup.
Variation Tip: Add a drizzle of taco seasoning.
Nutritional Information Per Serving:
Calories 218 | Fat 14g |Sodium 220mg | Carbs 22g | Fiber 2.4g | Sugar 1.2g | Protein 2.5g

Pig Candy

Prep time: 10 minutes.
Cook time: 20 minutes.
Serves: 4
Ingredients:
- ½ cup dark brown sugar
- ⅛ tsp. cayenne pepper
- 1 lb. thick cut bacon strips
- ¼ cup maple syrup

Preparation:
1. Mix cayenne pepper and brown sugar in a small bowl.
2. Drizzle this mixture over the bacon strips.
3. Place the cooking pot in the Ninja Foodi Grill then set a grill grate inside.
4. Select the "Grill" Mode, set the temperature to MED.
5. Use the arrow keys on the display to select the cooking time to 10 minutes.
6. Press the START/STOP button to initiate preheating.
7. Once preheated, place the bacon in the Ninja Foodi Grill.
8. Cover the hood and allow the grill to cook.
9. Brush the bacon with maple syrup and cook for 10 minutes more.
10. Serve.
Serving Suggestion: Serve the candy with zucchini chips.
Variation Tip: Drizzle maple syrup over the candy before serving.
Nutritional Information Per Serving:
Calories 85 | Fat 8g |Sodium 146mg | Carbs 25g | Fiber 0.1g | Sugar 0.4g | Protein 1g

Eggplant and Tomato Meal

Prep time: 10 minutes
Cook time: 14 minutes
Servings: 4
Ingredients
- 1 eggplant, sliced and ¼ inch thick
- ½ pound buffalo mozzarella, sliced into ¼ inch thick
- 2 heirloom tomatoes, cut into ¼ inch thick
- 12 large basil leaves
- 2 tablespoons canola oil
- Salt to taste
Preparation
1. Add eggplant, oil into a large-sized bowl.
2. Toss them well.
3. Pre-heat Ninja Foodi by pressing the "GRILL" option and setting it to "MAX.".
4. Let it pre-heat until you hear a beep.
5. Transfer eggplants to Grill Plant and lock lid.
6. Cook for 8-12 minutes.
7. Once done, top eggplant with one slice of tomato and mozzarella.
8. Lock lid and cook for 2 minutes more until cheese melts.
9. Once done, remove eggplant from the Grill.
10. Place 2-3 basil leaves on top of half stack.
11. Place remaining eggplant stacks on top with basil.
12. Season with salt and garnish with remaining basil.
13. Serve and enjoy!
Serving Suggestion: serve with basil.
Variation Tip: use chives for taste.
Nutritional Information per Serving:
Calories: 100| Fat: 19 g| Carbohydrates: 11 g| Fiber: 4 g| Sodium: 1555 mg| Protein: 32 g

Creamed Potato Corns

Prep time: 5-10 minutes
Cook time: 30-40 minutes
Servings: 4
Ingredients
- 1 and ½ tsp garlic salt
- ½ cup sour cream
- 1 jalapeno pepper, seeded and minced
- 1 tablespoon lime juice
- 1 tsp ground cumin
- ½ cup milk
- 2 pobiano pepper
- ¼ tsp cayenne pepper
- 2 sweet corn years
- 1 tablespoon cilantro, minced
- 3 tbsp olive oil
Preparation
1. Drain potatoes and rub them with oil.
2. Pre-heat your Ninja Foodi Grill with GRILL mode at MEDIUM heat.
3. Once you hear the beep, arrange poblano peppers over the grill grate.
4. Let them cook for 5 minutes, flip and cook for 5 minutes more.
5. Grill remaining veggies in the same way, giving 7 minutes to each side.
6. Take a bowl and whisk in the remaining Ingredients and prepare your vinaigrette.
7. Peel grilled corn and chop them.
8. Divide ears into small pieces and cut the potatoes.
Serving Suggestion: Serve grilled veggies with vinaigrette.
Variation Tip: use chopped dill for garnish.
Nutritional Information per Serving:
Calories: 344| Fat: 5 g| Carbohydrates: 51 g| Fiber: 3 g| Sodium: 600 mg| Protein: 5 g

Cob with Pepper Butter

Prep time: 15 minutes.
Cook time: 16 minutes.
Serves: 8

Ingredients:
- 8 medium ears sweet corn
- 1 cup butter, softened
- 2 tablespoons lemon-pepper seasoning

Preparation:
1. Season the corn cob with butter and lemon pepper liberally.
2. Preheat the Ninja Foodi Grill on the "Grill Mode" at LOW-temperature settings.
3. When the grill is preheated, open its hood and place the corn cobs in it.
4. Cover the grill's hood and grill for 15 minutes with grilling after every 5 minutes.
5. Grill the corn cobs in batches.
6. Serve warm.

Serving Suggestion: Serve the corn with parsley on top.
Variation Tip: Coat the corn with crushed cornflakes after grilling.
Nutritional Information Per Serving:
Calories 218 | Fat 22g |Sodium 350mg | Carbs 32.2g | Fiber 0.7g | Sugar 1g | Protein 4.3g

Tarragon Asparagus

Prep time: 15 minutes.
Cook time: 8 minutes.
Serves: 4

Ingredients:
- 2 lbs. fresh asparagus, trimmed
- 2 tablespoons olive oil
- 1 teaspoon salt

- ½ teaspoon black pepper
- ¼ cup honey
- 4 tablespoons fresh tarragon, minced

Preparation:
1. Liberally season the asparagus by tossing it with oil, salt, pepper, honey, and tarragon.
2. Preheat the Ninja Foodi Grill on the "Grill Mode" at MEDIUM-temperature settings.
3. When the grill is preheated, open its hood and place the asparagus in it.
4. Cover the grill's hood and grill for 4 minutes per side.
5. Serve warm.

Serving Suggestion: Serve the asparagus with crispy bacon.
Variation Tip: Coat the asparagus with breadcrumbs before cooking.
Nutritional Information Per Serving:
Calories 104 | Fat 3g |Sodium 216mg | Carbs 17g | Fiber 3g | Sugar 4g | Protein 1g

Honey Glazed Bratwurst

Prep time: 15 minutes.
Cook time: 10 minutes.
Serves: 4

Ingredients:
- 4 bratwurst links, uncooked
- ¼ cup Dijon mustard
- ¼ cup honey
- 2 tablespoons mayonnaise
- 1 teaspoon steak sauce
- 4 brat buns, split

Preparation:
1. First, mix the mustard with steak sauce and mayonnaise in a bowl.
2. Preheat the Ninja Foodi Grill on the "Grill Mode" at MEDIUM-temperature settings.
3. When the grill is preheated, open its hood and place the bratwurst in it.
4. Cover the grill's hood and grill for 5 minutes per side.
5. Serve with buns and mustard sauce on top.

Serving Suggestion: Serve the bratwurst with crumbled nacho chips on top and a cream cheese dip on the side.
Variation Tip: Toss bratwurst with shredded parmesan before serving.
Nutritional Information Per Serving:
Calories 173 | Fat 8g |Sodium 146mg | Carbs 18g | Fiber 5g | Sugar 1g | Protein 7g

Chicken Salad with Blueberry Vinaigrette

Prep time: 15 minutes.
Cook time: 14 minutes.
Serves: 4

Ingredients:
Salads:
- 1 package (10 oz.) salad greens
- 1 cup fresh blueberries
- ½ cup canned oranges
- 1 cup goat cheese, crumbled

Chicken:
- 2 boneless chicken breasts, halves
- 1 tablespoon olive oil
- 1 garlic clove, minced
- ¼ teaspoon salt
- ¼ teaspoon black pepper

Vinaigrette:
- ¼ cup olive oil
- ¼ cup blueberry preserves
- 2 tablespoons balsamic vinegar
- 2 tablespoons maple syrup
- ¼ teaspoon ground mustard
- ⅛ teaspoon salt
- Dash pepper

Preparation:
1. First, season the chicken liberally with garlic, salt, pepper, and oil in a bowl.
2. Cover to refrigerate for 30 minutes margination.
3. Preheat the Ninja Foodi Grill on the "Grill Mode" at MEDIUM-temperature settings.
4. When the grill is preheated, open its hood and place the chicken in it.
5. Cover the grill's hood and grill for 7 minutes per side.
6. Toss the remaining ingredients for salad and vinaigrette in a bowl.
7. Slice the grilled chicken and serve with salad.

Serving Suggestion: Serve the chicken salad with fresh berries on top.
Variation Tip: Add shredded cheese and strawberries to the salad.
Nutritional Information Per Serving:
Calories 140 | Fat 5g |Sodium 244mg | Carbs 16g | Fiber 1g | Sugar 1g | Protein 17g

Grilled Oysters with Chorizo Butter

Prep time: 15 minutes.
Cook time: 4 minutes.
Serves: 6

Ingredients:
- 4 ounces Mexican chorizo
- 1 ½ sticks butter, cut into cubes
- 2 tablespoons fresh lime juice
- Salt, to taste
- 18 Louisiana oysters, scrubbed
- Cilantro leaves and lime zest for garnish

Preparation:
1. Sauté chorizo with butter and lime juice and salt in a skillet for 8 minutes until brown.
2. Transfer the sautéed chorizo to a plate.
3. Preheat the Ninja Foodi Grill on the "Grill Mode" at MEDIUM-temperature settings.
4. When the grill is preheated, open its hood and place the oysters in it.
5. Cover the grill's hood and grill for 4 minutes.
6. Divide the chorizo on top of the grilled oysters.
7. Serve warm.

Serving Suggestion: Serve the oysters with garlic butter.
Variation Tip: Drizzle paprika on top for more spice.
Nutritional Information Per Serving:
Calories 201 | Fat 7g |Sodium 269mg | Carbs 15g | Fiber 4g | Sugar 12g | Protein 26g

Delicious Corn Dip

Prep time: 10 minutes
Cook time: 20 minutes
Serves: 6

Ingredients:
- 14 ounce can corn kernel, drained
- 1 teaspoon smoked paprika
- ¼ cup sour cream
- ⅓ cup mayonnaise
- 1 tablespoon green chilies, diced
- ½ bell pepper, diced
- ½ cup Cheddar cheese, shredded

Directions:
1. Place the cooking pot in the Ninja Foodi Grill main unit.
2. Add all ingredients into the bowl and mix until well combined.
3. Pour mixture into the greased baking dish.
4. Press Bake mode, set the temperature to 350°F, and set time to 20 minutes. Press Start.
5. Once a unit is preheated then place the baking dish in the cooking pot.
6. Cover with lid and cook for 20 minutes.

Serving Suggestion: Serve with tortilla chips.
Variation Tip: Add ¼ cup of chopped green onion.
Nutritional Information per Serving:
Calories 168 | Fat 10.2g |Sodium 354mg | Carbs 17.3g | Fiber 1.6g | Sugar 3.6g | Protein 4.7g

Creamy Chicken Dip

Prep time: 10 minutes
Cook time: 25 minutes
Serves: 6

Ingredients:
- 2 cups chicken, cooked and shredded
- 4 tablespoons hot sauce
- ¼ teaspoon garlic powder
- ½ cup sour cream
- 8 ouncesof cream cheese, softened

Directions:
1. Place the cooking pot in the Ninja Foodi Grill Main Unit.
2. Add all ingredients to a bowl and mix until well combined.
3. Transfer mixture in a greased baking dish.
4. Press Bake mode, set the temperature to 350°F, and set time to 25 minutes. Press Start.
5. Once a unit is preheated then place the baking dish in the cooking pot.
6. Cover with lid and cook for 25 minutes.

Serving Suggestion: Serve with tortilla chips.
Variation Tip: Add one tablespoon of dried parsley flakes.
Nutritional Information per Serving:
Calories 245 | Fat 18.7g |Sodium 405mg | Carbs 2.1g | Fiber 0g | Sugar 0.3g | Protein 17.1g

Spicy Cashews

Prep time: 10 minutes
Cook time: 10 minutes
Serves: 6

Ingredients:
- 3 cups cashews
- 1 teaspoon ground coriander
- 2 tablespoons olive oil
- 1 teaspoon ground cumin
- 1 teaspoon paprika
- 1 teaspoon salt

Directions:
1. Place the cooking pot in the Ninja Foodi Grill Main Unit then place the Foodi Crisper Basket in the pot.
2. Add cashews and remaining ingredients into the bowl and toss well.
3. Add cashews in the Ninja Foodi Crisper Basket.
4. Press Air Crisp mode, set the temperature to 330°F, and set time to 10 minutes.
5. Cover with lid and press Start.

Serving Suggestion: Allow to cool completely then serve.
Variation Tip: Add your choice of seasonings.
Nutritional Information per Serving:
Calories 436 | Fat 36.6g |Sodium 399mg | Carbs 22.7g | Fiber 2.2g | Sugar 3.5g | Protein 10.6g

Cheesy Chicken Dip

Prep time: 10 minutes
Cook time: 25 minutes
Serves: 8

Ingredients:
- 2 chicken breasts, cooked and shredded
- ½ cup hot sauce
- 8 ounces of cream cheese, softened
- 1 cup Mozzarella cheese, shredded
- ¼ cup Blue cheese, crumbled
- ½ cup ranch dressing
- 1 cup Cheddar cheese, shredded

Directions:
1. Place the cooking pot in the Ninja Foodi Grill main unit.
2. In a mixing bowl, add all ingredients and mix well.
3. Pour bowl mixture into the greased baking dish.
4. Press Bake mode, set the temperature to 350°F, and set time to 25 minutes. Press Start.
5. Once a unit is preheated then place the baking dish in the cooking pot.
6. Cover with lid and cook for 25 minutes.
Serving Suggestion: Serve with tortilla chips.
Variation Tip: Add ¼ cup of cooked and chopped bacon.
Nutritional Information per Serving:
Calories 256 | Fat 19.2g |Sodium 748mg | Carbs 2.2g | Fiber 0.1g | Sugar 0.7g | Protein 18.4g

Chicken Stuff Jalapenos

Prep time: 10 minutes
Cook time: 25 minutes
Serves: 12

Ingredients:
- 6 Jalapenos, cut in half and remove seeds
- ¼ teaspoon dried basil
- ½ cup chicken, cooked and shredded
- ¼ teaspoon garlic powder
- ¼ cup green onion, sliced
- ¼ cup Monterey jack cheese, shredded
- 4 ounces of cream cheese
- ¼ teaspoon dried oregano
- ¼ teaspoon salt

Directions:
1. Place the cooking pot in the Ninja Foodi Grill Main Unit.
2. Add all ingredients except Jalapeno pepper into the bowl and mix until well combined.
3. Spoon tablespoon mixture into each Jalapeno half and place into the baking dish.
4. Press Bake mode, set the temperature to 390°F, and set time to 25 minutes. Press Start.
5. Once a unit is preheated then place the baking dish in the cooking pot.
6. Cover with lid and cook for 25 minutes.
Serving Suggestion: Serve warm.
Variation Tip: Add ¼ teaspoon of Italian seasoning.
Nutritional Information per Serving:
Calories 52 | Fat 4g |Sodium 95mg | Carbs 0.5g | Fiber 0.1g | Sugar 0.1g | Protein 3g

Savory Roasted Almonds

Prep time: 10 minutes
Cook time: 12 minutes
Serves: 6

Ingredients:
- 2 cups almonds
- ½ teaspoon garlic powder
- 1 tablespoon olive oil
- 1 teaspoon Italian seasoning
- 2 teaspoons rosemary, chopped
- Salt

Directions:
1. Place the cooking pot in the Ninja Foodi Grill Main Unit.
2. In a bowl, toss almonds with remaining ingredients and transfer in the baking dish.
3. Press Bake mode, set the temperature to 350°F, and set time to 12 minutes. Press Start.
4. Once a unit is preheated then place the baking dish in the cooking pot.
5. Cover with lid and cook for 12 minutes.
Serving Suggestion: Allow to cool completely then serve.
Variation Tip: Add your choice of seasonings.
Nutritional Information per Serving:
Calories 208 | Fat 18.5g |Sodium 28mg | Carbs 7.3g | Fiber 4.2g | Sugar 1.5g | Protein 6.8g

Crispy Potato Wedges

Prep time: 10 minutes
Cook time: 15 minutes
Serves: 4

Ingredients:
- 2 potatoes, cut into wedges
- ½ teaspoon paprika
- 1 ½ tablespoon olive oil
- ⅛ teaspoonCayenne
- ¼ teaspoon garlic powder
- ¼ teaspoon pepper
- 1 teaspoonsea salt

Directions:
1. Place the cooking pot in the Ninja Foodi Grill Main Unit then place the Crisper Basket in the pot.
2. In a bowl, toss potato wedges with the remaining ingredients.
3. Add potato wedges in the Crisper Basket.
4. Press Air Crisp mode, set the temperature to 400°F, and set time to 15 minutes.
5. Cover with lid and press Start.
Serving Suggestion: Serve with your choice of dip.
Variation Tip: Add your choice of seasonings.
Nutritional Information per Serving:
Calories 120 | Fat 5.4g |Sodium 475mg | Carbs 17.1g | Fiber 2.7g | Sugar 1.3g | Protein 1.9g

Lemon Herb Carrots

Prep time: 10 minutes
Cook time: 15 minutes
Serves: 2

Ingredients:

- 2 carrots, cut into fries shape
- 2 tablespoons olive oil
- 2 tablespoons lemon-herb seasoning
Directions:
1. Place the cooking pot in the Ninja Foodi Grill Main unit then place the Ninja Foodi Crisper Basket in the pot.
2. In a bowl, toss carrot fries with seasoning and oil.
3. Add carrot fries in the Foodi Crisper Basket.
4. Press Air Crisp mode, set the temperature to 350°F, and set time to 15 minutes.
5. Cover with lid and press Start.
Serving Suggestion: Allow to cool completely then serve.
Variation Tip: Once done sprinkle some grated Parmesan cheese.
Nutritional Information per Serving:
Calories 145 | Fat 14g |Sodium 42mg | Carbs 6g | Fiber 1.5g | Sugar 3g | Protein 0.5g

Pesto Cheese Dip

Prep time: 10 minutes
Cook time: 12 minutes
Serves: 8

Ingredients:

- ⅓ cup basil pesto
- 1 cup Mozzarella cheese, shredded
- 8 ouncesof cream cheese, softened
- ¼ cup Parmesan cheese, grated
- ½ cup roasted peppers
Directions:

1. Place the cooking pot in the Ninja Foodi Grill Main Unit.
2. Add all ingredients into the bowl and mix until well-combined.
3. Pour mixture into the greased baking dish.
4. Press Bake mode, set the temperature to 350°F, and set time to 12 minutes. Press Start.
5. Once a unit is preheated then place the baking dish in the cooking pot.
6. Cover with lid and cook for 12 minutes.
Serving Suggestion: Serve warm.
Nutritional Information per Serving:
Calories 112 | Fat 10.6g |Sodium 133mg | Carbs 1.6g | Fiber 0.2g | Sugar 0.6g | Protein 3.3g

Grilled Kimchi

Prep time: 20 minutes.
Cook time: 6 minutes.
Serves: 4

Ingredients:
- ½ cup kochukaru
- 2 tsp. sauejeot
- 1 napa cabbage, cut into 2 inch pieces
- 8 oz daikon radish
- ½ cup kosher salt
- 4 medium scallions end trimmed, cut into 1-inch-long pieces
- ¼ cup fish sauce
- ¼ cup minced ginger
- 1 tbsp. of minced garlic cloves
- 1½ tsp. granulated sugar

Preparation:
1. Toss cabbage with salt and soak in water for 12 hours then drain.
2. Place the cooking pot in the Ninja Foodi Grill then set a Crisper Basket inside.
3. Select the "Air Crisp" Mode, set the temperature to 400 degrees F.
4. Use the arrow keys to set the cooking time to 6 minutes.
5. Press the START/STOP button to initiate preheating.
6. Once preheated, place the cabbage in the Ninja Foodi Grill.
7. Mix other ingredients in a bowl and stir in cabbage pieces then cover and refrigerate for 12 hours.
8. Serve.

Serving Suggestion: Serve the kimchi with bread.

Variation Tip: Add crushed red pepper on top.
Nutritional Information Per Serving:
Calories 132 | Fat 10g |Sodium 994mg | Carbs 13g | Fiber 0.4g | Sugar 3g | Protein 8g

Grilled Stuffed Mushrooms

Prep time: 10 minutes.
Cook time: 10 minutes.
Serves: 8

Ingredients:
- 8 portobello mushrooms
- cheddar cheese grated or shredded

Filling
- 4 slices bacon
- ½ lb. cream cheese
- 1 large red onion sliced
- 1 jalapeño peppers liked

Preparation:
1. Sear bacon slices in a skillet until crispy and keep them aside.
2. Mix jalapenos, cream cheese, bacon, and onion in a small bowl.
3. Stuff each mushroom with this cream cheese mixture.
4. Place the cooking pot in the Ninja Foodi Grill then set a grill grate inside.
5. Select the "Grill" Mode, set the temperature to MED.
6. Use the arrow keys to set the cooking time to 10 minutes.
7. Press the START/STOP button to initiate preheating.
8. Once preheated, place the mushrooms in the Ninja Foodi Grill.
9. Cover the hood and allow the grill to cook.
10. Drizzle cheese on top of the mushrooms and bake for 5 minutes.
11. Serve warm.

Serving Suggestion: Serve the mushrooms with crispy bacon crumbled on top.
Variation Tip: Add garlic salt on top for more taste.
Nutritional Information Per Serving:
Calories 449 | Fat 31g |Sodium 723mg | Carbs 22g | Fiber 2.5g | Sugar 2g | Protein 26g

Grilled Peach Salsa

Prep time: 15 minutes.
Cook time: 10 minutes.
Serves: 4
Ingredients:
- 4 peaches, halved and pitted
- 4 heirloom tomatoes diced
- 1 bunch cilantro
- 2 limes juiced
- 2 garlic cloves minced
- 2 tbsp. olive oil
- Sea salt to taste
- Black pepper to taste

Preparation:
1. Brush the peaches with oil.
2. Place the cooking pot in the Ninja Foodi Grill then set a grill grate inside.
3. Select the "Grill" Mode, set the temperature to MED.
4. Use the arrow keys to set the cooking time to 10 minutes.
5. Press the START/STOP button to initiate preheating.
6. Once preheated, place the fruits in the Ninja Foodi Grill.
7. Cover the hood and allow the grill to cook.
8. Dice the grilled peaches and mix with rest of the ingredients in a bowl.
9. Serve.

Serving Suggestion: Serve the salsa with the skewers.
Variation Tip: Add hot sauce to season for a tangy taste.
Nutritional Information Per Serving:
Calories 82 | Fat 6g |Sodium 620mg | Carbs 25g | Fiber 2.4g | Sugar 1.2g | Protein 12g

Bison Sliders

Prep time: 10 minutes.
Cook time: 12 minutes.
Serves: 4
Ingredients:
- 1 lb. ground buffalo meat
- 3 garlic cloves minced
- 2 tbsp. Worcestershire sauce
- 1 tsp. kosher salt
- 1 tsp. black pepper
- Cheese slices

For Serving
- Green onion thinly sliced
- Yellow mustard
- Tomato ketchup
- Lettuce
- Pickles

Preparation:
1. Mix meat with black pepper, salt and Worcestershire sauce in a large bowl.
2. Make 8 patties out of this mixture.
3. Place the cooking pot in the Ninja Foodi Grill then set a grill grate inside.
4. Select the "Grill" Mode, set the temperature to MED.
5. Use the arrow keys to set the cooking time to 10 minutes.
6. Press the START/STOP button to initiate preheating.
7. Once preheated, place the patties in the Ninja Foodi Grill.
8. Cover the hood and allow the grill to cook.
9. Grill the buns for 2 minutes per side.
10. Add each patty in between the two sides of the buns and add other veggies to the buns.
11. Serve warm.

Serving Suggestion: Serve the sliders with fresh greens.
Variation Tip: Add chopped spinach to the filling.
Nutritional Information Per Serving:
Calories 24 | Fat 1g |Sodium 236mg | Carbs 22g | Fiber 0.3g | Sugar 0.1g | Protein 31g

Grilled Honey Carrots

Prep time: 15 minutes
Cook time: 10 minutes
Servings: 4
Ingredients
- 6 carrots, cut lengthwise
- 1 tablespoon rosemary, chopped
- 2 tbsp melted butter

- 1 tablespoon parsley, chopped
- 1 tablespoon honey
- 1 tsp salt

Preparation

1. Take your Ninja Foodi Grill and open the lid.
2. Arrange grill grate and close top.
3. Pre-heat Ninja Foodi by pressing the "GRILL" option and setting it to "MAX."
4. Set the timer to 10 minutes.
5. Let it pre-heat until you hear a beep.
6. Arrange carrots over grill grate and spread the remaining Ingredients, and drizzle honey.
7. Lock lid and cook for 5 minutes.
8. Flip sausages and cook for 5 minutes more.

Serving Suggestion: Serve with dill garnishing or enjoy as it is.

Variation Tip: use chopped dill for garnish.

Nutritional Information per Serving:
Calories: 80| Fat: 4 g| Carbohydrates: 10 g| Fiber: 3 g| Sodium: 186 mg| Protein: 0.5 g

Lovely Seasonal Broccoli

Prep time: 10 minutes
Cook time: 10 minutes
Servings: 4

Ingredients

- ½ tsp salt
- ½ tsp red chili powder
- ¼ tsp spice mix
- 2 tbsp yogurt
- 1 tablespoon chickpea flour
- ¼ tsp turmeric powder
- 1pound broccoli, cut into florets

Preparation

1. Take your florets and wash them thoroughly.
2. Take a bowl and add listed Ingredients, except the florets.
3. Add broccoli and combine the mix well; let the mixture sit for 30 minutes.
4. Pre-heat your Ninja Foodi Grill to AIR CRISP mode at 390 degrees F and set the timer to 10 minutes.

5. Once you hear a beep, add florets and crisp for 10 minutes.

Serving Suggestion: Serve warm.

Variation Tip: use shredded cheese for taste.

Nutritional Information per Serving:
Calories: 111|Fat: 2 g| Carbohydrates: 12 g| Fiber: 1 g| Sodium: 024 mg| Protein: 7 g

Mammamia Banana Boats

Prep time: 19 minutes
Cook time: 6 minutes
Servings: 4

Ingredients

- ½ cup peanut butter chips
- ½ cup of chocolate chips
- 1 cup mini marshmallows
- 4 ripe bananas

Preparation

1. With the peel, slice a banana lengthwise and remember that not to cut all the way through.
2. Onward, reveal the inside of the banana by using your hand.
3. Press the "GRILL" option and set this in "MEDIUM" to pre-heat Ninja Foodi Grill with a 6 minutes timer.
4. Until you hear a beep, keep it in the pre-heat process.
5. Put the banana over the Grill Grate and lock the lid, let it cook for 4-6 minutes until chocolate melts and bananas are toasted.
6. Serve and Enjoy!

Serving Suggestion: Serve with melted chocolate.

Variation Tip: Uses condense milk as topping.

Nutritional Information per Serving:
Calories: 505| Fat: 18 g| Carbohydrates: 82 g| Fiber: 6 g | Sodium: 166 mg| Protein: 10 g

Grilled Sweet Honey Carrot

Prep time: 10 minutes
Cook time: 10 minutes
Servings: 6

Ingredients
- 1 tsp salt
- 1 tablespoon honey
- 1 tablespoon rosemary, chopped
- 1 tablespoon parsley, chopped
- 6 carrots, cut lengthwise
- 2 tbsp butter, melted

Preparation
1. Pre-heat your Ninja Foodi Grill to MAX with GRILL mode, set a timer for 10 minutes.
2. Once you hear the beep, arrange carrots over the grill grate.
3. Spread remaining Ingredients and drizzle honey.
4. Lock lid and cook for 5 minutes, flip and cook for 5 minutes more.

Serving Suggestion: Serve and enjoy.
Variation Tip: use chopped dill for garnish.
Nutritional Information per Serving:
Calories: 80| Fat: 4 g| Carbohydrates: 10 g|
Fiber: 3 g| Sodium: 186 mg| Protein: 0.5 g

Bacon Hot Dogs

Prep time: 15 minutes.
Cook time: 6 minutes.
Serves: 8

Ingredients:
- 12 bacon strips

- 8 beef hot dogs
- 8 hot dog buns, split and toasted
- ¼ cup chopped red onion
- 2 cups sauerkraut, rinsed and drained

Preparation:
1. Sear the bacon in a skillet until crispy from both sides.
2. Wrap a bacon strip around each hot dog and secure it by inserting a toothpick.
3. Preheat the Ninja Foodi Grill on the "Grill Mode" at MEDIUM-temperature settings.
4. When the grill is preheated, open its hood and place the hot dogs in it.
5. Cover the grill's hood and grill for 6 minutes, rotate after 3 minutes.
6. Cook all the hot dogs in batches, then remove the toothpick.
7. Serve warm in a hotdog bun with sauerkraut and onion.
8. Enjoy.

Serving Suggestion: Serve the hotdogs with tomato sauce or mayo dip.
Variation Tip: Add mustard sauce to hotdogs.
Nutritional Information Per Serving:
Calories 229 | Fat 5g |Sodium 510mg | Carbs 37g | Fiber 5g | Sugar 4g | Protein 11g

Complete Italian Squash

Prep time: 5-10 minutes
Cook time: 16 minutes
Servings: 4

Ingredients
- ¼ tsp black pepper
- 1 and ½ tsp dried oregano
- 1 tablespoon olive oil
- ½ tsp salt
- 1 tsp dried thyme
- 1 medium butternut squash, peeled, seeded, and cut into ½ inch slices

Preparation
1. Take a mixing bowl and add slices and other Ingredients, mix well.
2. Pre-heat your Ninja Foodi Grill with GRILL mode at MEDIUM heat and set the timer to 16 minutes.

3. Once you hear the beep, arrange squash slices over the grill grate.

4. Cook for 8 minutes, flip and cook for 8 minutes.

Serving Suggestion: Serve warm.

Variation Tip: use shredded cheese for extra taste.

Nutritional Information per Serving:

Calories: 238| Fat: 12 g| Carbohydrates: 36 g| Fiber: 3 g| Sodium: 128 mg| Protein: 15 g

Crispy Brussels

Prep time: 5-10 minutes

Cook time: 12 minutes

Servings: 4

Ingredients

- 1 pound Brussels sprouts, halved
- 6 slices bacon, chopped
- 2 tbsp olive oil, extra virgin
- 1 tsp salt
- ½ tsp ground black pepper

Preparation

1. Add Brussels, bacon, olive oil, salt, and pepper into a mixing bowl.

2. Pre-heat Ninja Foodi by pressing the "AIR CRISP" option and setting it to "390 degrees F.".

3. Set the timer to 12 minutes.

4. Let it pre-heat until you hear a beep.

5. Arrange Brussels over basket and lock lid.

6. Cook for 6 minutes.

7. Shake it generously and cook for 6 minutes more.

Serving Suggestion: Serve warm and crispy.

Variation Tip: use chopped dill for flavor.

Nutritional Information per Serving:

Calories: 279| Fat: 18 g| Carbohydrates: 12 g| Fiber: 4 g| Sodium: 874 mg| Protein: 14 g

Spice Lover's Cajun Eggplant

Prep time: 5-10 minutes

Cook time: 12 minutes

Servings: 4

Ingredients

- 2 small eggplants, cut into slices
- 3 tsp Cajun seasoning
- ¼ cup olive oil
- 2 tbsp lime juice

Preparation

1. Coat eggplant slices with oil, lemon juice, and Cajun seasoning in a mixing bowl.

2. Take your Ninja Foodi Grill and press "GRILL," and set to "MEDIUM" mode.

3. Set the timer to 10 minutes.

4. Let it pre-heat until you hear a beep.

5. Arrange eggplants over grill grate and lock lid.

6. Cook for 5 minutes.

7. Flip and cook for 5 minutes more.

Serving Suggestion: Serve with dill garnishing or enjoy as it is.

Variation Tip: use chopped dill for garnish.

Nutritional Information per Serving:

Calories: 362| Fat: 11 g| Carbohydrates: 16 g| Fiber: 1 g |Sodium: 694 mg| Protein: 8 g

Honey-Luscious Asparagus

Prep time: 5-10 minutes
Cook time: 15 minutes
Servings: 4
Ingredients
- 2pounds asparagus, trimmed
- 4 tbsp tarragon, minced
- ¼ cup honey
- 2 tbsp olive oil
- 1 tsp salt
- ½ tsp pepper
Preparation
1. Add asparagus, oil, salt, honey, pepper, tarragon into a mixing bowl.
2. Toss them well.
3. Pre-heat Ninja Foodi by pressing the "GRILL" option and setting it to "MED" heat.
4. Set the timer to 8 minutes.
5. Let it pre-heat until you hear a beep.
6. Arrange asparagus over grill grate and lock lid.
7. Cook for 4 minutes.
8. Flip the asparagus and cook for 4 minutes more.
Serving Suggestion: Serve with dill garnishing or enjoy as it is.
Variation Tip: use shredded cheese for fun.
Nutritional Information per Serving:
Calories: 240| Fat: 15 g| Carbohydrates: 31 g| Fiber: 1 g| Sodium: 103 mg| Protein: 7 g

Pineapple with Cream Cheese Dip

Prep time: 15 minutes.
Cook time: 8 minutes.
Serves: 4
Ingredients:
Pineapple
- 1 fresh pineapple
- ¼ cup packed brown sugar
- 3 tablespoons honey
- 2 tablespoons lime juice
Dip
- 3 oz. cream cheese softened
- ¼ cup yogurt
- 2 tablespoons honey
- 1 tablespoon brown sugar
- 1 tablespoon lime juice
- 1 teaspoon lime zest, grated
Preparation:
1. First, slice the peeled pineapple into 8 wedges, then cut each wedge into 2 spears.
2. Toss the pineapple with sugar, lime juice, and honey in a bowl, then refrigerate for 1 hour.
3. Meanwhile, prepare the lime dip by whisking all its ingredients together in a bowl.
4. Remove the pineapple from its marinade.
5. Preheat the Ninja Foodi Grill on the "Grill Mode" at MEDIUM-temperature settings.
6. When the grill is preheated, open its hood and place the pineapple chunks in it.
7. Cover the grill's hood and grill for 4 minutes per side.
8. Serve with lime dip.
Serving Suggestion: Serve the pineapple with cream cheese dip.
Variation Tip: Toss the grilled pineapples with berries.
Nutritional Information Per Serving:
Calories 282 | Fat 4g |Sodium 232mg | Carbs 47g | Fiber 1g | Sugar 0g | Protein 4g

Grilled Zucchini with Fresh Mozzarella

Prep time: 15 minutes.
Cook time: 10 minutes.
Serves: 6

Ingredients:
- 3 zucchinis, cut into slices
- 2 tablespoons olive oil
- Salt, to taste
- Black pepper, to taste
- ¼ teaspoon wine vinegar
- 1 garlic clove, minced
- 1 tablespoon parsley, chopped
- ½ pound fresh mozzarella, cut into thick slices

Preparation:
1. Toss zucchini with olive oil, black pepper, salt, wine vinegar, garlic, and parsley in a bowl.
2. Preheat the Ninja Foodi Grill on the "Grill Mode" at MEDIUM-temperature settings.
3. When the grill is preheated, open its hood and place the zucchini slices in it.
4. Cover the grill's hood and grill for 5 minutes per side.
5. Serve the zucchini slices with the cheese.
6. Enjoy.

Serving Suggestion: Serve the zucchini with yogurt dip.
Variation Tip: Coat the zucchini with breadcrumbs before cooking.
Nutritional Information Per Serving:
Calories 175 | Fat 16g |Sodium 255mg | Carbs 31g | Fiber 1.2g | Sugar 5g | Protein 24.1g

Tasty Cauliflower Tots

Prep time: 10 minutes
Cook time: 20 minutes
Serves: 6

Ingredients:
- 1 egg
- 2 cups cauliflower florets
- 1 small onion, minced
- ¼ cup breadcrumbs
- ½ cup Cheddar cheese, shredded
- ¼ cup bell pepper, minced
- ¼ cup Parmesan cheese, shredded
- Pepper
- Salt

Directions:
1. Place the cooking pot in the Ninja Foodi Grill Main Unit.
2. Boil cauliflower florets for five minutes. Drain well.
3. Add cauliflower florets into the food processor and blend.
4. Add blended cauliflower and remaining ingredients in a mixing bowl and mix until well combined.
5. Make small tots from cauliflower mixture and place into the baking dish.
6. Press Bake mode, set the temperature to 375°F, and set time to 20 minutes. Press Start.
7. Once a unit is preheated then place the baking dish in the cooking pot.
8. Cover with lid and cook for 20 minutes.

Serving Suggestion: Serve with ketchup.
Variation Tip: Add ¼ teaspoon of crushed red pepper flakes.
Nutritional Information per Serving:
Calories 81 | Fat 4g |Sodium 139mg | Carbs 6g | Fiber 1.4g | Sugar 1.9g | Protein 4.7g

Volcano Potatoes

Prep time: 15 minutes.
Cook time: 15 minutes.
Serves: 4

Ingredients:
- 4 russet potatoes
- 8 strips bacon
- 1 cup cheddar cheese shredded

Filling
- 2 cups cream cheese
- ½ green onion diced

Preparation:
1. Wrap the potatoes in a foil sheet.
2. Place the cooking pot in the Ninja Foodi Grill then set a grill grate inside.
3. Select the "Bake" Mode, set the temperature to 400 degrees F.
4. Use the arrow keys to set the cooking time to 10 minutes.

5. Press the START/STOP button to initiate preheating.
6. Once preheated, place the potatoes in the Ninja Foodi Grill.
7. Cover the hood and allow the grill to cook.
8. Allow the potatoes to cool, unwrap and scoop out the flesh from their center.
9. Mash the scooped out flesh in a bowl and stir in the rest of the ingredients except the bacon.
10. Stuff each potato shell with the mashed filling and wrap them with 2 bacon strips.
11. Once preheated, place the mixtures in the Ninja Foodi Grill.
12. Cover the Ninja Foodi Grill's hood, set the temperature to 350 degrees F and cook on the "BAKE Mode" for 10 minutes.
13. Drizzle cheese over the potatoes and broil for 5 minutes.
14. Serve warm.
Serving Suggestion: Serve the potatoes with tomato sauce.
Variation Tip: Drizzle lemon garlic butter on top before cooking.
Nutritional Information Per Serving:
Calories 56 | Fat 4g |Sodium 634mg | Carbs 43g | Fiber 1.4g | Sugar 1g | Protein 13g

Figs Stuffed with Cheese

Prep time: 10 minutes.
Cook time: 10 minutes.
Serves: 10
Ingredients:
- 20 ripe figs
- 4 oz soft goat cheese
- 2 tbsp. olive oil
- 2 tbsp. balsamic vinegar
- 1 tbsp. fresh rosemary, chopped
Preparation:
1. Cut a cross on top (about ¾ way down) of each fig.
2. Mix goat cheese, oil, vinegar and rosemary in a bowl.
3. Stuff each fig with the goat cheese mixture.
4. Place the cooking pot in the Ninja Foodi Grill then set a grill grate inside.
5. Select the "Grill" Mode, set the temperature to LOW.
6. Use the arrow keys to set the cooking time to 10 minutes.
7. Press the START/STOP button to initiate preheating.

8. Once preheated, place the figs in the Ninja Foodi Grill.
9. Cover the hood and allow the grill to cook.
10. Serve.
Serving Suggestion: Serve the figs with your favorite entrée.
Variation Tip: Drizzle crushed pork rind on top before grilling.
Nutritional Information Per Serving:
Calories 38 | Fat 7g |Sodium 316mg | Carbs 24g | Fiber 0.3g | Sugar 0.3g | Protein 3g

Cheese-Stuffed Grilled Peppers

Prep time: 15 minutes.
Cook time: 7 minutes.
Serves: 4
Ingredients:
- 1 cup ricotta cheese
- 1 cup cream cheese
- ½ cup Parmigiano-Reggiano cheese, grated
- Salt and black pepper, to taste
- 4 Anaheim or Cubanelle peppers
- 4 baby bell peppers
- 4 small poblano chiles
- Olive oil, for rubbing
Preparation:
1. Mix cream cheese, ricotta, black pepper, salt, and Parmigiano-Reggiano in a bowl.
2. Remove the top of the peppers and stuff them with ricotta mixture.
3. Preheat the Ninja Foodi Grill on the "Grill Mode" at MEDIUM-temperature settings.
4. When the grill is preheated, open its hood and place the peppers in it.
5. Cover the grill's hood and grill for 7 minutes while rotating after 4 minutes.
6. Serve warm.
Serving Suggestion: Serve the peppers with chili garlic sauce.
Variation Tip: Add pepperoni and sliced olives to the filling.
Nutritional Information Per Serving:
Calories 148 | Fat 12g |Sodium 710mg | Carbs 14g | Fiber 5g | Sugar 3g | Protein 11g

Grilled Butternut Squash

Prep time: 15 minutes.
Cook time: 16 minutes.
Serves: 4

Ingredients:
- 1 medium butternut squash
- 1 tablespoon olive oil
- 1 ½ teaspoons dried oregano
- 1 teaspoon dried thyme
- ½ teaspoon salt
- ¼ teaspoon black pepper

Preparation:
1. Peel and slice the squash into ½ inch thick slices.
2. Remove the center of the slices to discard the seeds.
3. Toss the squash slices with the remaining ingredients in a bowl.
4. Preheat the Ninja Foodi Grill on the "Grill Mode" at MEDIUM-temperature settings.
5. When the grill is preheated, open its hood and place the squash slices in it.
6. Cover the grill's hood and grill for 8 minutes per side.
7. Serve warm.

Serving Suggestion: Serve the squash with chili sauce or mayonnaise dip.

Variation Tip: Added shredded cheese on top of the grilled squash.

Nutritional Information Per Serving:
Calories 180 | Fat 9g |Sodium 318mg | Carbs 19g | Fiber 5g | Sugar 3g | Protein 7g

Ninja Foodi Corn Fritters

Prep time: 10 minutes
Cook time: 5 minutes
Serves: 8

Ingredients:
- ¾ cup cornmeal, finely ground
- ¾ cup flour
- 1 teaspoon baking powder
- 4 tablespoons green chilies
- ½ teaspoon paprika
- 4 cups frozen corn kernels
- ½ teaspoon garlic powder
- ½ teaspoon onion powder
- ½ cup chopped parsley
- 6 tablespoons almond milk
- Salt and pepper, to taste

Preparation:
1. In a Ninja Foodi Grill, press the "AIR CRISP" button and set the temperature to 375 degrees F and the time to 5 minutes.
2. To begin preheating, press START/STOP.
3. In a large mixing bowl, combine spices, flour, baking powder, cornmeal, and parsley. Mix thoroughly.
4. In a food processor, combine two cups corn, almond milk, salt, and pepper. Pulse until a smooth consistency is achieved.
5. Combine the corn and flour ingredients and thoroughly combine them.
6. Stir in the remaining corn kernels thoroughly.
7. When the Ninja Foodi Grill is shown "Add Food," spread the mixture in a pan and place it in the Ninja Foodi Grill.
8. Cook for about 5 minutes before serving.
9. Cut into slices and serve.

Serving Suggestions: Top with red chili powder before serving.

Variation Tip: You can use coconut milk.

Nutritional Information per Serving:
Calories: 184 |Fat: 3.9g|Sat Fat: 2.6g|Carbohydrates: 35.9g|Fiber: 3.9g|Sugar: 3.6g|Protein: 4.8g

Ninja Foodi Lemon Tofu

Prep time: 10 minutes
Cook time: 20 minutes
Serves: 4

Ingredients:
- 2 tablespoons tamari
- 3 tablespoons arrowroot powder
- 2 tablespoons lemon zest
- 2 pounds extra-firm tofu, drained, pressed and cubed
- ¾ cup lemon juice

- 1 cup water
- 4 tablespoons organic sugar

Preparation:
1. insert grill grate in the unit and close hood. Select GRILL, set temperature to MEDIUM, and set time to 15 minutes. Select START/STOP to begin preheating.
2. In a Ziploc bag, combine two teaspoons of arrowroot powder, tofu, and tamari.
3. Seal the Ziploc bag, give it a good shake, and leave it aside for 30 minutes.
4. Place the tofu mixture on the Ninja Foodi Grill when it says "Add Food" and cook for 15 minutes.
5. Remove the item and place it away.
6. In a skillet, combine the remaining arrowroot powder, lemon juice, lemon zest, water, and sugar.
7. Cook for 5 minutes on medium-low heat, then stir in the tofu mixture.
8. Remove the dish from the oven and serve.

Serving Suggestions: Top with oregano before serving.

Variation Tip: You can also add brown sugar in the sauce.

Nutritional Information per Serving:
Calories: 296 |Fat: 13.6g|Sat Fat: 1.6g|Carbohydrates: 24.6g|Fiber: 1.4g|Sugar: 14.4g|Protein: 23.8g

Ninja Foodi Mac n' Cheese

Prep time: 15 minutes
Cook time: 25 minutes
Serves: 8

Ingredients:
- 2 teaspoons cornstarch
- 4 cups dry macaroni
- 4 cups shredded cheddar cheese
- 4 cups heavy whipping cream

Preparation:
1. In a mixing bowl, combine three cups of cheese and cornstarch. Set aside after thoroughly mixing.
2. In a separate bowl, combine the remaining cheese, macaroni, and whipping cream. Mix thoroughly.

3. Transfer the macaroni mixture to a baking tray and cover with foil. Remove from the equation.
4. Meanwhile, in a Ninja Foodi Grill, prepare a "Crisper Basket" and press the "AIR CRISP" button. Preheat the oven to 310 degrees F and set the timer for 25 minutes.
5. To begin preheating, press START/STOP.
6. When it says "Add Food," insert the baking pan in the "Crisper Basket" and bake at 310 degrees F for 15 minutes.
7. Remove the foil and sprinkle the cornstarch mixture over the top.
8. Remove from the oven after 10 minutes of cooking.
9. Finally, serve and enjoy!

Serving Suggestions: Top with chopped mint leaves before serving.

Variation Tip: You can also mozzarella cheese to enhance taste.

Nutritional Information per Serving:
Calories: 593 |Fat: 41.6g|Sat Fat: 25.9g|Carbohydrates: 34.4g|Fiber: 1.4g|Sugar: 1.5g|Protein: 20.8g

Crispy Artichoke Hearts

Prep time: 10 minutes
Cook time: 13 minutes
Serves: 8

Ingredients:
- 1¾ pounds artichoke hearts, quartered
- 2 cups all-purpose flour
- 1 teaspoon paprika
- 2 cups almond milk
- 1 teaspoon garlic powder
- 3 cups bread crumbs
- Salt and black pepper, to taste

Preparation:
1. Insert grill grate in the unit and close hood. Select AIR CRISP, set temperature to 375°F, and set time to 13 minutes. Select START/STOP to begin preheating
2. Combine the dry ingredients in one basin and the liquid ingredients in a separate bowl. Make sure everything is well combined.
3. Dip artichoke hearts in wet ingredients first, then dry ingredients.
4. Place the artichoke hearts in the Ninja Foodi Grill when it shows "Add Food" and close the hood to let it cook.
5. Remove from the oven and serve immediately.

Serving Suggestions: Top with red chili flakes before serving.
Variation Tip: You can use onion powder instead of garlic powder.
Nutritional Information per Serving:
Calories: 500 |Fat: 17.1g|Sat Fat: 13.3g|Carbohydrates: 76.1g|Fiber: 14.1g|Sugar: 6.5g|Protein: 16.1g

Ninja Foodi Potato Croquettes

Prep time: 20 minutes
Cook time: 23 minutes
Serves: 8
Ingredients:
- 4 potatoes, peeled and cubed
- 1 cup grated parmesan cheese
- 4 tablespoons chives, minced
- 1 cup bread crumbs
- 4 tablespoons all-purpose flour
- 2 egg yolks
- 4 eggs
- 4 tablespoons vegetable oil
- Salt and black pepper, to taste

Preparation:
1. Place the potatoes in a pot of boiling water and simmer for 15 minutes.
2. In a large mixing bowl, mash them and set them aside to cool.
3. In a mixing bowl, combine the egg yolk, chives, flour, parmesan cheese, salt, and black pepper. Make sure everything is well combined.
4. Roll the mixture into cylindrical shapes and lay it aside.
5. Crack the eggs into a shallow bowl and thoroughly beat them.
6. In a separate bowl, combine bread crumbs and set them aside.
7. Dip the croquettes in the egg mixture first, then in the breadcrumbs.
8. Meanwhile, in the Ninja Foodi Grill cooking pot, arrange the "Crisper Basket" and press the "AIR CRISP" button. Preheat the oven to 390 degrees F and cook for 8 minutes.
9. Press START/STOP to begin preheating. Put croquettes in the "Crisper Basket" when the Ninja Foodi Grill shows "Add Food".
10. Put Cook for 8 minutes and take out.
11. Serve and enjoy!
Serving Suggestions: Serve with tomato sauce.
Variation Tip: You can add chopped cilantro to enhance taste.
Nutritional Information per Serving:
Calories: 258 |Fat: 11.8g|Sat Fat: 3.1g|Carbohydrates: 30g|Fiber: 3.3g|Sugar: 2.3g|Protein: 8.6g

Ninja Foodi Buffalo Chicken Wings

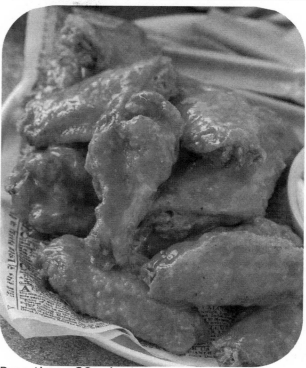

Prep time: 20 minutes
Cook time: 16 minutes
Serves: 10
Ingredients:
- 4 pounds frozen chicken wings
- 4 tablespoons buffalo sauce
- 4 tablespoons olive oil
- 1 teaspoon red pepper flakes
- Salt, to taste

Preparation:
1. In a Ninja Foodi Grill, arrange the "Crisper Basket" and push the "AIR CRISP" button. Preheat the oven to 390 degrees Fahrenheit and set the timer for 12 minutes.
2. To begin preheating, press START/STOP.
3. Drizzle olive oil over chicken wings and lay them in the "Crisper Basket."
4. Remove from the oven after 12 minutes at 390 degrees F.
5. In a large mixing bowl, combine buffalo sauce, red pepper flakes, and salt. Mix thoroughly.
6. Serve the wings dipped in the buffalo sauce mixture.
Serving Suggestions: Top with chopped mint leaves before serving.
Variation Tip: Barbeque sauce can also be used to enhance taste.
Nutritional Information per Serving:
Calories: 410 |Fat: 31.6g|Sat Fat: 8.1g|Carbohydrates: 0.9g|Fiber: 0.5g|Sugar: 0g|Protein: 29.2g

Ninja Foodi Italian Style Tofu

Prep time: 10 minutes
Cook time: 6 minutes
Serves: 8
Ingredients:
- 2 tablespoons tamari
- ½ teaspoon onion powder
- 1 teaspoon garlic powder
- 2 cups extra-firm tofu, pressed and cubed
- 1 teaspoon dried basil
- 1 teaspoon dried oregano
- Black pepper, to taste

Preparation:
1. In a Ninja Foodi Grill, press the "AIR CRISP" button. Preheat the oven to 400 degrees Fahrenheit and set the timer for 6 minutes.
2. To begin preheating, press START/STOP.
3. In a large mixing basin, combine all of the ingredients. Set aside for 20 minutes after thoroughly mixing.
4. Place the tofu in the Ninja Foodi Grill when it says "Add Food" and cook for around 6 minutes.
5. Remove the dish from the oven and serve immediately.
Serving Suggestions: Top with mayo sauce before serving.
Variation Tip: You can add red chili powder to enhance taste.
Nutritional Information per Serving:
Calories: 26 |Fat: 1.4g|Sat Fat: 0.1g|Carbohydrates: 1.2g|Fiber: 0.3g|Sugar: 0.3g|Protein: 2.8g

Ninja Foodi Roasted Cashews

Prep time: 5 minutes
Cook time: 5 minutes
Serves: 3
Ingredients:
- ½ teaspoon melted butter

- ¾ cups cashew nuts
- Salt and black pepper, to taste

Preparation:
1. In a mixing dish, combine the cashews, butter, salt, and pepper. Toss well to coat.
2. To begin preheating, press START/STOP.
3. Meanwhile, in a Ninja Foodi Grill, arrange the "Crisper Basket" and press the "AIR CRISP" button.
4. Preheat the oven to 355°F and set the timer for 5 minutes. When the Ninja Foodi Grill says "Add Food," put cashews in the "Crisper Basket."
5. Remove after 5 minutes of cooking.
6. Allow to cooling before serving.
Serving Suggestions: Top with maple syrup before serving.
Variation Tip: You can add honey to enhance taste.
Nutritional Information per Serving:
Calories: 202 |Fat: 16.5g|Sat Fat: 3.5g|Carbohydrates: 11.2g|Fiber: 1g|Sugar: 1.7g|Protein: 5.3g

Ninja Foodi Crispy Shrimp

Prep time: 20 minutes
Cook time: 20 minutes
Serves: 8
Ingredients:
- 2 cups coconut milk
- 1 cup bread crumbs
- 2 pounds shrimp, peeled and deveined
- 1 teaspoon cayenne pepper
- Salt and black pepper, to taste

Preparation:
1. In a large mixing bowl, combine the coconut milk, pepper, and salt. Mix thoroughly.
2. In a shallow dish, combine bread crumbs, salt, black pepper, and cayenne pepper. Mix thoroughly.
3. Toss the shrimp in the coconut milk mixture first, then in the bread crumb mixture. Remove from the equation.
4. Meanwhile, in a Ninja Foodi Grill, arrange "Crisper Basket" and push the "AIR CRISP " button. Preheat the oven to 350 degrees F and cook for 20 minutes.
5. To begin preheating, press START/STOP.
6. Place shrimp in the "Crisper Basket" and cook for 20 minutes at 350 degrees F when the Ninja Foodi Grill shown "Add Food."
7. Remove from the oven, serve, and enjoy!
Serving Suggestions: Top with barbeque sauce before serving.
Variation Tip: Cayenne pepper can be omitted.
Nutritional Information per Serving:
Calories: 327 |Fat: 17g|Sat Fat: 13.4g|Carbohydrates: 14.9g|Fiber: 2g|Sugar: 2.9g|Protein: 29g

Ninja Foodi Mozzarella Sticks

Prep time: 20 minutes
Cook time: 12 minutes
Serves: 6

Ingredients:
- 6 tablespoons white flour
- 6 tablespoons coconut milk
- 1 pound mozzarella cheese block, cut into 3 inch sticks
- 4 eggs
- 1 cup plain bread crumbs

Preparation:
1. In one dish, put flour, and in another, put bread crumbs.
2. In a small bowl, whisk together the eggs and milk. Beat the drums thoroughly.
3. Coat mozzarella sticks in flour, then in an egg mixture, and last in bread crumbs.
4. Place them on a cookie sheet and place them in the freezer for about 2 hours.
5. Meanwhile, in a Ninja Foodi Grill, arrange the "Crisper Basket" and press the "AIR CRISP" button.
6. Preheat the oven to 400 degrees F and cook for 12 minutes. Close the hood and wait for it to start cooking.
7. Remove from the oven and serve immediately.

Serving Suggestions: Top with red chopped mint leaves before serving.
Variation Tip: Coconut milk can be replaced with almond milk.
Nutritional Information per Serving:
Calories: 394 |Fat: 23.8g|Sat Fat: 13.9g|Carbohydrates: 23.1g|Fiber: 1.2g|Sugar: 2.1g|Protein: 29.1g

Lovely Rum Sundae

Prep time: 10 minutes
Cook time: 8 minutes
Servings: 4

Ingredients

- Vanilla ice cream for serving
- 1 pineapple, cored and sliced
- 1 tsp cinnamon, ground
- ½ cup brown sugar, packed
- ½ cup dark rum

Preparation:

1. Take a large deep bowl and add sugar, cinnamon, and rum.

2. Add the pineapple in the layer, dredge them properly and make sure that they are coated well.

3. Pre-heat your Foodi in "GRILL" mode with "MAX" settings, setting the timer to 8 minutes.

4. Once you hear the beep, strain any additional rum from the pineapple slices and transfer them to the grill rate of your appliance.

5. Press them down and grill for 6- 8 minutes. Make sure not to overcrowd the grill grate, Cook in batches if needed.

Serving Suggestion: Serve Top each of the ring with a scoop of your favorite ice cream, sprinkle a bit of cinnamon on top.

Variation Tip: use melted chocolate for extra taste.

Nutritional Information per Serving:

Calories: 240| Fat: 4 g| Carbohydrates: 43 g| Fiber: 8 g| Sodium: 85 mg| Protein: 2 g

The Healthy Granola Bites

Prep time: 10 minutes
Cook time: 15-20 minutes
Servings: 4

Ingredients

- Salt and pepper to taste
- 1 tablespoon coriander
- A handful of thyme, diced
- ¼ cup of coconut milk
- 3 handful of cooked vegetables, your choice
- 3 pounces plain granola

Preparation

1. Pre-heat your Ninja Foodi to 350 degrees F in AIR CRISP mode, set a timer to 20 minutes.

2. Take a bowl and add your cooked vegetables, granola.

3. Use an immersion blender to blitz your granola until you have a nice breadcrumb-like consistency.

4. Add coconut milk to the mix and mix until you have a nice firm texture.

5. Use the mixture to make granola balls and transfer them to your Ninja Foodi Grill.

6. Cook for 20 minutes.

7. Serve and enjoy!

Serving Suggestion: Serve and enjoy.

Variation Tip: add dates for sweetness.

Nutritional Information per Serving:

Calories: 140| Fat: 10 g| Carbohydrates: 14 g| Fiber: 4 g| Sodium: 215 mg| Protein: 2 g

Ninja Foodi Vanilla Donuts

Prep time: 10 minutes
Cook time: 3 minutes
Serves: 4

Ingredients:
- 1 cup powdered sugar
- ½ teaspoon vanilla extract
- 2 tablespoons whole milk
- 1 cup prepared biscuit dough
- ¼ teaspoon ground cinnamon

Preparation:
1. In a mixing dish, combine the milk, vanilla essence, and powdered sugar. Set aside after thoroughly mixing.
2. Form donuts out of the prepared biscuit dough and place them in the refrigerator for 5 minutes. Install grill grate in the unit and close hood. Select GRILL, set temperature to HIGH, and set time to 3 minutes. Select START/STOP to begin preheating.
3. When it says "Add Food," put the doughnuts in and cook for about 3 minutes.
4. Remove the pan from the oven and sprinkle with the cinnamon and vanilla extract mixture.
5. Finally, serve and enjoy!

Serving Suggestions: Put chocolate chips on the top before serving.

Variation Tip: You can omit cinnamon.

Nutritional Information per Serving:
Calories: 171 |Fat: 2.4g|Sat Fat: 0.9g|Carbohydrates: 36.7g|Fiber: 0.3g|Sugar: 30.9g|Protein: 1.3g

Rummy Pineapple Sunday

Prep time: 10 minutes
Cook time: 8 minutes
Servings: 4

Ingredients
- ½ cup dark rum
- ½ cup packed brown sugar
- 1 pineapple cored and sliced
- Vanilla ice cream, for serving

Preparation
1. Take a large-sized bowl and add rum, sugar, cinnamon.
2. Add pineapple slices, arrange them in the layer. Coat mixture then let them soak for 5 minutes, per side.
3. Preheat Ninja Foodie by pressing the "GRILL" option and setting it to "MAX" and timer to 8 minutes.
4. Let it preheat until you hear a beep.
5. Strain extra rum sauce from pineapple.
6. Transfer prepared fruit in grill grate in a single layer, press down fruit and lock lid.
7. Grill for 6-8 minutes without flipping, work in batches if needed.
8. Once done, remove and serve.

Serving Suggestion: top each pineapple ring with a scoop of ice cream, sprinkle cinnamon and serve Enjoy!

Variation Tip: use melted chocolate for taste.

Nutritional Information per Serving:
Calories: 240| Fat: 4 g| Carbohydrates: 43 g| Fiber: 3 g| Sodium: 32 mg| Protein: 2 g

Grilled Apples with Bourbon and Brown Sugar

Prep time: 20 minutes.
Cook time: 7 minutes.
Serves: 4

Ingredients
- 1 packet Brown Sugar Bourbon Marinade
- ½ cup oil
- ½cup water
- 2 tbsp apple cider vinegar
- 4 apples

- ½ tsp cinnamon
- 1 cup vanilla ice cream
- ¼ cup granola

Preparation

1. Prepare the Brown Sugar Bourbon Marinade by whisking together the water, oil, and apple cider vinegar. Pour the marinade into a large pan or zip top bag.
2. Remove the cores from the four apples with an apple corer.
3. Cut the apples horizontally into thick ½-inch slices. Discard the top and bottom. You should get 2-3 apple slices per apple depending on the size of your apples.
4. Place the apple slices in the marinade and turn or toss to gently coat. Cover and allow marinating for 15 minutes, but no longer than 30 minutes.
5. Preheat your Ninja Foodi grill at the "Grill" function to the "MAX" setting for 10 minutes.
6. Using tongs, place the apple slices onto the hot grill. Allow to grill for 2-3 minutes or until light brown grill marks appear on the bottoms.
7. Turn and grill an additional 2-3 minutes or until the apples are just fork-tender.
8. Remove to a plate and allow cooling a few minutes.

Serving Suggestion: Top the 2-3 slices of the warm apples with a sprinkle of cinnamon, a scoop of vanilla ice cream, and granola. Serve immediately.

Variation Tip: add pears and have unique deliciousness.

Nutritional Information Per Serving:
Calories 199 | Fat 5g | Carbohydrates 38g| Fiber 5g | Sodium 31mg | Protein 3g

Cute Marshmallow and Banana

Prep time: 19 minutes
Cook time: 6 minutes
Servings: 4

Ingredients
- 4 ripe bananas
- 1 cup mini marshmallows
- ½ cup of chocolate chips
- ½ cup peanut butter chips

Preparation

1. Slice a banana lengthwise, keeping its peel. Ensure not to cut all the way through.
2. Use your hands to open banana peel like a book, revealing the inside of a banana.
3. Divide marshmallow, chocolate chips, peanut butter among bananas, stuffing them inside.
4. Pre-heat Ninja Foodi by pressing the "GRILL" option and setting it to "MEDIUM" and timer to 6 minutes.
5. Let it pre-heat until you hear a beep.
6. Transfer banana to Grill Grate and lock lid, cook for 4-6 minutes until chocolate melts and bananas are toasted.

Serving Suggestion: Serve and enjoy.

Variation Tip: use chocolate shavings for little crunch.

Nutritional Information per Serving:
Calories: 505| Fat: 18 g| Carbohydrates: 82 g| Fiber: 6 g| Sodium: 103 mg| Protein: 10 g

Lemon Mousse

Prep time: 15 minutes
Cook time: 12 minutes
Servings: 2

Ingredients
- 4-ounce cream cheese softened
- ½ cup heavy cream
- ⅛ cup fresh lemon juice
- ½ tsp lemon liquid stevia
- 2 pinches salt

Preparation

1. Take a bowl and mix cream cheese, heavy cream, lemon juice, salt, and stevia.
2. Pour this mixture into the ramekins and transfer the ramekins in the pot of Ninja Foodi.
3. Select "BAKE" and bake for 12 minutes at 350 degrees F.

Serving Suggestion: Pour into the serving glasses and refrigerate for at least 3 hours and serve.

Variation Tip: use orange juice for flavor.

Nutritional Information per Serving:
Calories: 225| Fat: 17 g| Carbohydrates: 13 g| Fiber: 3 g| Sodium: 284 mg| Protein: 6 g

Marshmallow Roll-Up

Prep time: 15 minutes.
Cook time: 10 minutes.
Serves: 2

Ingredients:
- 1 flour tortilla
- 1 handful mini marshmallows
- 1 handful of chocolate chips
- 2 graham crackers

Preparation:
1. Spread a 12x12 inch foil on a working surface.
2. Place the tortilla over this sheet and top it with graham crackers, chocolate chips, and marshmallows.
3. Roll the tortilla tightly by rolling the foil sheet.
4. Preheat the Ninja Foodi Grill on the "Bake Mode" at 350 degrees F temperature.
5. When the grill is preheated, open its hood and place the tortilla rolls in it.
6. Cover the grill's hood and grill for 5 minutes per side.
7. Unwrap and slice in half.
8. Serve.

Serving Suggestion: Serve the rolls with chocolate syrup on top.
Variation Tip: Drizzle chocolate syrup on top of the rolls.
Nutritional Information Per Serving:
Calories 153 | Fat 1g |Sodium 8mg | Carbs 66g | Fiber 0.8g | Sugar 56g | Protein 1g

Chocolate-Cherry Sandwiches

Prep time: 15 minutes.
Cook time: 8 minutes.
Serves: 6

Ingredients:
- 12 (½-inch-thick) challah bread slices

- 3 tablespoons cherry preserves
- 2 (4-ounce) chocolate bars, each cut into thirds
- ⅓ cup unsalted butter, melted
- Confectioners' sugar, for garnish

Preparation:
1. Brush six bread slices with cherry preserves and divide the chocolate on top.
2. Place the remaining bread slices on top and brush the sandwiches with butter.
3. Preheat the Ninja Foodi Grill on the "Grill Mode" at MEDIUM-temperature settings.
4. When the grill is preheated, open its hood and place the sandwiches in it.
5. Cover the grill's hood and grill for 4 minutes per side.
6. Garnish with sugar and serve.

Serving Suggestion: Serve the sandwiches with chocolate dip.
Variation Tip: Add any fruit preserve for change of taste.
Nutritional Information Per Serving:
Calories 361 | Fat 10g |Sodium 218mg | Carbs 56g | Fiber 10g | Sugar 30g | Protein 14g

Berry Cobbler

Prep time: 15 minutes.
Cook time: 20 minutes.
Serves: 8

Ingredients:
- 2 cans (21 oz.) blueberry pie filling
- 1- ¼ cups water
- ½ cup canola oil
- 1 (8 oz.) package cake mix
- Vanilla ice cream

Preparation:
1. First, mix the cake mix with oil and water in a bowl until smooth.
2. Place the foil packet on a working surface and add pie filling.
3. Spread the cake mix on top of the filling.
4. Cover the foil packet and seal it.
5. Prepare and preheat the Ninja Foodi Grill at 350 degrees F.
6. When the grill is preheated, open its hood and place the cobbler packet in it.

7. Cover the grill's hood and cook on the "Bake Mode" for 20 minutes.
8. Serve fresh with vanilla ice cream on top.
Serving Suggestion: Serve the cobbler with blueberry syrup on top.
Variation Tip: Add crushed walnuts or pecans to the filling.
Nutritional Information Per Serving:
Calories 198 | Fat 14g |Sodium 272mg | Carbs 34g | Fiber 1g | Sugar 9.3g | Protein 1.3g

Cinnamon Grilled Peaches

Prep time: 15 minutes.
Cook time: 8 minutes.
Serves: 4
Ingredients:
- ¼ cup salted butter
- 1 tablespoon 1 teaspoon granulated sugar
- ¼ teaspoon cinnamon
- 4 ripe peaches, halved and pitted
- vegetable oil
Preparation:
1. Mix sugar with butter and cinnamon in a bowl until smooth.
2. Preheat the Ninja Foodi Grill on the "Grill Mode" at MEDIUM-temperature settings.
3. When the grill is preheated, open its hood and place the peaches in it.
4. Cover the grill's hood and grill for 1 minutes per side.
5. Serve the peaches with cinnamon butter on top.
6. Enjoy.
Serving Suggestion: Serve the peaches with chocolate syrup on top.
Variation Tip: Add dried raisins to garnish the grilled peaches.
Nutritional Information Per Serving:
Calories 203 | Fat 8.9g |Sodium 340mg | Carbs 24.7g | Fiber 1.2g | Sugar 11.3g | Protein 5.3g

Grilled Apples a la Mode

Prep time: 10 minutes.
Cook time: 6 minutes.
Serves: 4
Ingredients:
- 2 tart-sweet apples, sliced
- 2 tbsp. butter, melted
- 2 tbsp. brown sugar
- 2 tbsp. white sugar
- 1 tsp. cinnamon
- ¼ tsp. ginger
- ¼ tsp. nutmeg
- For serving: Vanilla ice cream
Preparation:
1. Mix sugars, butter, cinnamon, nutmeg and ginger in a suitable bowl.
2. Toss in butter, and apples mix well and leave for 5 minutes.
3. Place the cooking pot in the Ninja Foodi Grill then set a grill grate inside.
4. Select the "Grill" Mode, set the temperature to MED.
5. Use the arrow keys to set the cooking time to 6 minutes.
6. Press the START/STOP button to initiate preheating.
7. Once preheated, place the apple in the Ninja Foodi Grill.
8. Cover the hood and allow the grill to cook.
9. Flip the apple slices once cooked halfway through.
10. Serve with an ice-cream scoop on top.
Serving Suggestion: Serve the apples with fresh blueberries on top.
Variation Tip: Add crushed nuts on top of the apples.
Nutritional Information Per Serving:
Calories 255 | Fat 21g |Sodium 152mg | Carbs 36g | Fiber 2g | Sugar 15g | Protein 3.6g

Grilled Pears with Cinnamon Drizzle

Prep time: 15 minutes.
Cook time: 8 minutes.
Serves: 3

Ingredients:
- 3 ripe pears
- 2 tablespoons honey
- 1 tablespoon cinnamon
- ¼ cup pecans, chopped
- coconut oil
- sea salt

Preparation:
1. Peel and cut the pears into quarters.
2. Toss pears with honey, cinnamon, and coconut oil.
3. Preheat the Ninja Foodi Grill on the "Bake Mode" at 375 degrees F temperature.
4. When the grill is preheated, open its hood and place the pears in it.
5. Cover the grill's hood and grill for 7 minutes per side.
6. Garnish with pecans and sea salt.
7. Serve.

Serving Suggestion: Serve the pears with fresh berries on top.
Variation Tip: Add crushed nuts to give the pears a crunchy texture.
Nutritional Information Per Serving:
Calories 118 | Fat 20g |Sodium 192mg | Carbs 23.7g | Fiber 0.9g | Sugar 19g | Protein 5.2g

Marshmallow Stuffed Banana

Prep time: 15 minutes.
Cook time: 4 minutes.
Serves: 2

Ingredients:

- ¼ cup of chocolate chips
- 1 banana
- ¼ cup mini marshmallows

Preparation:
1. Place a peeled banana over a 12 x 12-inch foil sheet.
2. Make a slit in the banana lengthwise and stuff this slit with chocolate chips and marshmallows.
3. Wrap the foil around the banana and seal it.
4. Preheat the Ninja Foodi Grill on the "Bake Mode" at 375 degrees F temperature.
5. When the grill is preheated, open its hood and place the banana packet in it.
6. Cover the grill's hood and grill for 5 minutes per side.
7. Unwrap and serve.

Serving Suggestion: Serve the marshmallows with a scoop of vanilla cream on top.
Variation Tip: Add chopped nuts to the marshmallows.
Nutritional Information Per Serving:
Calories 248 | Fat 16g |Sodium 95mg | Carbs 38.4g | Fiber 0.3g | Sugar 10g | Protein 14.1g

Apricots with Brioche

Prep time: 15 minutes.
Cook time: 8 minutes.
Serves: 8

Ingredients:
- 8 ripe apricots
- 2 tablespoon butter
- 2 tablespoon sugar
- 4 slice brioches, diced
- 2 tablespoon Honey
- 2 cup vanilla ice cream

Preparation:
1. Toss the apricot halves with butter and sugar.
2. Preheat the Ninja Foodi Grill on the "Grill Mode" at LOW-temperature settings.
3. When the grill is preheated, open its hood and place the brioche slices in it.
4. Cover the grill's hood and grill for 2 minutes per side.
5. Now grill the apricots in the same grill for 2 minutes per side.
6. Top these slices with apricot slices, honey, and a scoop of vanilla ice cream.
7. Serve.

Serving Suggestion: Serve the apricot brioche with chocolate or apple sauce.
Variation Tip: Dip the brioche in maple syrup.
Nutritional Information Per Serving:
Calories 117 | Fat 12g |Sodium 79mg | Carbs 24.8g | Fiber 1.1g | Sugar 18g | Protein 5g

Chocolate Cheesecake

Prep time: 15 minutes
Cook time: 15 minutes
Servings: 4
Ingredients
- 2 cups cream cheese, softened
- 2 eggs
- 2 tsp cocoa powder
- 1 tsp pure vanilla extract
- ½ cup Swerve
Preparation
1. Add in eggs, cocoa powder, vanilla extract, swerve, cream cheese in an immersion blender and blend until smooth.
2. Pour the mixture evenly into mason jars.
3. Put the mason jars in the insert of Ninja Foodi Grill and close the lid.
4. Select "BAKE" and bake for 15 minutes at 360 degrees F.
5. Refrigerate for at least 2 hours.
Serving Suggestion: Serve and enjoy.
Variation Tip: use chopped nuts for garnish.
Nutritional Information per Serving:
Calories 244| Total Fat 24 g| Carbohydrates2.1 g| Fiber 0.1 g| Sodium 204 mg| Protein 4 g

Marshmallow Banana Boat

Prep time: 19 minutes
Cook time: 6 minutes
Servings: 4
Ingredients
- 4 ripe bananas
- 1 cup mini marshmallows
- ½ cup of chocolate chips
- ½ cup peanut butter chips
Preparation
1. Slice a banana lengthwise, keeping its peel.
2. Use your hands to open banana peel like a book, revealing the inside of a banana.
3. Divide marshmallow, chocolate chips, peanut butter among bananas, stuffing them inside.
4. Preheat Ninja Foodie by pressing the "GRILL" option and setting it to "MEDIUM" and timer to 6 minutes let it preheat until you hear a beep.
5. Transfer banana to Grill Grate and lock lid, cook for 4-6 minutes until chocolate melts and bananas are toasted.
Serving Suggestion: Serve and enjoy.
Variation Tip: use nuts for crunch.
Nutritional Information per Serving:
Calories: 505| Fat: 18 g| Carbohydrates: 82| Fiber: 6 g| Sodium: 103 mg| Protein: 10 g

Fruit Kabobs

Prep time: 15 minutes.
Cook time: 7 minutes.
Serves: 4
Ingredients:
- 1 tablespoon butter
- ½ cup apricot preserves
- 1 tablespoon water
- ⅛ teaspoon ground cinnamon
- ⅛ teaspoon ground nutmeg
- 3 nectarines, quartered
- 3 peaches, quartered
- 3 plums, quartered
- 1 loaf (10-3/4 oz.) pound cake, cubed
Preparation:
1. Take the first five ingredients in a small saucepan and stir cook for 3 minutes on medium heat.
2. Alternately thread the pound cake and fruits on the skewers.

3. Brush these skewers with the apricot mixture.
4. Preheat the Ninja Foodi Grill on the "Grill Mode" at LOW-temperature settings.
5. When the grill is preheated, open its hood and place the fruit skewers in it.
6. Cover the grill's hood and grill for 2 minutes per side.
7. Cook the skewers in batches.
8. Serve.
Serving Suggestion: Serve the fruits with cream cheese dip
Variation Tip: Soak the cake cubes in orange juice before grilling.
Nutritional Information Per Serving:
Calories 159 | Fat 3g |Sodium 277mg | Carbs 21g | Fiber 1g | Sugar 9g | Protein 2g

Banana Skewers

Prep time: 15 minutes.
Cook time: 6 minutes.
Serves: 2
Ingredients:
- 1 loaf (10 3/4 oz.) cake, cubed
- 2 large bananas, one-inch slices
- ¼ cup butter, melted
- 2 tablespoons brown sugar
- ½ teaspoon vanilla extract
- ⅛ teaspoon ground cinnamon
- 4 cups butter pecan ice cream
- ½ cup butterscotch ice cream topping
- ½ cup chopped pecans, toasted
Preparation:
1. Thread the cake and bananas over the skewers alternately.
2. Whisk butter with cinnamon, vanilla, and brown sugar in a small bowl.
3. Brush this mixture over the skewers liberally.
4. Preheat the Ninja Foodi Grill on the "Grill Mode" at LOW-temperature settings.
5. When the grill is preheated, open its hood and place the banana skewers in it.
6. Cover the grill's hood and grill for 3 minutes per side.
7. Serve with ice cream, pecan, and butterscotch topping on top.
Serving Suggestion: Serve the skewers with maple syrup on top.
Variation Tip: Add crushed chocolate on top of the skewers.
Nutritional Information Per Serving:
Calories 245 | Fat 14g |Sodium 122mg | Carbs 23.3g | Fiber 1.2g | Sugar 12g | Protein 4.3g

Grill Pineapple Slices

Prep time: 10 minutes
Cook time: 8 minutes
Serves: 6
Ingredients:
- 6 pineapple slices
- ½ teaspoon ground cinnamon
- ¼ cup brown sugar

Directions:
1. Place the cooking pot in the Ninja Foodi Grill Main Unit then place the grill plate in the pot.
2. Toss pineapple slices with brown sugar and cinnamon.
3. Press Grill mode, set the temperature to HIGH, and set time to 8 minutes. Press Start.
4. Once a unit is preheated then place pineapple slices on the grill plate.
5. Cover with lid and cook for 8 minutes. Turn halfway through.
Serving Suggestion: Allow to cool completely then serve.
Variation Tip: None
Nutritional Information per Serving:
Calories 83 | Fat 0g |Sodium 2mg | Carbs 21g | Fiber 1g | Sugar 19g | Protein 0g

Moist Carrot Muffins

Prep time: 10 minutes
Cook time: 20 minutes
Serves: 6
Ingredients:
- 1 egg
- ¼ cup brown sugar
- ¼ cup sugar

- 1 cup all-purpose flour
- ¾ cup grated carrots
- 1 teaspoon vanilla
- ¼ cup applesauce
- ½ tablespoon canola oil
- 1 ½ teaspoon baking powder
- ¼ teaspoon nutmeg
- 1 teaspoon cinnamon
- ¼ teaspoon salt

Directions:
1. Place the cooking pot in the Ninja Foodi Grill Main Unit.
2. Add all ingredients into the bowl and mix until well combined.
3. Pour batter into the greased silicone muffin molds.
4. Press Bake mode, set the temperature to 350°F, and set time to 20 minutes. Press Start.
5. Once a unit is preheated then place muffin molds in the cooking pot.
6. Cover with lid and cook for 20 minutes.

Serving Suggestion: Allow to cool completely then serve.
Variation Tip: Add melted butter if you don't have canola oil.
Nutritional Information per Serving:
Calories 165 | Fat 2.2g | Sodium 120mg | Carbs 33.7g | Fiber 1.3g | Sugar 16.2g | Protein 3.2g

Delicious Chocolate Brownie

Prep time: 10 minutes
Cook time: 20 minutes
Serves: 8
Ingredients:
- 2 eggs
- ½ cup chocolate chips
- 2 cup all-purpose flour
- 2 teaspoons baking powder
- 1 teaspoon vanilla
- 1 ¼ cup brown sugar
- 1 cup butter, melted
- ½ teaspoon salt

Directions:
1. Place the cooking pot in the Ninja Foodi Grill Main Unit.
2. In a bowl, mix butter and sugar.
3. Add vanilla and eggs and mix well.
4. Add flour, baking powder and salt and mix until well combined.
5. Add chocolate chips and stir well.
6. Pour batter into the greased baking dish.
7. Press Bake mode, set the temperature to 350°F, and set time to 20 minutes. Press Start.

8. Once a unit is preheated then place the baking dish in the cooking pot.
9. Cover with lid and cook for 20 minutes.
Serving Suggestion: Slice and serve.
Variation Tip: None
Nutritional Information per Serving:
Calories 478 | Fat 27.5g | Sodium 343mg | Carbs 53.1g | Fiber 1.2g | Sugar 27.6g | Protein 5.7g

S'mores Pizza

Prep time: 15 minutes.
Cook time: 17 minutes.
Serves: 6
Ingredients:
- 1 pizza crust dough
- ⅓ cup nutella
- 3 graham crackers, broken into large pieces
- 1 tbsp. honey
- 8 marshmallows

Preparation:
1. Spread the dough in a baking pan.
2. Place the cooking pot in the Ninja Foodi Grill.
3. Select the Bake Mode and set the temperature to 350 degrees F.
4. Use the Arrow keys to set the time to 12 minutes.
5. Press the Start/Stop button to initiate preheating.
6. Once preheated, place the pan in the Ninja Foodi Grill.
7. Cover the hood and allow the grill to cook.
8. Add nutella and rest of the ingredients on top of the crust.
9. Cover the hood and bake for 5 minutes.
10. Serve.
Serving Suggestion: Serve the pizza with chocolate sauce on top.
Variation Tip: Add chopped nuts to the toppings.
Nutritional Information Per Serving:
Calories 248 | Fat 16g | Sodium 95mg | Carbs 24g | Fiber 0.3g | Sugar 10g | Protein 14.1g

Easy Scalloped Pineapple

Prep time: 10 minutes
Cook time: 30 minutes
Serves: 6

Ingredients:
- 3 eggs, lightly beaten
- 8 ounces can pineapple, crushed
- 1 ½ cup sugar
- 4 cups of bread cubes
- ¼ cup milk
- ½ cup butter, melted
- ½ cup brown sugar

Directions:
1. Place the cooking pot in the Ninja Foodi Grill Main Unit.
2. In a bowl, mix eggs, milk, pineapple, butter, brown sugar and sugar.
3. Add bread cubes and stir until well coated.
4. Pour mixture into the greased baking dish.
5. Press Bake mode, set the temperature to 350°F, and set time to 30 minutes. Press Start.
6. Once a unit is preheated then place the baking dish in the cooking pot.
7. Cover with lid and cook for 30 minutes.
Serving Suggestion: Serve warm.
Variation Tip: None
Nutritional Information per Serving:
Calories 492 | Fat 17g |Sodium 281mg | Carbs 80g | Fiber 0g | Sugar 66g | Protein 3.4g

Moist Lemon Cupcakes

Prep time: 10 minutes
Cook time: 15 minutes
Serves: 6
Ingredients:

- 1 egg
- 1 cup flour
- ¾ teaspoon baking powder
- ½ teaspoon vanilla
- ½ cup milk
- 2 tablespoons canola oil
- ¼ teaspoon baking soda
- 1 teaspoon lemon zest, grated
- ½ cup sugar
- ½ teaspoon salt

Directions:
1. Place the cooking pot in the Ninja Foodi Grill Main Unit.
2. In a bowl, whisk egg, vanilla, milk, oil and sugar until creamy.
3. Add remaining ingredients and stir until well combined.
4. Pour batter into the silicone muffin molds.
5. Press Bake mode, set the temperature to 350°F, and set time to 15 minutes. Press Start.
6. Once a unit is preheated then place muffin molds in the cooking pot.
7. Cover with lid and cook for 15 minutes.
Serving Suggestion: Allow to cool completely then serve.
Variation Tip: Add melted butter if you don't have canola oil.
Nutritional Information per Serving:
Calories 202 | Fat 6g |Sodium 267mg | Carbs 34g | Fiber 0.6g | Sugar 17.8g | Protein 3.8g

Grilled Chocolate Sandwiches

Prep time: 15 minutes.
Cook time: 10 minutes.
Serves: 4

Ingredients:
- ¼ cup seedless raspberry preserves
- 8 (¼ -inch) Portuguese bread slices
- 12 (.53-oz.) packages dark chocolate squares
- 8 tsp. butter

Preparation:
1. Top each of the 4 bread slices with 2 chocolate squares, and ¼ raspberry preserves.
2. Place the other bread slices on top and brush the top with butter.
3. Place the cooking pot in the Ninja Foodi Grill then set a grill grate inside.
4. Select the "Grill" Mode, set the temperature to MED.
5. Use the arrow keys to set the cooking time to 10 minutes.
6. Press the START/STOP button to initiate preheating.
7. Once preheated, place the sandwiches in the Ninja Foodi Grill.
8. Cover the hood and allow the grill to cook.
9. Flip the sandwiches once cooked halfway through.

10. Serve.
Serving Suggestion: Serve the sandwiches with sliced strawberries on top.
Variation Tip: Add crushed nuts on top.
Nutritional Information Per Serving:
Calories 159 | Fat 3g |Sodium 277mg | Carbs 29g | Fiber 1g | Sugar 9g | Protein 2g

Grilled Pineapple Pizza

Prep time: 15 minutes.
Cook time: 20 minutes.
Serves: 6
Ingredients:
- 1 pizza dough crust
- 3 tbsp. light brown sugar
- ⅛ tsp. ground cinnamon
- 1 fresh pineapple
- 1 (8-oz.) package cream cheese, softened
- 3 tbsp. light brown sugar
- ⅛ tsp. ground cinnamon
- Caramel topping
- Toasted pecans
- Fresh mint sprigs
Preparation:
1. Flour the pizza crust evenly in a baking pan.
2. Place the cooking pot in the Ninja Foodi Grill.
3. Select the "Grill" Mode, set the temperature to MED.
4. Use the arrow keys to set the cooking time to 10 minutes.
5. Press the START/STOP button to initiate preheating.
6. Once preheated, place the pineapple in the Ninja Foodi Grill.
7. Cover the hood and allow the grill to cook.
8. Meanwhile, mix rest of the ingredients in a bowl and spread over the pizza crust then top with pineapple.
9. Cover the hood and cook on "Bake Mode" for 10 minutes.
10. Serve.
Serving Suggestion: Serve the pizza with chocolate syrup on top.
Variation Tip: Add crushed cashews to the pizza.

Nutritional Information Per Serving:
Calories 153 | Fat 1g |Sodium 8mg | Carbs 26g | Fiber 0.8g | Sugar 56g | Protein 1g

Grilled Pound Cake

Prep time: 15 minutes.
Cook time: 5 minutes.
Serves: 4
Ingredients:
- 2 large peaches, sliced
- 2 tbsp. pomegranate molasses
- 2 tbsp. brandy
- ½ tsp. sugar
- 4 1-in.-thick pound cake slices
- About ¼ cup whipped cream
Preparation:
1. Mix peaches with sugar, brandy, and molasses in a bowl.
2. Place the cooking pot in the Ninja Foodi Grill then set a grill grate inside.
3. Select the "Grill" Mode, set the temperature to MED.
4. Use the arrow keys to set the cooking time to 5 minutes.
5. Press the START/STOP button to initiate preheating.
6. Once preheated, place the cake slices in the Ninja Foodi Grill.
7. Cover the hood and allow the grill to cook.
8. Flip the cake slices once cooked halfway through.
9. Top the cake slices with the peach mixture.
10. Garnish with almonds and whipped cream.
11. Serve.
Serving Suggestion: Serve the pound cake with melted chocolate on top.
Variation Tip: Add crushed nuts to the cake.
Nutritional Information Per Serving:
Calories 118 | Fat 20g |Sodium 192mg | Carbs 26g | Fiber 0.9g | Sugar 19g | Protein 5.2g

Chocolate Chip Bars

Prep time: 10 minutes
Cook time: 30 minutes
Serves: 12
Ingredients:
- 2 eggs, lightly beaten
- 1 ½ cup all-purpose flour
- 1 teaspoon vanilla
- 1 ½ cups chocolate chips
- ½ teaspoon baking soda
- ½ cup sugar
- ½ cup brown sugar
- 1 stick butter

Directions:
1. Place the cooking pot in the Ninja Foodi Grill Main Unit.
2. In a bowl, beat butter with sugar, vanilla and brown sugar until fluffy.
3. Add eggs and vanilla and beat well.
4. In a separate bowl, mix flour and baking soda.
5. Add flour mixture into the egg mixture and mix until just combined.
6. Add 1 cup chocolate chips and fold well.
7. Pour batter into the greased baking dish.
8. Sprinkle remaining chocolate chips on top.
9. Press Bake mode, set the temperature to 350°F, and set time to 30 minutes. Press Start.
10. Once a unit is preheated then place baking dish in the cooking pot.
11. Cover with lid and cook for 30 minutes.
Serving Suggestion: Slice and serve.
Variation Tip: None
Nutritional Information per Serving:
Calories 302 | Fat 14g |Sodium 135mg | Carbs 38g | Fiber 1g | Sugar 25g | Protein 4g

Pumpkin Muffins

Prep time: 10 minutes
Cook time: 35 minutes
Serves: 12
Ingredients:
- 2 eggs
- 2 cups all-purpose flour
- 1 cup pumpkin puree
- ½ cup olive oil
- ½ cup maple syrup
- ½ cup of chocolate chips
- 1 teaspoon pumpkin pie spice
- 1 teaspoon baking soda
- ½ teaspoon salt

Directions:
1. Place the cooking pot in the Ninja Foodi Grill Main Unit.
2. In a bowl, mix flour, baking soda, pumpkin pie spice and salt.
3. In a separate bowl, whisk eggs, pumpkin puree, oil and maple syrup.
4. Add flour mixture into the egg mixture and mix until well combined.
5. Add chocolate chips and fold well. Pour batter into the muffin molds.
6. Press Bake mode, set the temperature to 350°F, and set time to 35 minutes. Press Start.
7. Once a unit is preheated then place muffin molds in the cooking pot.
8. Cover with lid and cook for 35 minutes.
Serving Suggestion: Allow to cool completely then serve.
Variation Tip: None
Nutritional Information per Serving:
Calories 237 | Fat 11.5g |Sodium 219mg | Carbs 30.7g | Fiber 1.4g | Sugar 12.2g | Protein 3.8g

Fudgy Brownie

Prep time: 10 minutes
Cook time: 45 minutes
Serves: 16
Ingredients:
- 4 eggs
- 1 cup all-purpose flour
- 1 ¼ cups butter
- 1 ½ cups cocoa powder
- 2 ½ cups sugar
- 1 teaspoon vanilla
- 1 cup chocolate chips
- 2 teaspoons baking powder
- ½ tsp Kosher salt

Directions:

1. Place the cooking pot in the Ninja Foodi Grill Main Unit.
2. Add butter, cocoa powder and sugar in a microwave-safe bowl and microwave for one minute. Stir well.
3. Add eggs and stir until well combined.
4. Add flour, baking powder and salt and stir well.
5. Add chocolate chips and fold well.
6. Pour batter into the greased baking dish.
7. Press Bake mode, set the temperature to 325°F, and set time to 45 minutes. Press Start.
8. Once a unit is preheated then place the baking dish in the cooking pot.
9. Cover with lid and cook for 45 minutes.
Serving Suggestion: Slice and serve.
Variation Tip: None
Nutritional Information per Serving:
Calories 364 | Fat 19.7g |Sodium 202mg | Carbs 48.3g | Fiber 3g | Sugar 36.9g | Protein 4.6g

Strawberry Cobbler

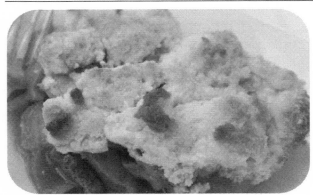

Prep time: 10 minutes
Cook time: 45 minutes
Serves: 6
Ingredients:
- 2 cups strawberries, diced
- 1 cup self-rising flour
- 1 ¼ cup sugar
- 1 teaspoon vanilla
- ½ cup butter, melted
- 1 cup milk

Directions:
1. Place the cooking pot in the Ninja Foodi Grill Main Unit.
2. In a bowl, mix flour and one cup sugar. Add milk and whisk until smooth.
3. Add vanilla and butter and mix well.
4. Pour mixture into the baking dish and sprinkle with strawberries and top with remaining sugar.
5. Press Bake mode, set the temperature to 350°F, and set time to 45 minutes. Press Start.
6. Once a unit is preheated then place the baking dish in the cooking pot.
7. Cover with lid and cook for 45 minutes.
Serving Suggestion: Allow to cool completely then serve.
Variation Tip: You can also add some fresh chopped raspberries.
Nutritional Information per Serving:
Calories 405 | Fat 16.5g |Sodium 129mg | Carbs 63.4g | Fiber 1.5g | Sugar 46g | Protein 4g

Pecan Kabobs

Prep time: 15 minutes.
Cook time: 10 minutes.
Serves: 4
Ingredients:
- 1 loaf (10- ¾ oz.) pound cake, cubed
- 2 large bananas, cut into 1-inch slices
- ¼ cup butter, melted
- 2 tbsp. brown sugar
- ½ tsp. vanilla extract
- ⅛ tsp. ground cinnamon
- 4 cups butter pecan ice cream
- ½ cup butterscotch ice cream topping
- ½ cup chopped pecans, toasted

Preparation:
1. Thread cake and banana pieces on the wooden skewers.
2. Mix butter with cinnamon, vanilla and brown sugar.
3. Brush this mixture over the skewers.
4. Place the cooking pot in the Ninja Foodi Grill.
5. Select the Bake Mode and set the temperature to 350 degrees F.
6. Use the Arrow keys to set the time to 10 minutes.
7. Press the Start/Stop button to initiate preheating.
8. Once preheated, place the skewers in the Ninja Foodi Grill.
9. Cover the hood and allow the grill to cook.
10. Serve the skewers with ice cream and, butterscotch topping.
11. Garnish with pecans.
12. Serve.
Serving Suggestion: Serve the kabobs with whipped cream on top.
Variation Tip: Add crushed walnuts or pecans to the kebabs.
Nutritional Information Per Serving:
Calories 203 | Fat 8.9g |Sodium 340mg | Carbs 22g | Fiber 1.2g | Sugar 11.3g | Protein 5.3g

Banana Muffins

Prep time: 10 minutes
Cook time: 15 minutes
Serves: 10
Ingredients:
- 1 egg
- ¾ cup self-rising flour
- ⅓ cup olive oil
- 2 ripe bananas, mashed
- 1 teaspoon cinnamon
- 1 teaspoon vanilla
- ½ cup brown sugar

Directions:
1. Place the cooking pot in the Ninja Foodi Grill Main Unit.
2. In a bowl, mix egg with mashed bananas, oil, vanilla and brown sugar until well combined.
3. Add flour and cinnamon and mix until well combined.
4. Spoon mixture into the silicone muffin molds.
5. Press Bake mode, set the temperature to 320°F, and set time to 15 minutes. Press Start.
6. Once a unit is preheated then place muffin molds in the cooking pot.
7. Cover with lid and cook for 15 minutes.
Serving Suggestion: Allow to cool completely then serve.
Variation Tip: None
Nutritional Information per Serving:
Calories 148 | Fat 7.3g |Sodium 9mg | Carbs 19.9g | Fiber 1g | Sugar 10g | Protein 1.8g

Dessert Nachos

Prep time: 10 minutes.
Cook time: 9 minutes.
Serves: 8
Ingredients:
- 8 flour tortillas
- ¼ cup sugar
- 1 tbsp. cinnamon
- 1 cup caramel sauce
- 6 oz. chocolate chips
- 6 oz. white chocolate, grated
- ½ cup heavy cream
- 1 cup pecans, chopped
Preparation:
1. Cut tortillas in 8 wedges.
2. Place the cooking pot in the Ninja Foodi Grill.
3. Select the Bake Mode and set the temperature to 350 degrees F.
4. Use the Arrow keys to set the time to 10 minutes.
5. Press the Start/Stop button to initiate preheating.
6. Once preheated, place the wedges in the Ninja Foodi Grill.
7. Cover the hood and allow the grill to cook.
8. Spread the rest of the ingredients on top of the tortilla wedges.
9. Cover the hood and bake for 3 minutes.
10. Serve.
Serving Suggestion: Serve the nachos with creamy frosting on top.
Variation Tip: Add crushed pecans to the muffins.
Nutritional Information Per Serving:
Calories 195 | Fat 3g |Sodium 355mg | Carbs 27g | Fiber 1g | Sugar 25g | Protein 1g

Moist Raspberry Muffins

Prep time: 10 minutes
Cook time: 20 minutes
Serves: 12
Ingredients:
- 1 egg
- 1 cup raspberries
- 1 ¾ cups all-purpose flour
- 1 teaspoon baking powder
- ⅓ cup sugar
- ½ cup canola oil
- 6 ounces of yogurt
- ½ teaspoon baking soda
- ½ teaspoon salt

Directions:

1. Place the cooking pot in the Ninja Foodi Grill Main Unit.
2. In a bowl, mix all dry ingredients.
3. In a small bowl, whisk egg, oil and yogurt.
4. Add egg mixture and raspberries into the dry mixture and mix until well combined.
5. Spoon mixture into the silicone muffin molds.
6. Press Bake mode, set the temperature to 400°F, and set time to 20 minutes. Press Start.
7. Once a unit is preheated then place muffin molds in the cooking pot.
8. Cover with lid and cook for 20 minutes.
Serving Suggestion: Allow to cool completely then serve.
Variation Tip: None
Nutritional Information per Serving:
Calories 189 | Fat 9.9g |Sodium 165mg | Carbs 21.9g | Fiber 1.2g | Sugar 7.1g | Protein 3.3g

Donut Ice Cream Sandwich

Prep time: 15 minutes.
Cook time: 14 minutes.
Serves: 4
Ingredients:
- 4 whole donuts
- 2 cups fresh blueberries
- 1 cup fresh blackberries
- ¾ cup water
- 1 tsp. lemon zest
- ¼ cup honey
Preparation:
1. Toss berries with water, honey, and lemon zest in a baking pan.
2. Place the cooking pot in the Ninja Foodi Grill.
3. Select the Bake Mode and set the temperature to 350 degrees F.
4. Use the Arrow keys to set the time to 10 minutes.
5. Press the Start/Stop button to initiate preheating.
6. Once preheated, place the pan in the Ninja Foodi Grill.
7. Cover the hood and allow the grill to cook.
8. Slice the donuts in half and grill them in the Ninja Foodi Smart Grill for 2 minutes per side.
9. Add ice cream scoop and berries mixture to the donut halves.
10. Serve.
Serving Suggestion: Serve the donuts with chocolate syrup on top.
Variation Tip: Add crushed walnuts or pecans to the filling.
Nutritional Information Per Serving:
Calories 198 | Fat 14g |Sodium 272mg | Carbs 27g | Fiber 1g | Sugar 9.3g | Protein 1.3g

Ninja Foodi Grilled Pineapple Sundaes

Prep time: 5 minutes
Cook time: 4 minutes
Serves: 2
Ingredients:
- 2 scoops vanilla ice cream
- 2 pineapple slices
- 1 tablespoon sweetened coconut, toasted and shredded
Preparation:
1. Install grill grate in the unit and close hood. Select GRILL, set temperature to HIGH, and set time to 4 minutes. Select START/STOP to begin preheating.
2. When it shows "Add Food", place pineapple slices in it and cook for 4 minutes, flipping halfway through.
3. When the unit beeps to signify it has preheated, place pineapple slices on the grill grate, gently pressing them down to maximize grill marks.
4. When cooking is complete, remove pineapple and top with vanilla ice cream and shredded coconut.
5. Serve
Serving Suggestions: Serve with pineapple syrup on the top.
Variation Tip: You can add vanilla extract.
Nutritional Information per Serving:
Calories: 228 |Fat: 8g|Sat Fat: 5.3g|Carbohydrates: 38g|Fiber: 3g|Sugar: 30.4g|Protein: 3.3g

Ninja Foodi S'mores Roll-Up

Prep time: 10 minutes
Cook time: 5 minutes
Serves: 4
Ingredients:
- 8 graham crackers
- 4 cups mini marshmallows
- 4 cups chocolate chips

- 4 flour tortillas

Preparation:
1. Install grill grate in the unit and close hood. Select GRILL, set temperature to HIGH, and set time to 5 minutes. Select START/STOP to begin preheating
2. Arrange marshmallows, crackers, and chocolate chips on tortillas in the meantime. Wrap them tightly in plastic wrap and set them aside.
3. Place wrapped tortillas in Ninja Foodi Grill when it shows "Add Food" and cook for 5 minutes, flipping halfway through.
4. Remove from the oven, serve, and enjoy!

Serving Suggestions: Serve with whipped cream on the top.

Variation Tip: Add honey to enhance taste.

Nutritional Information per Serving:
Calories: 1161 |Fat: 53.4g|Sat Fat: 35.5g|Carbohydrates: 154.4g|Fiber: 8g|Sugar: 108.7g|Protein: 16.4g

Ninja Foodi Grilled Food Skewers

Prep time: 5 minutes
Cook time: 12 minutes
Serves: 5

Ingredients:
- 1½ cups sliced strawberries
- ¾ cup pineapple, cubed
- 1½ tablespoons honey
- 4 peaches, sliced
- 1½ tablespoons olive oil
- 5 skewers, soaked
- Salt, to taste

Preparation:
1. Install grill grate in the unit and close hood. Select GRILL, set temperature to MAX, and set time to 12 minutes. Select START/STOP to begin preheating
2. Skewer strawberries, pineapple, and peach slices. Remove from the equation.
3. Season with salt and oil, then add to the Ninja Foodi Grill when the "Add Food" button appears.
4. Grill for 12 minutes, then serve with honey on top.
5. Finally, serves and enjoy!

Serving Suggestions: Serve with white chocolate chips on the top.

Variation Tip: You can add more fruits if you want.

Nutritional Information per Serving:
Calories: 312 |Fat: 16.2g|Sat Fat:

2.2g|Carbohydrates: 45.7g|Fiber: 5.4g|Sugar: 40.4g|Protein: 2.4g

Ninja Foodi Grilled Donut Ice Cream Sandwich

Prep time: 5 minutes
Cook time: 3 minutes
Serves: 2

Ingredients:
- 4 scoops vanilla ice cream
- ½ cup whipped cream
- 2 glazed donuts, halved
- 2 cherries

Preparation:
1. Install grill grate in the unit and close hood. Select GRILL, set temperature to MAX, and set time to 3 minutes for medium-cooked donuts. Select START/STOP to begin preheating
2. When it shows "Add Food," put the doughnuts in and cook for 3 minutes.
3. Place each donut sandwich on a plate and top with vanilla ice cream.
4. Garnish with cherries and whipped cream.
5. Finally, serve and enjoy!

Serving Suggestions: Top with chocolate syrup before serving.

Variation Tip: Cherries can be omitted.

Nutritional Information per Serving:
Calories: 637 |Fat: 33.3g|Sat Fat: 16.8g|Carbohydrates: 77.6g|Fiber: 2.4g|Sugar: 28g|Protein: 7.5g

Ninja Foodi Chocolate Marshmallow Banana

Prep time: 10 minutes
Cook time: 5 minutes
Serves: 4

Ingredients:
- 2 cups chocolate chips

- 2 cups mini marshmallows
- 4 bananas, sliced lengthwise

Preparation:
1. Install grill grate in the unit and close hood. Select GRILL, set temperature to MAX, and set time to 5 minutes. Select START/STOP to begin preheating
2. In the meantime, lay banana slices on foil paper and stuff them with marshmallows and chocolate chips. Wrap it up securely.
3. When the Ninja Foodi Grill shown "Add Food," put the banana wraps in and cook for 5 minutes.
4. Remove the dish from the oven, unwrap it, and serve.

Serving Suggestions: Top with chocolate syrup before serving.

Variation Tip: Sugar can also be added for sweeter taste.

Nutritional Information per Serving:
Calories: 600 |Fat: 25.3g|Sat Fat: 17.6g|Carbohydrates: 88g|Fiber: 5.9g|Sugar: 64.3g|Protein: 7.8g

Ninja Foodi Bloomin' Grilled Apples

Prep time: 5 minutes
Cook time: 30 minutes
Serves: 2

Ingredients:
- 4 tablespoons maple cream caramel sauce
- 2 apples
- 2 scoops vanilla ice cream
- 6 teaspoons chopped pecans

Preparation:
1. Install grill grate in the unit and close hood. Select GRILL, set temperature to MAX, and set time to 30 minutes. Select START/STOP to begin preheating
2. In the meantime, slice the tops of the apples and scoop out the core.
3. Place pecans and maple cream caramel sauce in the center of the apples and wrap foil around them.
4. Place apples in the Ninja Foodi Grill when it says "Add Food" and cook for half an hour.
5. Serve with vanilla ice cream scoops on top.
6. Finally, serve and enjoy!

Serving Suggestions: Top with chocolate chips before serving.

Variation Tip: You can also use applesauce to enhance taste.

Nutritional Information per Serving:
Calories: 636 |Fat: 62.4g|Sat Fat: 9.5g|Carbohydrates: 67.8g|Fiber: 10.4g|Sugar: 53.7g|Protein: 8.4g

Ninja Foodi Banana Split

Prep time: 10 minutes
Cook time: 14 minutes
Serves: 4

Ingredients:
- 1½ tablespoons coconut oil
- ¼ cup corn flour
- 2 bananas, halved lengthwise
- ¼ teaspoon ground cinnamon
- ½ cup bread crumbs
- 1 egg
- 1½ tablespoons sugar
- 1 tablespoon chopped walnuts

Preparation:
1. In a pan, heat the coconut oil and bread crumbs. Cook for 4 minutes before transferring the mixture to a shallow dish. Remove from the equation.
2. Separate the corn flour from the egg into two bowls. Remove from the equation.
3. Toss the bananas in the corn flour mixture, then in the egg mixture, and finally in the bread crumb mixture.
4. Meanwhile, in a Ninja Foodi Grill, position the "Crisper Basket," select "AIR CRISP," and set the temperature to 280 degrees F. Set the timer for 10 minutes.
5. To begin preheating, press START/STOP.
6. When it says "Add Food," add the bananas and cook for 10 minutes.
7. Remove from the oven and top with cinnamon, sugar, and walnuts.
8. Finally, serve and enjoy!

Serving Suggestions: Top with whipped cream before serving.

Variation Tip: More cinnamon can be added.

Nutritional Information per Serving:
Calories: 383 |Fat: 22.1g|Sat Fat: 16.9g|Carbohydrates: 45.7g|Fiber: 2.9g|Sugar: 24.7g|Protein: 4.8g

Ninja Foodi Cherry Clafoutis

Prep time: 10 minutes
Cook time: 25 minutes
Serves: 2

Ingredients:
- ¾ cup fresh cherries, pitted
- 2 tablespoons flour
- 1 egg
- 2 tablespoons powdered sugar
- 1½ tablespoons vodka
- ¼ cup sour cream
- Salt, to taste

Preparation:
1. In a separate bowl, combine the cherries and the vodka. Mix thoroughly.
2. Combine salt, sugar, and flour in a separate basin. Mix thoroughly.
3. Combine the egg and sour cream in a mixing bowl. To make a dough, combine all of the ingredients in a mixing bowl until a dough is formed.
4. Cover the dough with the cherry mixture and leave it aside.
5. Meanwhile, in a Ninja Foodi Grill, arrange "Crisper Basket" and push the "AIR CRISP" button.
6. Preheat the oven to 355°F and set the timer for 25 minutes.
7. To begin preheating, press START/STOP.
8. When it says "Add Food," put the dough in and bake for 25 minutes at 355 degrees F.
9. Remove the pan from the oven and set it aside to cool for about 10 minutes.
10. Finally, serve and enjoy!

Serving Suggestions: Top with cherries before serving.

Variation Tip: Butter can also be added in the dough.

Nutritional Information per Serving:
Calories: 273 |Fat: 8.3g|Sat Fat: 4.4g|Carbohydrates: 23.1g|Fiber: 0.4g|Sugar: 8.1g|Protein: 4.6g

Ninja Foodi Banana Mug Cake

Prep time: 10 minutes
Cook time: 30 minutes
Serves: 2

Ingredients:
- ½ cup all-purpose flour
- ½ teaspoon baking soda
- 1 cup mashed banana
- 2 tablespoons melted butter
- ½ teaspoon vanilla extract
- ¼ teaspoon ground cinnamon
- 4 tablespoons sugar
- 2 egg yolks
- Salt, to taste

Preparation:
1. In a mixing basin, combine the cinnamon, flour, baking soda, and salt. Mix thoroughly.
2. In a separate bowl, combine the mashed banana, butter, egg yolk, vanilla extract, and sugar. Make sure everything is well combined.
3. Combine the two recipes in a mixing bowl, well combine, and pour into buttered ramekins. Remove from the equation.
4. In the Ninja Foodi Grill, arrange the "Crisper Basket," select "AIR CRISP," and set the temperature to 350 degrees F. Make the timer 30 minutes long.
5. To begin preheating, press START/STOP.
6. When "Add Food" appears, add the ramekins and simmer for around half an hour.
7. Remove from the oven and set aside to cool.
8. Finally, serve and enjoy!

Serving Suggestions: Top with banana slices before serving.

Variation Tip: You can use maple syrup to enhance taste.

Nutritional Information per Serving:
Calories: 430 |Fat: 16.6g|Sat Fat: 9g|Carbohydrates: 66g|Fiber: 2.9g|Sugar: 33.5g|Protein: 6.9g

4 Weeks Meal Plan

Week 1

Day 1:
Breakfast: Grilled Bruschetta
Lunch: Honey Carrot Dish
Snack: Chicken Stuff Jalapenos
Dinner: Barbecued Turkey
Dessert: Rummy Pineapple Sunday

Day 2:
Breakfast: Cinnamon Oatmeal
Lunch: Grilled Cauliflower with Miso Mayo
Snack: Mammamia Banana Boats
Dinner: Teriyaki-Marinated Salmon
Dessert: Chocolate Cheesecake

Day 3:
Breakfast: Energetic Bagel Platter
Lunch: Cool Rosemary Potatoes
Snack: Crispy Brussels
Dinner: Grilled Beef Burgers
Dessert: Grilled Chocolate Sandwiches

Day 4:
Breakfast: Breakfast Skewers
Lunch: Potatoes in a Foil
Snack: Tasty Cauliflower Tots
Dinner: Avocado Salsa Steak
Dessert: Banana Muffins

Day 5:
Breakfast: Ninja Foodi Breakfast Sausages
Lunch: Cheesy Cauliflower Casserole
Snack: Ninja Foodi Corn Fritters
Dinner: Shrimp with Tomatoes
Dessert: Moist Raspberry Muffins

Day 6:
Breakfast: Bistro Breakfast Sandwiches
Lunch: Grilled Smashed Potatoes
Snack: Volcano Potatoes
Dinner: Chicken Kebabs with Currants
Dessert: Grilled Pound Cake

Day 7:
Breakfast: Zesty Grilled Ham
Lunch: Grilled Brussels Sprouts with Bacon
Snack: Grilled Oysters with Chorizo Butter
Dinner: Peruvian Chicken Skewers
Dessert: Ninja Foodi Grilled Pineapple Sundaes

Week 2

Day 1:
Breakfast: Delicious Banana Bread
Lunch: Vegetable Orzo Salad
Snack: Pineapple with Cream Cheese Dip
Dinner: Lettuce Cheese Steak
Dessert: Banana Skewers

Day 2:
Breakfast: Grilled French Toast
Lunch: Southwestern Potato Salad
Snack: Lemon Herb Carrots
Dinner: Grilled Seafood Platter
Dessert: Delicious Chocolate Brownie

Day 3:
Breakfast: Morning Frittata
Lunch: Parmesan Zucchini and Squash
Snack: Grilled Peach Salsa
Dinner: Grilled Chicken with Banana Pepper Dip
Dessert: Marshmallow Stuffed Banana

Day 4:
Breakfast: Delicious Berry Oatmeal
Lunch: Baked Parmesan Zucchini
Snack: Grilled Stuffed Mushrooms
Dinner: Piri Piri Chicken
Dessert: Moist Lemon Cupcakes

Day 5:
Breakfast: Breakfast Potato Casserole
Lunch: Hearty Spinach Olive
Snack: Grilled Sweet Honey Carrot
Dinner: Grilled Fish Tacos
Dessert: Pumpkin Muffins

Day 6:
Breakfast: Ninja Foodi Bean
Lunch: Baked Apple and Sweet Potatoes
Snack: Lovely Seasonal Broccoli
Dinner: Steak with Salsa Verde
Dessert: Grilled Apples a la Mode

Day 7:
Breakfast: Sausage with Eggs
Lunch: Zucchini with Parmesan
Snack: Savory Roasted Almonds
Dinner: Easy BBQ Roast Shrimp
Dessert: Grilled Pineapple Pizza

Week 3

Day 1:
Breakfast: Portobello Mushrooms Bruschetta
Lunch: Ninja Foodi Stuffed Tomatoes
Snack: Grilled Kimchi
Dinner: Huli Huli Chicken Wings
Dessert: Strawberry Cobbler

Day 2:
Breakfast: Kale and Sausage Delight
Lunch: Air Grilled Brussels
Snack: Grilled Honey Carrots
Dinner: Paprika Grilled Shrimp
Dessert: Grill Pineapple Slices

Day 3:
Breakfast: Avocado Eggs
Lunch: Balsamic Vegetables
Snack: Chicken Salad with Blueberry Vinaigrette
Dinner: Sausage and Pepper Grinders
Dessert: Ninja Foodi S'mores Roll-Up

Day 4:
Breakfast: Banana Oat Muffins
Lunch: Rosemary Potatoes
Snack: Spice Lover's Cajun Eggplant
Dinner: Pistachio Pesto Shrimp
Dessert: Donut Ice Cream Sandwich

Day 5:
Breakfast: Stuffed up Bacon and Pepper
Lunch: Grilled Veggies with Vinaigrette
Snack: Ninja Foodi Mac n' Cheese
Dinner: Grilled Chicken with Grapes
Dessert: Ninja Foodi Cherry Clafoutis

Day 6:
Breakfast: Ninja Foodi Breakfast Frittata
Lunch: Cajun Green Beans
Snack: Ninja Foodi Buffalo Chicken Wings
Dinner: Spinach Salad with Steak & Blueberries
Dessert: Ninja Foodi Vanilla Donuts

Day 7:
Breakfast: Mushroom Pepper
Lunch: Grilled Greens and Cheese on Toast
Snack: Crispy Potato Wedges
Dinner: Baked Coconut Chicken
Dessert: Fudgy Brownie

Week 4

Day 1:
Breakfast: Greek Egg Muffins
Lunch: Delicious Broccoli and Arugula
Snack: Ninja Foodi Roasted Cashews
Dinner: Shrimp Stuffed Sole
Dessert: Moist Carrot Muffins

Day 2:
Breakfast: Ninja Foodi Swiss-Cheese Sandwiches
Lunch: Mustard Green Veggie Meal
Snack: Grilled Butternut Squash
Dinner: Bourbon Pork Chops
Dessert: Berry Cobbler

Day 3:
Breakfast: Grilled Honeydew
Lunch: Honey Dressed Asparagus
Snack: Figs Stuffed with Cheese
Dinner: Grilled Orange Chicken
Dessert: Apricots with Brioche

Day 4:
Breakfast: Spinach Tater Tot Casserole
Lunch: Ninja Foodi Tofu with Orange Sauce
Snack: Cheesy Chicken Dip
Dinner: Alfredo Chicken Apples
Dessert: Easy Scalloped Pineapple

Day 5:
Breakfast: Bacon-Herb Grit
Lunch: Charred Asparagus Tacos
Snack: Complete Italian Squash
Dinner: Blackened Salmon
Dessert: Marshmallow Banana Boat

Day 6:
Breakfast: Veggie Packed Egg Muffin
Lunch: Sweet Grilled Pickles
Snack: Honey-Luscious Asparagus
Dinner:
Dessert: Chocolate Chip Bars

Day 7:
Breakfast: Ninja Foodi Cinnamon Buttered Toasts
Lunch: Grilled Potato Rounds
Snack: Ninja Foodi Lemon Tofu
Dinner: Chipotle-Raspberry Pork Chops
Dessert: Ninja Foodi Grilled Food Skewers

The Ninja Foodi Grill is an electric power grill, so it is safe for indoor use. The grill comes with a compact design and easily fits over your kitchen countertop. It grills and roasts your favorite food without filling your kitchen with smoke. The Ninja Foodi cooks your food with perfection by distributing the even heat thoroughly around the food and gives even cooking results. It perfectly handles your frozen food directly without defrosting it. The Ninja Foodi One-Touch Button Control Panel is easy to operate and comes with five cooking functions. It also allows you to choose four different temperature settings from low, medium, high and max. It allows you to cook most of the delicious food in less than 25 minutes.

Appendix Measurement Conversion Chart

VOLUME EQUIVALENTS(DRY)

US STANDARD	METRIC (APPROXIMATE)
1/8 teaspoon	0.5 mL
1/4 teaspoon	1 mL
1/2 teaspoon	2 mL
3/4 teaspoon	4 mL
1 teaspoon	5 mL
1 tablespoon	15 mL
1/4 cup	59 mL
1/2 cup	118 mL
3/4 cup	177 mL
1 cup	235 mL
2 cups	475 mL
3 cups	700 mL
4 cups	1 L

VOLUME EQUIVALENTS(LIQUID)

US STANDARD	US STANDARD (OUNCES)	METRIC (APPROXIMATE)
2 tablespoons	1 fl.oz.	30 mL
1/4 cup	2 fl.oz.	60 mL
1/2 cup	4 fl.oz.	120 mL
1 cup	8 fl.oz.	240 mL
1 1/2 cup	12 fl.oz.	355 mL
2 cups or 1 pint	16 fl.oz.	475 mL
4 cups or 1 quart	32 fl.oz.	1 L
1 gallon	128 fl.oz.	4 L

WEIGHT EQUIVALENTS

US STANDARD	METRIC (APPROXIMATE)
1 ounce	28 g
2 ounces	57 g
5 ounces	142 g
10 ounces	284 g
15 ounces	425 g
16 ounces (1 pound)	455 g
1.5 pounds	680 g
2 pounds	907 g

TEMPERATURES EQUIVALENTS

FAHRENHEIT(F)	CELSIUS(C) (APPROXIMATE)
225 °F	107 °C
250 °F	120 °C
275 °F	135 °C
300 °F	150 °C
325 °F	160 °C
350 °F	180 °C
375 °F	190 °C
400 °F	205 °C
425 °F	220 °C
450 °F	235 °C
475 °F	245 °C
500 °F	260 °C